The Liberal Approach to the Past

The Liberal
Approach to the Past:
A Reader

Edited and with an introduction by
Michael J. Douma

CATO INSTITUTE
WASHINGTON, DC

Print ISBN: 978-1-952223-10-5
eBook ISBN: 978-1-948647-83-0

Printed in the United States of America.

CATO INSTITUTE
1000 Massachusetts Avenue NW
Washington, DC 20001
www.cato.org

CONTENTS

CONTENTS

Introduction

This reader contains a carefully selected collection of writings on historical methods and the philosophy of history penned by liberal historians.

What do we mean by "liberalism" or "liberal history"? It seems that every scholar in the social sciences would like to define liberalism in his or her own way. Certainly, plenty of room exists for differences of opinion on this matter. But defining any "-ism" requires circumscribing a set of beliefs, or drawing lines in such a way as to connect ideas that we believe form a coherent tradition.

A common path toward defining liberalism, for example, is to list thinkers for whom there is general agreement that they fit the tradition: Benedetto Croce, Thomas Jefferson, Immanuel Kant, John Locke, John Stuart Mill, Thomas Paine, Max Weber, and so forth. Generally, however, this list includes social thinkers, political theorists, and economists but neglects historians and the historical writings of such polymaths as David Hume or Wilhelm von Humboldt, who are included for their other, nonhistorical contributions. For this reason, existing works on the history of liberalism are typically of little value for understanding the liberal approach to the past.

Liberal history is primarily concerned with ideas and with the reasons why individuals acted as they did in the past. Liberal historians prefer to study themes of power and liberty, particularly as they relate to the rise and fall of political systems that protect liberties and individual rights. In the 19th century, liberals proposed various stadial theories of history, which were often based on race and geography. These early liberals shared a belief that liberty was emerging in history, and some even thought that this pattern was natural and unstoppable.[1] Liberal historians in the 20th century, however, generally took the opposite position, rejecting historical inevitability and any grand scheme of history. They also abandoned deterministic theories of race and geography. From a certain perspective then, a discontinuity exists in what constitutes liberal theorizing about history.

The writings collected here indicate, however, that self-identified liberal historians from the 19th century to the present day have held fairly consistently to a core set of positions in the methods and theory of history:

1. The belief that historical writing should aim to describe reality, that a real world existed before and outside the mind of the historian, and that evidence of this world can be reliable for producing historical accounts.

2. The view that historical knowledge is different from the knowledge of the natural sciences and social sciences, and that history is an autonomous discipline, with its own methods.

3. An opposition to proposed laws of history and any kind of historical determinism that devalues the free action of individuals. Liberals prefer instead a historicism that supports the uniqueness and incommensurability of each historical event, culture, or period.

4. The rejection of sociological concepts as actors, that is, nations as agents or abstractions such as the *Volksgeist* being responsible for historical change.

The first point—essential to the liberal view of history—might be confused for a universal premise of modern historiography, but that owes something to the influence of liberal thought on mainline Western historical thought. Not every historian aims to describe reality through the evidence. Some schools of historical thought explicitly reject that such a thing is possible, or even desirable. Some historians revel in paradox or esotericism, or they deny that historical writing can ever present a true description of the real world. History, they say, is nothing but a language game that we play to give power to one group or person over another. History, in this view, is a form of politics.

On the second point, this reader indicates that the anti-scientific strain of liberal history has always been quite strong, even if it has appeared in different guises. One problem here is that the adjective "scientific" applied to historical methods has multiple meanings. In one instance, it means a spirit of accuracy, thorough observation, and rational argumentation with professional standards. No liberal historian (or modern historian of any kind I suppose) opposes that kind of scientific history. But liberals have taken issue with the idea that history is a protoscience, and that, like physicists, historians can deduce a set of laws from observations.

Before scientific history was the old tradition of literary history, or history as an art, which required imagination and creativity; its purpose was education and moral insight. This view was still the school of Lord Acton and his followers like G. M. Trevelyan, whose essay "Clio, a Muse" related its history. Trevelyan contrasted this school of thought with the new, scientific history: "There is no utilitarian value in knowledge of the past," he wrote, "and there is no way of scientifically deducing causal laws about the action of human beings in the mass. In short, the value of history is not scientific. Its true value is educational. It can educate the minds of men by causing them to reflect on the past."[2]

In 19th-century Germany as well, liberal historians defended the independence of history from science by defining history as a part of the *Geisteswissenschaften*, or human sciences. At issue was whether historical understanding was something different from scientific explanation. Liberals argue, then and now, that human behavior cannot be explained and is not predictable in the scientific sense because humans have free will, they respond uniquely to each circumstance, and there is no path toward replication.

The most influential thinker in this regard was the German Wilhelm Dilthey, who argued that the aim of the human sciences was not to isolate actions as examples of a universal law, but to understand the relationship between the part and the whole, or, as historians might phrase it, the event in context. Combined with the view that one could not isolate historical facts and treat them as separate abstract instances of natural laws, Dilthey defended the historicist view that experience and even rationality are conditioned by historical circumstances.

The debate about the autonomy of history is at the root of the divide between mainline liberal historicists and many of the 20th-century social science historians inspired by sociology, Progressivism, and Marxism. Left-liberals influenced by anthropology more than Comtean sociological or logical positivism, however, tend to also defend a version of historicism, wherein they emphasize the uniqueness of each culture and individual, as well as the uniqueness and irreproducibility of historical events.

As the selections in this reader show, the liberal approach to the past is generally skeptical of laws of history and suggestions of historical determinism, noted above as the third point. Liberalism is a wide tradition, and it must be noted that there are examples of liberals—like the father of scientific history, Henry Thomas Buckle—who sought laws of history. Those who defend causal laws of history sometimes argue that we come to historical explanations by seeing them as particular instances of general laws. Yet this appears to be a distinctly minority position among liberals. In fact, it is precisely on this point of laws and determinism where many a liberal will fall or stand. Sidney Hook, for example, switched from being a communist to a social democrat, partly, as he explains in his book *The Hero in History*, because he could not stomach historical determinism.

Arguments against "laws" of history appear in the following selections from Froude, Maitland, Crump, Collingwood, Hayek, Geyl, Commager, and Hartwell. But why is liberal history so strongly linked with this anti-scientific or anti-positivistic view of history? To liberal ears, any defense of "laws of history" suggests that the behavior of individuals is limited or determined. It seems that to retain our moral judgment, both as historians and as historical actors, we require at a minimum the freedom to think and act. Liberals also want to draw a distinction between mind and nature, or mental and physical processes.

What has been the liberal answer to historical determinism? One response comes from the Austrian-born economist Joseph Schumpeter. Schumpeter was keenly aware of the empirical problems of history, and specifically those of economic history. He knew that historians study cause and effect, but that they can't always isolate casual factors. Schumpeter, therefore, taught historians to seek the entrepreneur in history, the actor who changes the status quo. This was the "creative response" that determined the direction of history. He wrote:

> First, from the standpoint of the observer who is in full possession of all relevant facts, it can always be understood *ex post*; but it can practically never be understood *ex ante*; that is to say, it cannot be predicted by applying the ordinary rules of interference from the pre-existing facts. This is why the "how" in what has been called the "mechanisms" must be investigated in each case. Secondly, creative response shapes the whole course of subsequent events and their "long-run" outcome. It is not true that both types of responses dominate only what

the economist loves to call "transitions," leaving the ultimate outcome to be determined by the initial data. Creative response changes social and economic situations for good, or, to put it differently, it creates situations from which there is no bridge to those situations that might have emerged in its absence. This is why creative response is an essential element in the historical process; no deterministic credo avails against this.[3]

Schumpeter's position, then, is that history takes place in the context of material conditions, but it is primarily driven and shaped by ideas. Creativity is almost synonymous with liberty in the liberal mind. Benedetto Croce shares thoughts similar to Schumpeter's when he writes: "Whatever the spheres of these activities may be, the principle of liberty animates them all: it is synonymous with the activity or spirituality, that is, of the creations of life. A forced creation, a mechanical creation, creation to order, or in chains, has never yet been tried and is impossible to imagine: these are, in fact, a series of words devoid of sense."[4]

A fourth consistent theme in liberals' writings about the methods and philosophy of history is an opposition to sociological concepts or categories as actors, or, in other words, a defense of strict methodological individualism, the view that only individuals can act. The French historians Seignobos and Langlois, in their influential treatise on historical methods from 1898, defend and define methodological individualism when they criticize historians' use of concepts like *Volksgeist* and *âme nationale* as actors in the past.

A world of imaginary beings has thus been created behind the historical facts, and has replaced Providence in the explanation of them. For our defence against this deceptive mythology, a single rule will suffice: Never seek the causes of an historical fact without having first expressed it concretely in terms of acting and thinking individuals. If abstractions are used, every metaphor must be avoided which would make them play the part of living beings.[5]

The same complaint formed the core of Croce's opposition to "writers who devise and theorize on the concept of France, of Germany, of Spain, of England, and of Russia, Switzerland and Belgium, which being particular and transient and therefore clearly not definable concepts . . ." The "worst in these matters," continued Croce, "occurs when substance is given to things, and when they are given a reality and a value which strictly belong to the activities of the spirit, to its political and moral, scientific and artistic works."[6]

Intentions, or thoughts, are precisely what liberal historians hope to reveal in their research. The concept of methodological individualism does not deny the usefulness of such collective entities in everyday speech; however, it seeks to explain any collective action by looking for the underlying motivations or intentions of individual action.

Methodological individualism has been more useful (and more controversial) in economics, where neoclassical and Austrian economists defend reducing macroeconomic ideas to microeconomic foundations. The doctrine has been less problematic for historians, probably because they already mostly agree with it. It seems to be in the nature of historians to focus on the unique and the individual in history, while expressing skepticism of the generalization of sociologists and the general models of the positivist economists. This, I suggest, is the result of the thoroughgoing historicism that still reigns in mainline historical thinking.

Historical explanations (unlike social scientific explanations) are often clearly explained by reference to a particular individual action (or the actions of multiple individuals) so that appeals to generalities are not needed. That is to say, the problems historians tend to focus on are individual in nature, whereas sociologists and economists tend seek answers to general problems. At the same time, historians tend to be open to new theories and may have no difficulty accepting historical insights from, say, Marxist and liberal historians, even when those insights are fundamentally contradictory and arise from incompatible theoretical foundations. When historians encounter multiple explanations for a historical problem, they do not necessarily see a theoretical debate that must be sorted out. Rather, they see a richer landscape with perhaps deeper meaning and more understanding of the possible ways that the past could have been.

The four positions outlined here are the philosophical foundations of liberal history. They provide a framework for what it means to write liberal history, but they don't define or determine the further methods of inquiry, the personal or political goals of the history, or the positions that historians must arrive at. The liberal approach prescribes certain views about the world, but it does not demand full agreement. In fact, if one were to add a fifth element to the list of what makes a historian liberal, it is the openness to other views and to disagreement that lies at the heart of liberalism.

Historical and Geographical Coverage

This reader has a clear preference for English and American writers. It is to some extent a reflection of the contingent origins and spread of liberal historical methods. Liberal views of history emerged in England, France, and Germany at roughly the same time, and historians in those countries certainly influenced one another. But the torch of liberal history burned brightest in England and the United States. Most historians who wrote in the liberal tradition penned no statement of historical methods or theories, but left their approach to historical scholarship implicit in their work. That of course makes it more difficult to boil down the essential elements of what they believed about historical methods.

Many 18th- and 19th-century British historians of the highest pedigree were liberals. James Anthony Froude and Frederic William Maitland are examples in this book, but one could also include Edward Augustus Freeman, David Hume, John Millar, Thomas Babington Macaulay (whom Lord Acton called the greatest of the liberals), and a host of others who participated in a long historiographical conflict over the origins of English liberties. These historians were heavily invested in the question of who protected English freedoms, and what was the role of the constitution, the Parliament, the king, and the church in bringing about these freedoms and maintaining them.

Freedom (and especially national freedom) was also a major theme in 19th-century German historiographical writing, with such luminaries as Kant and Hegel weighing in. Some French liberal historians, like Augustin Thierry, Benjamin Constant, and Raymond Aron, were read in the Anglo-American world, but they made little influence on historical methods.

Although these historians were sometimes familiar with one another, we should not draw too fine of a line connecting them all. They did not share all of same views on historical methods, nor did they write a single manifesto of liberal history. One might say that these historians—in their work at the archives, in their thoughtful hours at their desks—arrived at or "discovered" similar answers about the nature of history and historical methods. It might be said that modern historical scholarship, emerging in the 19th century, was an attempt to find common ground and common methods. History was a tool to unite nations under a common history, but history also hoped for a universality, a "universal history" that would connect mankind across all times and places. Universal history was a predecessor to approaches today known as world history, global history, and big history. The liberal international attempt to create a common history required certain norms of research to maintain trust in the product of historical research. Liberal history motivated professional standards in the field. At the same time, the liberal milieu that gave rise to professional history also enabled a tolerance for argument about methods.

A recent article by Samuel Hammond argues that liberal principles have been "repeatedly discovered throughout history." Hammond explains, "Whenever liberal ideas emerge in history, it is in the context of a pragmatic need to unite different peoples, races and creeds under broadly acceptable norms, giving liberal constitutions their characteristic 'thinness.'" Hammond's observations about the discovery of liberal ideas might have some value for thinking about the development of liberal history. He writes, "At some point, a liberal norm goes from being merely pragmatic to being an internalized value that transcends time and place."[7]

It is my contention that many of the basic elements of modern historical research—source analysis, historiography as contested but working toward a common understanding, reasoned debate, and so forth—all emerged in the 19th century with a strong liberal imprint. The inherent empiricism, historicism, aversion to a priori theorizing, distrust of the attempts of other disciplines to colonize history, and so forth, form the mainline historical discipline from which new developments in Marxist history, social history, postmodern history, and others diverge.

It would also be unfair to overly politicize the motivations and sets of beliefs of professional historians of the past two centuries. Although plenty of liberals, like Augustin Thierry in France, thought of themselves as political essayists first and historians second, many historians called themselves liberals whose historical work bears little or no trace of any ideology. For the large number of historians who border on antiquarians, simply studying the past for its own sake, or satisfying their collecting fetish, there isn't time for politics or much concern with theory. But for those who were consciously liberal and wished to outline their thoughts on historical method, there is plenty of overlap to demonstrate a tradition at work.

Who are the liberals? The liberals were the heirs of the Enlightenment. The liberal historians helped define what that meant. They set the tone for the new understanding of how society was changing, and what changes might be possible. For the 18th-century *philosophes*, history was to be used to create new societies. Historian Carl Becker provides some clarification of what "we" (liberals) stand for: "What we seek to know is how [society] may be set right; and we look to the past for light, not on the origins of society, but on its future state. We wish neither to break with the past nor to hold fast to it, but to make use of it."[8] Liberals hold a number of assumptions or beliefs about the world: There are individuals. They have rights. They can act on their own. Societies flourish best when people are free. These are the beginnings of liberal history.

How then can we succinctly describe the liberal approach to the past? In some ways, liberal history is an anti-theory of history: in general, it posits no prime mover; it promises no utopian end. It is skeptical of grand claims and opposes inevitability. The liberal approach to the past is grounded in the reality of the free individual. Without minds, without morality, without free choice and the interaction between mind and matter, there is no history, per se, there is only an endless stream of determined cause and effect.

An injection of explicitly liberal methods may be healthful for the field of history today. It could help refocus history as the history of individuals across time and space, without placing artificial limits or borders on our study of their lives. World historians too often forget that although they have stopped categorizing people into nation-states, they still have a tendency to categorize them into all sorts of other groups, or to defend certain kinds of geographical determinism. The groups then become convenient proxies for having to get down to the gritty level of the individual. Historians of all kinds need to be reminded that the setting of a story (i.e., the factors that influence historical change) is not the source of action and does not explain action. Methods books are typically written at the end of a career. That fact reflects the idea that methods and philosophy come after history. But in truth, philosophical ideas about history and historical methods often precede historical research and writing. At best, I think, ideas about proper historical methods are discovered in the process of researching and writing history.

Many of the selections chosen for this book are little known and are difficult to find in print. I have reproduced original footnotes only in the articles where such notes seemed necessary for understanding the argument of the piece.

1

James Anthony Froude

*"The Science of History," a lecture delivered
at the Royal Institution, February 5, 1864,
reprint, Ten Cent Pocket Series no. 175,
Haldeman-Julius Company, Girard, KS
(undated, probably early 1920s)*

James Anthony Froude (1818–1894) was a novelist, lecturer, editor, and historian. Educated at Oxford, he served as the Regius Professor of Modern History from 1892 to 1894, following Edward Augustus Freeman, Froude's adversary. He wrote biographies of Luther, Erasmus, Caesar, Bunyan, Disraeli, and Thomas Carlyle; historical and travel accounts of English colonies; and a 12-volume history of England to which he devoted 20 years of research and writing. In his politics and in his writing, Froude was a polemicist, a friend and follower of Thomas Carlyle, whose idea of the hero in history had much influence on Froude. Froude himself has been the subject of a number of biographies, but his fame and impact in his own day appear to have been much greater than his legacy.[9]

In this essay, Froude squares off against Henry Thomas Buckle's cause-and-effect naturalism, in which man acts only from nature, like an animal, subject only to natural laws. Buckle was himself a liberal in religion and a supporter of laissez faire economics who, as a historian, was interested in themes of progress and liberty. It is telling that Froude's methodological argument here was against another liberal, since liberals then dominated historical writing.

Liberal history was of course not codified, and never has been, so liberals then and now could disagree on some points of historical method and theory. At question in Froude's mind was whether history could become a science, with laws or at least general tendencies. By the end of the 19th century, this was decidedly the view of the positivists and it dominated sociological thinking. But liberals, standing opposite the socialists and the planners, moved in the other direction, more in support of Froude than Buckle, it seems.

Men, Froude declares, are more than just products of their environments. They have volition, and with volition, there can be no science of history, at least not a science of prediction. Some of Froude's statements anticipate Ludwig von Mises and others in this tradition: "History is but the record of individual action"; and "All actions arise from self-interest," citing Adam Smith in support. Froude provides criticism of historical determinism and the grand philosophies of history, which come and go in fashion. He defends individual action and choice against the reducibility of all behavior to laws.

But in this speech, his own theory of history remains a bit obscured, hidden behind poetry and references to characters from literature. And yet that seems to have been Froude's intention, to show that history is more an art than a science, more concerned with sympathy for characters than predictions of nature.

Among late 19th-century English liberals, Froude was far from the only writer to debate whether history could approach a science.[10] His lecture, however, appears to have been among the better-known examples of the period. A common response is that Froude overstated Buckle's historical determinism, and that history did have the possibility to be or perhaps become a science with general but not exact predictions.

Ladies and Gentlemen,—I have undertaken to speak to you this evening on what is called the science of history. I fear it is a dry subject, and there seems, indeed, something incongruous in the very connection of such words as science and history. It is as if we were to talk of the color of sound, or the longitude of the rule-of-three. Where it is so difficult to make out the truth on the commonest disputed fact in matters passing under our very eyes, how can we talk of a science in things long past, which comes to us only through books? It often seems to me as if history was like a child's box of letters, with which we can spell any word we please. We have only to pick out such letters as we want, arrange them as we like, and say nothing about those which do not suit our purpose.

First, however, I wish to say a word or two about the eminent person whose name is connected with this way of looking at history, and whose premature death struck us all with such a sudden sorrow. Many of you, perhaps, recollect Mr. Buckle as he stood not so long ago in this place. He spoke more than an hour without a note,—never repeating himself, never wasting words; laying out his matter as easily and as pleasantly as if he had been talking to us at his own fireside. We might think what we pleased of Mr. Buckle's views, but it was plain enough that he was a man of uncommon power; and he had qualities also—qualities to which he, perhaps, himself attached little value—as rare as they were admirable.

Most of us, when we have hit on something which we are pleased to think important and original, feel as if we should burst with it. We come out into the book-market with our wares in hand, and ask for thanks and recognition. Mr. Buckle, at an early age, conceived the thoughts which made him famous, but he took the measure of his abilities. He knew that whenever he pleased he could command personal distinction, but he cared more for his subject than for himself. He was contented to work with patient reticence, unknown and unheard of, for twenty years; and then, at middle life, he produced a work which was translated at once into French and German, and, of all places in the world, fluttered the dove-cotes of the Imperial Academy of St. Petersburg.

Goethe says somewhere, that as soon as a man has done any thing remarkable there seems to be a general conspiracy to prevent him from doing it again. He is feasted, feted, caressed; his time is stolen from him by breakfasts, dinners, societies, idle businesses of a thousand kinds. Mr. Buckle had his share of all this; but there are also more dangerous enemies that wait upon success like his. He had scarcely won for himself the place which he deserved, than his health was found shattered by his labors. He had but time to show us how large a man he was; time just to sketch the outlines of his philosophy, and he passed away as suddenly as he appeared. He went abroad to recover strength for his work, but his work was done with and over. He died of a fever at Damascus, vexed only that he was compelled to leave it uncompleted. Almost his last conscious words were: "My book, my book! I shall never finish my book!" He went away as he had lived, nobly careless of himself, and thinking only of the thing which he had undertaken to do.

But his labor had not been thrown away. Disagree with him as we might, the effect which he had already produced was unmistakable, and it is not likely to pass away. What he said was not essentially new. Some such interpretation of human things is as early as the beginning of thought. But Mr. Buckle, on the one hand, had the art which belongs to men of genius: he could present his opinions with peculiar distinctness; and, on the other hand, there is much in the mode of speculation at present current among us for which those opinions have an unusual fascination. They do not please us, but they excite and irritate us. We are angry with them; and we betray, in being so, an uneasy misgiving that there may be more truth in those opinions than we like to allow.

Mr. Buckle's general theory was something of this kind: When human creatures began first to look about them in the world they lived in, there seemed to be no order in any thing. Days and nights were not the same length. The air was sometimes hot and sometimes cold. Some of the stars rose and set like the sun; some described circles round a central star above the north horizon. The planets went on principles of their own; and in the elements there seemed nothing but caprice. Sun and moon would at times go out in eclipse. Sometimes the earth itself would shake under men's feet; and they could only suppose that earth and air and sky and water were inhabited and managed by creatures as wayward as themselves.

Time went on, and the disorder began to arrange itself. Certain influences seemed beneficent to men, others malignant and destructive; and the world was supposed to be animated by good spirits and evil spirits, who were continually fighting against each other, in outward nature and in human creatures themselves. Finally, as men observed more and imagined less, these interpretations gave way also. Phenomena the most opposite in effect were seen to be the result of the same natural law. The fire did not burn the house down if the owners of it were careful, but remained on the hearth and boiled the pot; nor did it seem inclined to burn a bad man's house down than a good man's, provided the badness did not take the form of negligence. The phenomena of nature were found for the most part to proceed in an orderly, regular way, and their variations to be such as could be counted upon. From observing the order of things, the step was easy to cause and effect. An eclipse, instead of being a sign of the anger of Heaven, was found to be the necessary and innocent result of the relative position of sun, moon and earth. The comets become bodies in space, unrelated to the beings who had imagined that all creation was watching them and their doings. By degrees caprice, volition, all symptoms of arbitrary action, disappeared out of the universe; and almost every phenomenon in earth or heaven was found attributable to some law, either understood or perceived to exist. Thus nature was reclaimed from the imagination. The first fantastic conception of things gave way before the moral; the moral in turn gave way before the natural; and at last there was left but one small tract of jungle where the theory of law had failed to penetrate,—the doings and characters of human creatures themselves.

There, and only there, amidst the conflicts of reason and emotion, conscience and desire, spiritual forces were still conceived to exist. Cause and effect were not traceable when there was a free volition to disturb the connection. In all other things, from a given set of conditions the consequences necessarily followed. With man the word "law" changed its meaning; and instead of a fixed order, which he could not choose but follow, it become a moral precept, which he might disobey if he dared.

This it was which Mr. Buckle disbelieved. The economy which prevailed throughout nature, he thought it very unlikely should admit of this exception. He considered that human beings acted necessarily from the impulse of outward circumstances upon their mental and bodily condition at any given moment. Every man, he said, acted from a motive; and his conduct was determined by the motive which affected him most powerfully. Every man naturally desires what he supposes to be good for him; but, to do well, he must know well. He will eat poison, so long as he does not know that it is poison. Let him see that it will kill him, and he will not touch it. The question was not of moral right and wrong. Once let him be thoroughly made to feel that the thing is destructive, and he will leave it alone by the law of his nature. His virtues are the result of knowledge; his faults, the necessary consequence of the want of it. A boy desires to draw. He knows nothing about it; he draws men like trees or houses, with their centre of gravity anywhere. He makes mistakes because he knows no better. We do not blame him. Till he is better taught, he cannot help it. But his instruction begins. He arrives at straight lines; then at solids; then at curves. He learns perspective, and light and shade. He observes more accurately the forms which he wishes to represent. He perceives effects, and he perceives the means by which they are produced. He has learned what to do; and, in part, he has learned how to do it. His after-progress will depend on the amount of force which his nature possesses; but all this is as natural as the growth of an acorn. You do not preach to the acorn that it is its duty to become a large tree; you do not preach to the art-pupil that it is his duty to become a Holbein. You plant your acorn in favorable soil, where it can have light and air, and be sheltered from the wind; you remove the superfluous branches, you train the strength into the leading shoots. The acorn will then become as fine a tree as it has vital force to become. The difference between men and

22

other things is only in the largeness and variety of man's capacities; and in this special capacity, that he alone has the power of observing the circumstances favorable to his own growth, and can apply them for himself, yet, again, with this condition,—that he is not, as is commonly supposed, free to choose whether he will make use of these appliances or not. When he knows what is good for him, he will choose it; and he will judge what is good for him by the circumstances which have made him what he is.

And what he would do, Mr. Buckle supposed that he always had done. His history had been a natural growth as much as the growth of the acorn. His improvement had followed the progress of his knowledge; and, by a comparison of his outward circumstances with the condition of his mind, his whole proceedings on this planet, his creeds and constitutions, his good deeds and his bad, his arts and his sciences, his empires and his revolutions, would be found all to arrange themselves into clear relations of cause and effect.

If, when Mr. Buckle pressed his conclusions, we objected the difficulty of finding what the truth about past times really was, he would admit it candidly as far as concerned individuals; but there was not the same difficulty, he said, with masses of men. We might disagree about the character of Julius or Tiberius Caesar, but we could know well enough the Romans of the Empire. We had their literature to tell us how they thought; we had their laws to tell us how they governed; we had the broad face of the world, the huge mountainous outline of their general doings upon it, to tell us how they acted. He believed it was all reducible to laws, and could be made as intelligible as the growth of the chalk or the coal measures.

And thus consistently Mr. Buckle cared little for individuals. He did not believe (as some one has said) that the history of mankind is the history of its great men. Great men with him were but larger atoms, obeying the same impulses with the rest, only perhaps a trifle more erratic. With them or without them, the course of things would have been much the same.

As an illustration of the truth of his view, he would point to the new science of political economy. Here already was a large area of human activity in which natural laws were found to act unerringly. Men had gone on for centuries trying to regulate trade on moral principles. They would fix wages according to some imaginary rule of fairness; they would fix prices by what they consider things ought to cost; they encouraged one trade or discouraged another, for moral reasons. They might as well have tried to work a steam-engine on moral reasons. The great statesmen whose names were connected with these enterprises might have as well legislated that water should run up-hill. There were natural laws, fixed in the conditions of things; and to contend against them was the old battle of the Titans against the gods.

As it was with political economy, so it was with all other forms of human activity; and as the true laws of political economy explained the troubles which people fell into in old times because they were ignorant of them, so the true laws of human nature, as soon as we knew them, would explain their mistakes in more serious matters, and enable us to manage better for the future. Geographical position, climate, air, soil, and the like, had their several influences. The northern nations are hardy and industrious, because they must till the earth if they would eat the fruits of it, and because the temperature is too low to make an idle life enjoyable. In the south, the soil is more productive, while less food is wanted and fewer clothes; and, in the exquisite air, exertion is not needed to make the sense of existence delightful. Therefore, in the south we find men lazy and indolent.

True, there are difficulties in these views; the home of the languid Italian was the home also of the sternest race of whom the story of mankind retains a record. And again, when we are told that the Spaniards are superstitious because Spain is a country of earthquakes, we remember Japan, the spot in all the world where earthquakes are most frequent, and where at the same time there is the most serene disbelief in any supernatural agency whatsoever.

Moreover, if men grow into what they are by natural laws, they cannot help being what they are; and if they cannot help being what they are, a good deal will have to be altered in our general view of human obligations and responsibilities.

That, however, in these theories there is a great deal of truth, is quite certain, were there but a hope that those who maintain them would be contented with that admission. A man born in a Mahometan country grows up a Mahometan; in a Catholic country, a Catholic; in a Protestant country, a Protestant. His opinions are like his language: he learns to think as he learns to speak; and it is absurd to suppose him responsible for being what nature makes him. We take pains to educate children. There is a good education and a bad education; there are rules well ascertained by which characters are influenced; and, clearly enough, it is no mere matter for a boy's free will whether he turns out well or ill. We try to train him into good habits; we keep him out of the way of temptations; we see that he is well taught; we mix kindness and strictness; we surround him with every good influence we can command. These are what are termed the advantages of good education; and if we fail to provide those under our care with it, and if they go wrong, the responsibility we feel is as much ours as theirs. This is at once an admission of the power over us of outward circumstances.

In the same way, we allow for the strength of temptations, and the like. In general, it is perfectly obvious that men do necessarily absorb, out of the influences in which they grow up, something which gives a complexion to their whole after-character. When historians have to relate great social or speculative changes, the overthrow of a monarchy, or the establishment of a creed, they do but half their duty if they merely relate the events. In an account, for instance, of the rise of Mahometanism, it is not enough to describe the character of the Prophet, the ends which he set before him, the means which he made use of, and the effect which he produced; the historian must show what there was in the condition of the Eastern races which enabled Mahomet to act upon them so powerfully; the existing beliefs, their existing moral and political condition.

In our estimate of the past, and in our calculations of the future, in the judgments which we pass upon one another, we measure responsibility, not by the thing done, but by the opportunities which people have had of knowing better or worse. In the efforts which we make to keep our children from bad associations or friends, we admit that external circumstances have a powerful effect in making men what they are.

But are circumstances every thing? That is the whole question. A science of history, if it is more than a misleading name, implies that the relation between cause and effect holds in human things as completely as in all others; that the origin of human actions is not to be looked for in mysterious properties of the mind, but in influences which are palpable and ponderable. When natural causes are liable to be set aside and neutralized by what is called volition, the word science is out of place. If it is free to man to choose what he will do or not do, there is no adequate science of him. If there is a science of him, there is no free choice, and the praise or blame with which we regard one another are impertinent and out of place.

I am trespassing upon these ethical grounds because, unless I do, the subject cannot be made intelligible. Mankind are but an aggregate of individuals; history is but the record of individual action: and what is true of the part is true of the whole.

We feel keenly about such things, and, when the logic becomes perplexing, we are apt to grow rhetorical about them. But rhetoric is only misleading. Whatever the truth may be, it is best that we should know it; and for truth of any kind we should keep our heads and hearts as cool as we can.

I will say at once, that, if we had the whole case before us; if we were taken, like Leibnitz' Tarquin, into the council-chamber of Nature, and were shown what we really were, where we came from, and where we were going, however unpleasant it might be for some of us to find ourselves, like Tarquin, made into villains, from the subtle necessities of "the best of all possible worlds,"—nevertheless, some such theory as Mr. Buckle's might possibly turn out to be true. Likely enough, there is some great "equation of the universe" where the value of the unknown quantities can be determined. But we must treat things in relation to our own powers and positions, and the question is, whether the sweep of those vast curves can be measured by the intellect of creatures of a day like ourselves.

The "Faust" of Goethe, tired of the barren round of earthly knowledge, calls magic to his aid. He desires first, to see the spirit of the Macrocosmos, but his heart fails him before he ventures that tremendous experiment, and he summons before him, instead, the spirit of his own race. There he feels himself at home. The stream of life and the storm of action, the ever-lasting ocean of existence, the web and the woof, and the roaring loom of Time,—he gazes upon them all, and in passionate exultation claims fellowship with the awful thing before him. But the majestic vision fades, and a voice comes to him,—"Thou art fellow with the spirits which thy mind can grasp, not with me."

Had Mr. Buckle tried to follow his principle into detail it might have fared no better with him than with Faust.

What are the conditions of a science, and when may any subject be said to enter the scientific stage? I suppose when the facts begin to resolve themselves into groups; when phenomena are no longer isolated experiences but appear in connection and order; when, after certain antecedents, certain consequences are uniformly seen to follow; when facts enough have been collected to furnish a basis for conjectural explanation; and when conjectures have so far ceased to be utterly vague that it is possible in some degree to foresee the future by the help of them.

Till a subject has advanced as far as this, to speak of a science of it is an abuse of language. It is not enough to say that there must be a science of human things because there is a science of all other things. This is like saying the planets must be inhabited because the only planet of which we have any experience is inhabited. It may or may not be true, but it is not a practical question; it does not affect the practical treatment of the matter in hand.

Let us look at the history of astronomy.

So long as sun, moon, and planets were supposed to be gods or angels; so long as the sword of Orion was not a metaphor, but a fact; and the groups of stars which inlaid the floor of heaven were the glittering trophies of the loves and wars of the Pantheon,—so long there was no science of astronomy. There was fancy, imagination, poetry, perhaps reverence, but no science. As soon, however, as it was observed that the stars retained their relative places; that the times of their rising and setting varied with the seasons; that sun, moon, and planets moved along them in a plane, and the belt of the Zodiac was marked out and divided,—then a new order of things began. Traces of the earlier stage remained in the names of the signs and constellations, just as the Scandinavian mythology survives now in the names of the days of the week; but, for all that, the understanding was now at work on the thing; science had begun, and the first triumph of it was the power of foretelling the future. Eclipses were perceived to recur in cycles of nineteen years, and philosophers were able to say when an eclipse was to be looked for. The periods of the planets could be calculated with moderate certainty by them. The very first result of the science, in its most imperfect stage, was a power of foresight; and this was possible before any one true astronomical law had been discovered.

We should not therefore question the possibility of a science of history because the explanations of its phenomena were rudimentary or imperfect: that they might be, and long continue to be, and yet enough might be done to show that there was such a thing, and that it was not entirely without use. But how was it that in those rude days, with small knowledge of mathematics, and with no better instruments than flat walls and dialplates, those first astronomers made progress so considerable? Because, I suppose, the phenomena which they were observing recurred, for the most part, within moderate intervals; so that they could collect large experience within the compass of their natural lives; because days and months and years were measurable periods, and within them the more simple phenomena perpetually repeated themselves. But how would it have been if, instead of turning on its axis once in twenty-four hours, the earth had taken a year about it; if the year had been nearly four hundred years; if man's life had been no longer than it is, and for the initial steps of astronomy there had been nothing to depend upon except observations recorded in history? How many ages would have passed, had this been our condition, before it would have occurred to any one, that, in what they saw night after night, there was any kind of order at all?

We can see to some extent how it would have been, by the present state of those parts of the science which in fact depend on remote recorded observations. The movements of the comets are still extremely uncertain. The times of their return can be calculated only with the greatest vagueness.

And yet such a hypothesis as I have suggested would but inadequately express the position in which we are in fact placed toward history. There the phenomena never repeat themselves. There we are dependent wholly on the record of things said to have happened once, but which never happen or can happen a second time. There no experiment is possible; we can watch for no recurring fact to test the worth of our conjectures. It has been suggested fancifully, that, if we consider the universe to be infinite, time is the same as eternity, and the past is perpetually present. Light takes nine years to come to us from Sirius: those rays which we may see tonight, when we leave this place, left Sirius nine years ago; and could the inhabitants of Sirius see the earth at this moment, they would see the English army in the trenches before Sebastopol, Florence Nightingale watching at Scutari over the wounded at Enkermann, and the peace of England undisturbed by "Essays and Reviews."

As the stars recede into distance, so time recedes with them; and there may be, and probably are, stars from which Noah might be seen stepping into the ark, Eve listening to the temptation of the serpent, or that older race, eating the oysters and leaving the shell-heaps behind them, when the Baltic was an open sea.

Could we but compare notes, something might be done: but of this there is no present hope, and without it there will be no science of history. Eclipses, recorded in ancient books, can be verified by calculations, and lost dates can be recovered by them;

and we can foresee, by the laws which they follow, when there will be eclipses again. Will a time ever be when the lost secret of the foundation of Rome can be recovered by historic laws? If not, where is our science? It may be said that this is a particular fact, that we can deal satisfactorily with general phenomena affecting eras and cycles. Well, then, let us take some general phenomenon: Mahometanism, for instance, or Buddhism. Those are large enough. Can you imagine a science which would have* *foretold* such movements as those? The state of things out of which they rose is obscure; but, suppose it not obscure, can you conceive that, with any amount of historical insight into the old Oriental beliefs, you could have seen that they were about to transform themselves into those particular forms and no other?

It is not enough to say, that, after the fact, you can understand partially how Mahometanism came to be. All historians worth the name have told us something about that. But when we talk of science, we mean something with more ambitious pretences, we mean something which can foresee as well as explain; and, thus looked at, to state the problem is to show its absurdity. As little could the wisest man have foreseen this mighty revolution, as thirty years ago such a thing as Mormonism could have been anticipated in America; as little as it could have been foreseen that table-turning and spirit-rapping would have been an

---

* It is objected that geology is a science; yet that geology cannot foretell the future changes of the earth's surface. Geology is not a century old, and its periods are measured by millions of years. Yet, if geology cannot foretell future facts, it enabled Sir Roderick Murchison to foretell the discovery of Australian gold.

outcome of the scientific culture of England in the nineteenth century.

The greatest of Roman thinkers, gazing mournfully at the seething mass of moral putrefaction round him, detected and deigned to notice among its elements a certain detestable super-stition, so he called it, rising up amidst the offscouring of the Jews, which was named Christianity. Could Tacitus have looked forward nine centuries to the Rome of Gregory VII, could he have beheld the representative of the majesty of the Caesars hold-ing the stirrup of the Pontiff of that vile and execrated sect, the spectacle would scarcely have appeared to him the fulfilment of a national expectation, or an intelligible result of the causes in operation round him. Tacitus, indeed, was born before the science of history; but would M. Comte have seen any more clearly?

Nor is the case much better if we are less hard upon our phi-losophy; if we content ourselves with the past, and require only a scientific explanation of that. First, for the facts themselves. They come to us through the minds of those who recorded them, neither machines nor angels, but fallible creatures, with human passions and prejudices. Tacitus and Thucydides were perhaps the ablest men who ever gave themselves to writing history; the ablest, and also the most incapable of conscious falsehood. Yet even now, after all these centuries, the truth of what they relate is called in question. Good reasons can be given to show that neither of them can be confidently trusted. If we doubt with these, whom are we to believe?

Or, again, let the facts be granted. To revert to my simile of the box of letters, you have but to select such facts as suit you,

you have but to leave alone those which do not suit you, and let your theory of history be what it will, you can find no difficulty in providing facts to prove it. You may have your Hegel's philosophy of history, or you may have your Schlegel's philosophy of history; you may prove from history that the world is governed in detail by a special Providence; you may prove that there is no sign of any moral agent in the universe, except man; you may believe, if you like it, in the old theory of the wisdom of antiquity; you may speak, as was the fashion in the fifteenth century, of "our fathers, who had more wit and wisdom than we;" or you may talk of "our barbarian ancestors," and describe their wars as the scuffling of kites and crows.

You may maintain that the evolution of humanity has been an unbroken progress toward perfection; you may maintain that there has been no progress at all, and that man remains the same poor creature that he ever was; or, lastly, you may say, with the author of the "Contract Social," that men were purest and best in primeval simplicity,—

"When wild in woods the noble savage ran."

In all or any of these views, history will stand your friend. History, in its passive irony, will make no objection. Like Jarno, in Goethe's novel, it will not condescend to argue with you, and will provide you with abundant illustrations of any thing which you may wish to believe.

"What is history," said Napoleon, "but a fiction agreed upon?" "My friend," said Faust to the student, who was growing enthusiastic about the spirit of past ages,—"my friend, the times which are gone are a book with seven seals; and what you call the spirit of past ages is but the spirit of this or that worthy gentleman in whose mind those ages are reflected." One lesson, and only one, history may be said to repeat with distinctness: that the world is built somehow on moral foundations; that, in the long run, it is ill with the wicked. But this is no science; it is no more than the old doctrine taught long ago by the Hebrew prophets. The theories of M. Comte and his disciples advance us, after all, not a step beyond the trodden and familiar ground. If men are not entirely animals, they are at least half animals, and are subject in this aspect of them to the conditions of animals. So far as those parts of man's doings are concerned, which neither have, nor need have, anything moral about them, so far the laws of him are calculable. There are laws for his digestion, and laws of the means by which his digestive organs are supplied with matter. But pass beyond them, and where are we? In a world where it would be as easy to calculate men's actions by laws like those of positive philosophy as to measure the orbit of Neptune with a foot-rule, or weigh Sirius in a grocer's sale.

And it is not difficult to see why this should be. The first principle, on which the theory of a science of history can be plausibly argued, is that all actions whatsoever arise from self-interest. It may be enlightened self-interest, it may be unenlightened; but it is assumed as an axiom, that every man, in whatever he does, is aiming at something which he considers will promote his happiness. His conduct is not determined by his will; it is determined by the object of his desire. Adam Smith, in laying the foundations of political economy, expressly eliminates every other motive. He does not say that men never act on other motives; still less, that they never ought to act on other motives. He asserts merely that, as far as the arts of production are concerned, and of buying and selling, the action of self-interest may be counted upon as uniform. What Adam Smith says of political economy, Mr. Buckle would extend over the whole circle of human activity.

Now, that which especially distinguishes a high order of man from a low order of man—that which constitutes human goodness, human greatness, human nobleness—is surely not the degree of enlightenment with which men pursue their own advantage: but it is self-forgetfulness, it is self-sacrifice; it is the disregard of personal pleasure, personal indulgence, personal advantages remote or present, because some other line of conduct is more right.

We are sometimes told that this is but another way of expressing the same thing; that, when a man prefers doing what is right, it is only because to do right gives him a higher satisfaction. It appears to me, on the contrary, to be a difference in the very heart and nature of things. The martyr goes to the stake, the patriot to the scaffold, not with a view to any future reward to themselves, but because it is a glory to fling away their lives for truth and freedom. And so through all phases of existence, to the smallest details of common life, the beautiful character is the unselfish character. Those whom we most love and admire are those to whom the thought of self seems never to occur; who do simply and with no ulterior aim—with no thought whether it will be pleasant to themselves or unpleasant—that which is good and right and generous.

Is this still selfishness, only more enlightened? I do not think so. The essence of true nobility is neglect of self. Let the thought of self pass in, and the beauty of a great action is gone, like a bloom from a soiled flower. Surely it is a paradox to speak of the self-interest of a martyr who dies for a cause, the triumph of which he will never enjoy; and the greatest of that great company in all ages would have done what they did, had their personal prospects closed with the grave. Nay, there have been those so zealous for some glorious principle as to wish themselves blotted out of the book of Heaven if the cause of Heaven could succeed.

And out of this mysterious quality, whatever it be, arise the higher relations of human life, the higher modes of human obligation. Kant, the philosopher, used to say that there were two things which overwhelmed him with awe as he thought of them. One was the star-sown deep of space, without limit and without end; the other was, right and wrong. Right, the sacrifice of self to good; wrong, the sacrifice of good to self,—not graduated objects of desire, to which we are determined by the degrees of our knowledge, but wide asunder as pole and pole, as light and darkness: one the object of infinite love; the other, the object of infinite detestation and scorn. It is in this marvelous power in men to do wrong (it is an old story, but none the less true for that),—it is in this power to do wrong—wrong or right, as it lies somehow with ourselves to choose,—that the impossibility stands of forming scientific calculations of what men will do before the fact, or scientific explanations of what they have done after the fact. If men were consistently selfish, you might analyze their motives; if they were consistently noble, they would express in their conduct the laws of the highest perfection. But so long as two natures are mixed together, and the strange creature which results from the combination is now under one influence and now under another, so long you will make nothing of him except from the old-fashioned moral—or, if you please, imaginative—point of view.

Even the laws of political economy itself cease to guide us when they touch moral government. So long as labor is a chattel to be bought and sold, so long, like other commodities, it follows the condition of supply and demand. But if, for his misfortune, an employer considers that he stands in human relations toward his workmen; if he believes, rightly or wrongly, that he is responsible for them; that in return for their labor he is bound to see that their children are decently taught, and they and their families decently fed and clothed and lodged; that he ought to care for them in sickness and in old age,—then political economy will no longer direct him, and the relations between himself and his dependents will have to be arranged on quite other principles. So long as he considers only his own material profit, so long supply and demand will settle every difficulty; but the introduction of a new factor spoils the equation.

And it is precisely in this debatable ground of low motives and noble emotions; in the struggle, ever failing yet ever renewed, to carry truth and justice into the administration of human society; in the establishment of states and in the overthrow of tyrannies; in the rise and fall of creeds; in the world of ideas; in the character

and deeds of the great actors in the drama of life, where good
and evil fight out their everlasting battle, now ranged in opposite
camps, now and more often in the heart, both of them, of each
living man,—that the true human interest of history resides. The
progress of industries, the growth of material and mechanical
civilization, are interesting; but they are not the most interesting.
They have their reward in the increase of material comforts; but,
unless we are mistaken about our nature, they do not highly concern us after all. Once more: not only is there in men this baffling
duality of principle, but there is something else in us which still
more defies scientific analysis.

Mr. Buckle would deliver himself from the eccentricities of this
and that individual by a doctrine of averages. Though he cannot
tell whether A, B, or C will cut his throat, he may assure himself
that one man in every fifty thousand, or thereabout (I forget the
exact proportion), will cut his throat, and with this he consoles
himself. No doubt it is a comforting discovery. Unfortunately, the
average of one generation need not be the average of the next.
We may be converted by the Japanese, for all that we know, and
the Japanese methods of taking leave of life may become fashionable among us. Nay, did not Novalis suggest that the whole race
of men would at last become so disgusted with their impotence,
that they would extinguish themselves by a simultaneous act of
suicide, and make room for a better order of beings? Anyhow, the
fountain out of which the race is flowing perpetually changes;
no two generations are alike. Whether there is a change in the
organization itself we cannot tell; but this is certain,—that, as the
planet varies with the atmosphere which surrounds it, so each new

generation varies from the last, because it inhales as its atmosphere the accumulated experience and knowledge of the whole past of the world. These things form the spiritual air which we breathe as we grow; and, in the infinite multiplicity of elements of which that air is now composed, it is forever a matter of conjecture what the minds will be like which expand under its influence.

From the England of Fielding and Richardson to the England of Miss Austen, from the England of Miss Austen to the England of railways and free trade, how vast the change! Yet perhaps Sir Charles Grandison would not seem so strange to us now as one of ourselves will seem to our great-grandchildren. The world moves faster and faster; and the difference will probably be considerably greater.

The tempter of each new generation is a continual surprise. The Fates delight to contradict our most confident expectations. Gibbon believed that the era of conquerors was at an end. Had he lived out the full life of man, he would have seen Europe at the feet of Napoleon. But a few years ago we believed the world had grown too civilized for war, and the Crystal Palace in Hyde Park was to be the inauguration of a new era. Battles bloody as Napoleon's are now the familiar tale of every day; and the arts which have made greatest progress are the arts of destruction. What next? We may strain our eyes into the future which lies beyond this waning century; but never was conjecture more at fault. It is blank darkness, which even the imagination fails to people.

What, then, is the use of history, and what are its lessons? If it can tell us little of the past, and nothing of the future, why waste our time over so barren a study?

First, it is a voice forever sounding across the centuries the laws of right and wrong. Opinions alter, manners change, creeds rise and fall, but the moral law is written on the tablets of eternity. For every false word or unrighteous deed, for cruelty and oppression, for lust or vanity, the price has to be paid at last, not always by the chief offenders, but paid by someone. Justice and truth alone endure and live. Injustice and falsehood may be long-lived, but doomsday comes at last to them, in French revolutions and other terrible ways.

That is one lesson of history. Another is, that we should draw no horoscope; that we should expect little, for what we expect will not come to pass. Revolutions, reformations,—those vast movements into which heroes and saints have flung themselves, in the belief that they were the dawn of the millennium,—have not borne the fruit which they looked for. Millenniums are still far away. These great convulsions leave the world changed,—perhaps improved, but not improved as the actors in them hoped it would be. Luther would have gone to work with less heart, could he have foreseen the Thirty Years' War, and in the distance the theology of Tubingen. Washington might have hesitated to draw the sword against England, could he have seen the country which he made as we see it now.*

The most reasonable anticipations fail us, antecedents the most apposite mislead us, because the conditions of human problems never repeat themselves. Some new feature alters every thing,— some element which we detect only in its after-operation. But this,

* February 1864.

41

it may be said, is but a meagre outcome. Can the long records of humanity, with all its joys and sorrows, its sufferings and its conquests, teach us more than this? Let us approach the subject from another side.

If you were asked to point out the special features in which Shakespeare's plays are so transcendently excellent, you would mention perhaps, among others, this—that his stories are not put together, and his characters are not conceived, to illustrate any particular law or principle. They teach many lessons, but not any one prominent above another; and when we have drawn from them all the direct instruction which they contain, there remains still something unresolved,—something which the artist gives, and which the philosopher cannot give.

It is in this characteristic that we are accustomed to say Shakespeare's supreme *truth* lies. He represents real life. His drama teaches as life teaches,—neither less nor more. He builds his fabrics, as Nature does, on right and wrong; but he does not struggle to make Nature more systematic than she is. In the subtle interflow of good and evil; in the unmerited sufferings of innocence; in the disproportion of penalties to desert; in the seeming blindness with which justice, in attempting to assert itself, overwhelms innocent and guilty in a common ruin,—Shakespeare is true to real experience. The mystery of life he leaves as he finds it; and, in his most tremendous positions, he is addressing rather the intellectual emotions than the understanding,—knowing well that the understanding in such things is at fault, and the sage as ignorant as the child.

Only the highest order of genius can represent Nature thus. An inferior artist produces either something entirely immoral, where

good and evil are names, and nobility of disposition is supposed
to show itself in the absolute disregard of them, or else, if he is a
better kind of man, he will force on Nature a didactic purpose;
he composes what are called moral tales, which may edify the
conscience, but only mislead the intellect.

The finest work of this kind produced in modern times is
Lessing's play of "Nathan the Wise." The object of it is to teach
religious toleration. The doctrine is admirable, the mode in which
it is enforced is interesting; but it has the fatal fault that it is not
true. Nature does not teach religious toleration by any such direct
method; and the result is—no one knew it better than Lessing
himself—that the play is not poetry, but only splendid manufac-
ture. Shakespeare is eternal; Lessing's "Nathan" will pass away
with the mode of thought which gave it birth. One is based on
fact; the other seems at first sight to contain the most immediate
instruction; but it is not really so.

Cibber and others, as you know, wanted to alter Shakespeare.
The French King, in "Lear," was to be got rid of; Cordelia was to
marry Edgar, and Lear himself was to be rewarded for his sufferings by a golden old age. They could not bear that Hamlet
should suffer for the sins of Claudius. The wicked king was to die,
and the wicked mother; and Hamlet and Ophelia were to make a
match of it, and live happily ever after. A common novelist would
have arranged it thus; and you would have had your comfortable
moral that wickedness was fitly punished, and virtue had its due
reward, and all would have been well. But Shakespeare would
not have it so. Shakespeare knew that crime was not so simple in
its consequences, or Providence so paternal. He was contented to

take the truth from life; and the effect upon the mind of the most correct theory of what life ought to be, compared to the effect of the life itself, is infinitesimal in comparison.

Again, let us compare the popular historical treatment of remarkable incidents with Shakespeare's treatment of them. Look at "Macbeth." You may derive abundant instruction from it,—instruction of many kinds. There is a moral lesson of profound interest in the steps by which a noble nature glides to perdition. In more modern fashion you may speculate, if you like, on the political conditions represented there, and the temptation presented in absolute monarchies to unscrupulous ambition; you may say, like Doctor Slop, these things could not have happened under a constitutional government: or, again, you may take up your parable against superstition; you may dilate on the frightful consequences of a belief in witches, and reflect on the superior advantages of an age of schools and newspapers. If the bare facts of the story had come down to us from a chronicler, and an ordinary writer of the nineteenth century had undertaken to relate them, his account, we may depend upon it, would have been put together upon one or other of these principles. Yet, by the side of that unfolding of the secrets of the prison-house of the soul, what lean and shriveled anatomies the best of such descriptions would seem! Shakespeare himself, I suppose, could not have given us a theory of what he meant; he gave us the thing itself, on which we might make whatever theories we pleased. Or, again, look at Homer.

The "Iliad" is from two to three thousand years older than "Macbeth," and yet it is as fresh as if it had been written yesterday. We have there no lessons save in the emotions which rise in us as we read. Homer had no philosophy; he never struggles to press upon us his views about this or that; you can scarcely tell, indeed, whether his sympathies are Greek or Trojan; but he represents to us faithfully the men and women among whom he lived. He sang the tale of Troy, he touched his lyre, he drained the golden beaker in the halls of men like those on whom he was conferring immortality. And thus, although no Agamemnon, king of men, ever led a Grecian fleet to Ilium; though no Priam sought the midnight tent of Achilles; though Ulysses and Diomede and Nestor were but names, and Helen but a dream, yet, through Homer's power of representing men and women, those old Greeks will still stand out from amidst the darkness of the ancient world with a sharpness of outline which belongs to no period of history except the most recent. For the mere hard purposes of history, the "Iliad" and "Odyssey" are the most effective books which ever were written. We see the hall of Menelaus, we see the garden of Alcinus, we see Nausicaa among her maidens on the shore, we see the mellow monarch sitting with ivory scepter in the market-place dealing out genial justice. Or, again, when the wild mood is on, we can hear the crash of the spears, the rattle of the armor as the heroes fall, and the plunging of the horses among the slain. Could we enter the palace of the old Ionian lord, we know what we should see there; we know the words in which he would address us. We could meet Hector as a friend. If we could choose a companion to spend an evening with over a fireside, it would be the man of many counsels, the husband of Penelope.

I am not going into the vexed question whether history or poetry is the more true. It has been sometimes said that poetry is the more true, because it can make things more like what our moral sense would prefer they should be. We hear of poetic justice and the like, as if nature and fact were not just enough.

I entirely dissent from that view. So far as poetry attempts to improve on truth in that way, so far it abandons truth, and is false to itself. Even literal facts, exactly as they were, a great poet will prefer whenever he can get them. Shakespeare in the historical plays is studious, wherever possible, to give the very words which he finds to have been used; and it shows how wisely he was guided in this, that those magnificent speeches of Wolsey are taken exactly, with no more change than the metre makes necessary, from Cavendish's Life. Marlborough read Shakespeare for English history, and read nothing else. The poet only is not bound, when it is inconvenient, to what may be called the accidents of facts. It was enough for Shakespeare to know that Prince Hal in his youth had lived among loose companions, and the tavern in Eastcheap came in to fill out his picture; although Mrs. Quickly and Falstaff and Poins and Bardolph were more likely to have been fallen in with by Shakespeare himself at the Mermaid, than to have been comrades of the true Prince Henry. It was enough for Shakespeare to draw real men, and the situation, whatever it might be, would sit easy on them. In this sense only it is that poetry is truer than history,—that it can make a picture more complete. It may take liberties with time and space, and give the action distinctness by throwing it into more manageable compass. But it may not alter the real conditions of things, or represent life as other than it is. The greatness of the poet depends on his being true to Nature, without insisting that Nature shall theorize with him, without making her more just, more philo-sophical, more moral than reality; and, in difficult matters, leaving much to reflection which cannot be explained.

And if this be true of poetry—if Homer and Shakespeare are what they are from the absence of every thing didactic about them—may we not thus learn something of what history should be, and in what sense it should aspire to teach?

If poetry must not theorize, much less should the historian theorize, whose obligations to be true to fact are even greater than the poet's. If the drama is grandest when the action is least explicable by laws, because then it best resembles life, then history will be grandest also under the same conditions. "Macbeth," were it literally true, would be perfect history; and so far as the historian can approach to that kind of model, so far as he can let his story tell itself in the deeds and words of those who act it out, so far is he most successful. His work is no longer the vapor of his own brain, which a breath will scatter; it is the thing itself, which will have interest for all time. A thousand theories may be formed about it,—spiritual theories, pantheistic theories, cause and effect theories—but each age will have its own philosophy of history, and all these in turn will fail and die. Hegel falls out of date, Schlegel falls out of date, and Comte in good time will fall out of date; the thought about the thing must change as we change; but the thing itself can never change; and a history is durable or perishable as it contains more or less of the writer's own speculations. The splendid intellect of Gibbon for the most part kept him true to the right course in this; yet the philosophical chapters for which he has been most admired or censured may hereafter be thought the least interesting of his work. The time has been when they would not have been comprehended; the time may come when they will seem commonplace.

It may be said that, in requiring history to be written like a drama, we require an impossibility.

For history to be written with the complete form of a drama, doubtless is impossible; but there are periods, and these the periods, for the most part, of greatest interest to mankind, the history of which may be so written that the actors shall reveal their characters in their own words; where mind can be seen matched against mind, and the great passions of the epoch not simply be described as existing, but be exhibited at their white heat in the souls and hearts possessed by them. There are all the elements of drama—drama of the highest order—where the huge forces of the times are as the Grecian destiny, and the power of the man is seen either stemming the stream till it overwhelms him, or ruling while he seems to yield to it.

It is Nature's drama,—not Shakespeare's, but a drama none the less.

So at least it seems to me. Wherever possible, let us not be told about this man or that. Let us hear the man himself speak, let us see him act, and let us be left to form our own opinions about him. The historian, we are told, must not leave his readers to themselves. He must not only lay the facts before him; he must tell them what he himself thinks about those facts. In my opinion, this is precisely what he ought not to do. Bishop Butler says somewhere, that the best book which could be written would be a book consisting only of premises, from which the readers should draw conclusions for themselves. The highest poetry is the very thing which Butler requires, and the highest history ought to be. We should no more ask for a theory of this or that period of history, than we should ask for a theory of "Macbeth" or "Hamlet." Philosophies of history, sciences of history,—all these there will continue to be: the fashions of them will change, as our habits of thought will change; each new philosopher will find his chief employment in showing that before him no one understood anything; but the drama of history is imperishable, and the lessons of it will be like what we learn from Homer or Shakespeare,— lessons for which we have no words.

The address of history is less to the understanding than to the higher emotions. We learn in it to sympathize with what is great and good; we learn to hate what is base. In the anomalies of fortune we feel the mystery of our mortal existence; and in the companionship of the illustrious natures who have shaped the fortunes of the world, we escape from the littlenesses which cling to the round of common life, and our minds are turned in a higher and nobler key.

For the rest, and for those large questions which I touched in connection with Mr. Buckle, we live in times of disintegration, and none can tell what will be after us. What opinions, what convictions, the infant of today will find prevailing on the earth, if he and it live out together to the middle of another century, only a very bold man would undertake to conjecture. "The time will come," said Lichtenberg, in scorn at the materializing tendencies of modern thought,—"the time will come when the belief in God will be as the tales with which old women frighten children; when the world will be a machine, the ether a gas, and God will be a force." Mankind, if they last long enough on the earth, may develop strange things out of themselves; and the growth of what is called the Positive Philosophy is a curious commentary on Lichtenberg's prophecy. But whether the end be seventy years hence, or seven hundred,—be the close of the mortal history of humanity as far distant in the future as its shadowy beginnings seem now to lie behind us,—this only we may foretell with confidence,—that the riddle of man's nature will remain unsolved. There will be that in him yet which physical laws will fail to explain,—that something, whatever it be, in himself and in the world, which science cannot fathom, and which suggests the unknown possibilities of his dread,—be the close of the mortal history of origin and his destiny. There will remain yet

> Those obstinate questionings
> Of sense and outward things;
> Falling from us, vanishing;
> Blank misgivings of a creature
> Moving about in worlds not realized;
> High instincts, before which our moral nature
> Doth tremble like a guilty thing surprised.

There will remain

> Those first affections.
> Those shadowy recollections,
> Which, be they what they may,

Are yet the fountain-light of all our day,—
Are yet the master-light of all our seeing,—
Uphold us, cherish, and have power to make
Our noisy years seem moments in the being
Of the Eternal Silence.

2

Frederic William Maitland

Extract from "The Body Politic," in Frederic William Maitland, A Historical Sketch of Liberty and Equality *(Indianapolis: Liberty Fund, c. 2000)*

Frederic William Maitland (1850–1906)—a preeminent English legal historian and professor at the University of Cambridge, published often in his career—was perhaps best known for his book (with Frederick Pollock) *History of English Law before the Time of Edward I* (Cambridge: Cambridge University Press, 1895).

The history of progress was a grand theme of 19th-century liberal historiography. In this selection, Maitland explains that the discipline of history had been long in the shadow of the natural sciences, which led the way in progress. Maitland was skeptical, however, of history's following the natural sciences too closely. He argued that historical understanding is indeed like science in that it involves generalizing from particulars, but, he warned, overgeneralizations in historical thought could lead historians in the wrong directions.

It is popular in our current day to say that one account of the past has as much truth as another, or that all interpretations are valid, so long as they correspond to the sources. But Maitland believed that in his century real progress had been made in historical writing, just as there had been progress in civilization. Indeed, the two things were linked, he believed. By "progress," he meant greater historical understanding, not just more viewpoints or interpretations. In another place, Maitland wrote, "History is lengthening and widening and deepening," by which he was referring, respectively, to chronological distance, geographical area, and depth of understanding particular episodes.[11] Greater understanding of our history, he thought, helped us better understand current society, while progress in society meant more time for collecting, studying, and writing about records of the past.

In this historiography of progress, Maitland was confident that historical accounts were getting better. This reflected the liberal belief that the world was knowable, that facts could be right or wrong, that hypotheses were generally testable, and that history could be known, not perfectly, but to some comfortable level of accuracy.

I hope that you will forgive me for choosing a subject which lies very near to that which Sidgwick[12] discussed at our last meeting. I had thought of it before I heard his paper, and though to my great delight he said some things which I had long wanted to hear said, his object was not quite that which I have in view. He spoke of the means, the very inadequate means, that we have of foretelling the future of bodies politic. I wish to speak of the means, the very inadequate means as some people seem to think them, that we have of filling up the gaps that at present exist in our knowledge of the past history of these political organisms. The two processes, that of predicting the future and that of reconstructing the past are essentially similar, both are processes of inference and generalization. Of course when the historian tells us a single fact, for example, gives the date of a battle, inference and generalization are already at work. He has got this supposed fact from (let us say) some chronicler or some tombstone, and he has come to the conclusion that about such a matter this chronicler's or this tombstone's word may be trusted. But when he goes on to represent as usual or rare some habit or custom or mode of thought or of conduct he is very obviously drawing general conclusions from particular instances, and is, if I may so say, predicting the past.

Sidgwick drew a distinction between empirical and scientific predictions. I will apply this distinction to postdictions. I did not gather from him that he meant to draw a hard and accurate line between the empirical and the scientific. Certainly for my purpose I could not draw it with a firm hand. But still though we have before us a matter of degree the distinction is real and important. The historian of the old-fashioned type who does not talk about scientific method or law of nature is drawing inferences and making generalizations, but these do not as a general rule go far outside the country and the time that he is studying. We may compare him to the chancellor of the exchequer who is estimating the produce of next year's taxes. Sometimes the two procedures are very strictly comparable, as when the historian who thinks that he has examined enough accounts ventures on a general statement about the revenue of Henry II or George III. Now in a certain sense it is true that the method employed in these cases ought to be a scientific method, that is to say, it ought to be the method best adapted to the purpose in hand. Still it is only scientific in the sense in which the method of a Sherlock Holmes would be scientific. The end of it all is a story, a causally connected story tested and proved at every point. Also it must I think be allowed that history of this old-fashioned kind is successfully standing one of those tests of a science that Sidgwick mentioned last time. No historian dreams of beginning the work all over again. Even if he has a taste for paradox and a quarrelsome temper he accepts what is after all the great bulk of his predecessor's results. Men are disputing now whether the forged decretals were concocted in the east or in the west of France, whether they shall be dated a little after or before 850; the man who attributed them to the popes whose names they bear would be in much the same position as that which is assigned to the man who says that the world is flat; he would be taking up arms against an organized body of knowledge. I should doubt whether books about the most rapidly advancing of the physical sciences become antiquated more rapidly than those books about history which do not belong to the very first class.

Now to this progress I do not think that we can set any narrow limits. During the present century there has been a rapid acceleration. Tracts which were dark are now fairly well lit and neglected and remote pieces of the story are being systematically explored. Of course, I am including under the name of history what some people call archaeology; for to my mind an archaeology that is not history is somewhat less than nothing, and a Special Board for History and Archaeology is like a Special Board for Mathematics and the Rule of Three. Whether we fix our eyes on the east or the west, the ancient or modern times, we see that new truths are being brought in and secured, and this in that gradual fashion in which a healthy body of knowledge grows, the new truth generally turning out to be but a quarter-truth and yet one which must modify the whole tale.

But this process, rapid as it seems to me (for I am comparing it with the growth of historical knowledge in the last century), seems far too slow to some who compare it with the exploits of the natural sciences. They want to have a science of history comparable to some of those sciences, and, for choice, to biology. A desire of this kind there has been for a long time past; in our own day it has become very prominent and there are many writers and readers who seem to think that we are within a measurable distance of a sociology or an inductive political science which shall take no shame when set beside the older sciences. Having a science of the body natural we are at last to have a similar science of the body politic. The comparison of a state or nation to a living body is of course ancient enough. The Herbert Spencer of the twelfth century worked it out with grotesque medieval detail; the John of Salisbury of our own century teaches us that the comparison is just about to become strictly scientific since we have at last an evolutionary biology. Now the suggestions derived from this comparison have been of inestimable value to mankind at large and to historians in particular. I wish once for all to make a very large admission about this matter. But for the comparison, the vocabulary of the historian and of the political theorist would be exceedingly meagre, and I need not say that a rich, flexible, delicate vocabulary is necessary if there is to be accurate thinking and precise description. For the presentation—nay, for the perception—of unfamiliar truth we have need of all the metaphors that we can command, and any source of new and apt metaphors is a source of new knowledge. The language of any and every science must be in the eyes of the etymologist a mass of metaphors and of very mixed metaphors. I am also very far from denying that popularization of its results, will supply the historian and the political theorist with new thoughts, and with new phrases which will make old thought truer. I can conceive that a century hence political events will be currently described in a language borrowed from biology, or, for this also is possible, from some science of which no one has yet laid the first stone. But I think that at present the man studying history will do well not to hand himself over body and soul to the professor of any science; that if in one sentence he has spoken of political germs or embryos or organisms, he will not be ashamed to speak in the next of political machinery and checks and balances. He may write of the decay, death, dissolution of the Roman empire, but at times he will not contemn the classical decline and fall. . . .

Life is short; history is the longest of all the arts; a minute division of labour is necessary. No one man will ever write of even a short period of that full history which should be written if we are to see in all completeness the play of those many forces which shape the life of man, even of man regarded as a political animal.

And therefore I think it is that some of the best because the truest history books are those which are professedly fragmentary, those which by their every page impress upon the reader that he has only got before him a small part of the whole tale. That is the reason why, though history may be an art, it is falling out of the list of fine arts and will not be restored thereto for a long time to come. It must aim at producing not aesthetic satisfaction but intellectual hunger.

All this by the way. The faculty, so it seems to me, of the would-be scientific procedure of our sociologists lies in the too frequent attempt to obtain a set of "laws" by the study of only one class of phenomena, the attempt for example encouraged by this University to fashion an inductive political science. Too often it seems to be thought that you can detach one kind of social phenomena from all other kinds and obtain by induction a law for the phenomena of that class. For example, it seems to be assumed that *the* history of *the* family can be written and that it will come out in some such form as this: We start with promiscuity, the next stage is "mother right," the next "father right," and so forth. Or again take the history of property—land is owned first by the tribe or horde, then by the house-community, then by the village-community, then by the individual.

Now I will not utterly deny the possibility of some such science of the very early stages in human progress. I know too little about the materials to do that. But even in this region I think it plain that our scientific people have been far too hasty with their laws. When this evidence about barbarians gets into the hands of men who have been trained in a severe school of history and who have been taught by experience to look upon all the social phenomena as interdependent it begins to prove far less than it used to prove. Each case begins to look very unique and a law which deduces that "mother right" cannot come after "father right," or that "father right" cannot come after "mother right," or which would establish any other similar sequence of "states" begins to look exceedingly improbable. Our cases, all told, are not many and very rarely indeed have we any direct evidence of the passage of a barbarous nation from one state to another. My own belief is that by and by anthropology will have the choice between being history and being nothing.

3

William Torrey Harris

Preface to B. A. Hinsdale, How to Study and
Teach History, with Particular Reference to
the History of the United States *(New York:
D. Appleton and Company, 1912 [originally
published 1893])*

A New Englander by birth and education, William Torrey Harris (1835–1909) had worked in the St. Louis public schools—first as an elementary school teacher and eventually as superintendent—before becoming the U.S. commissioner of education from 1889 to 1906. Previously, he had also taught philosophy at a small college in St. Louis. He was particularly interested in the views on freedom, reason, and self-determination that he found in the philosophy of Georg Wilhelm Friedrich Hegel and other idealist German philosophers.

Harris can be described as a supporter of public schools and an egalitarian who believed education served to link individuals to their societies, to promote Christian moral improvement, and to perpetuate the good of Western civilization and the accumulated wisdom of the past. These views led him to support compulsory education for all Americans, including American Indians who might not have otherwise attended traditional Western schools. Despite his support of public education and democracy, Harris was frequently an opponent of Progressive ideas in education.

An article on Harris describes how he linked education and freedom: "The educative process was conceived to be inseparable from the quest for freedom; hence, the school and society, in the view of Harris, were engaged in a common progress toward rational freedom."[13]

A man of many accomplishments and influence, Harris's hand can be found everywhere steering turn-of-the-century American educational theory and practice. Among his published works are books titled *Introduction to the Study of Philosophy* (New York: Appleton, 1889) and *Hegel's Logic: A Book on the Genesis of the Categories of the Mind* (New York: Kraus, 1890).[14]

Burke Aaron Hinsdale was a professor of the science and art of teaching at the University of Michigan. He also worked as president of Hiram College and superintendent of Cleveland Public Schools.

In Harris's preface to Hinsdale's history, we see liberal themes of freedom, reason, and progress expressed in Hegelian terms and applied to U.S. national history. Harris's views on race and religion will strike some as old-fashioned today. However, his belief in the importance of culture and institutions—more than geography—in shaping history is consistent with the long run of liberal thought about history.

The present volume belongs to the fourth division of works included in this series. It relates to the art of education, and comes under the first subdivision of that head—namely, methods of instruction.* There is no branch of educational literature of more importance than that which treats of methods of instruction. I might add, too, that the method of teaching history, as contrasted with the methods of teaching mathematics or geology, or other branches of natural science, even including biology, has a peculiar importance of its own. For history deals with the will power of man and moves chiefly in the province of mere mechanical causation.

While it is important to study the theater of action and to understand the problems presented by land and water, by mountain ranges, deserts, rivers, climates, and soil, yet these and all circumstances of the environment belong only to the category of means and agencies which man as a self-active being has learned to use—or will learn how to use. They are the stuff which he is to work up into patterns according to his ideals. The material world is the quarry in which we may help ourselves to whatever can

---

* The scheme includes works under four general heads:
  I.   History of Education.
  II. Criticisms of Education, mostly written by educational reformers.
  III. Systematic Works presenting the Theory of Education.
  IV. Art or Practice of Education.

serve to realize our inner aims. Civilization is the conquest over material nature by the organization of human society according to ideals of justice and beneficence. Justice returns the deed upon the doer; but beneficence, philanthropy, loving-kindness, or grace, as this moral sensibility is called, seeks to bring good to the doer in place of the evil that he sends forth, and consequently prefers to accept pain and suffer from discommoding when it may thereby help an evil doer to grow into righteousness and goodness. Righteousness and goodness are the ideas that the Hebrew sacred writings have given to mankind as the essential attributes of the Divine Being. As righteous, He holds men responsible for their actions and returns their deeds upon them; as goodness, however, He shows tenderness toward sinful and erring humanity and is eternally forgiving—thus suffering and bearing evil in this world in order that He may nurture self-active beings potentially in his image into the realization of his image.

This Hebrew idea adopted into our civilization is the essence of history, because it is at once the cause of civilization and the measure of it. In proportion as a people organize institutions that realize righteousness and goodness, or what is the same thing, justice and mercy, they achieve civilization.

History is an account of this progress, and Hegel has well said, in his Introduction to the Philosophy of History, that "the theme of world history is the onward progress into the consciousness of freedom."* The steps to this insight are, first, man's self-activity; second,

---

* Page 24, 3d ed.: "Die Weltgeschichte ist der Fortschritt im Bewusstseyn der Freiheit."

the religious idea that God is perfect self-activity; third, that perfect self-activity is moral;[†] fourth, moral freedom, being the divine form and image, man's destiny is to grow into it; and hence, fifth, the measure of progress in history is this development into the consciousness of freedom, or into clear insight into what is divine and eternal, and the *use* of the earth to celebrate this consciousness and make it perpetual. For this consciousness can never be fully achieved except through the conquest of nature for spiritual uses; nor except through a completed natural science which will reveal all provinces of matter and force and life as progressive steps in the development of free individuality—mineral, plant, animal, man, being the four chief stadia. The world in time and space, according to this religious theory, is a cradle for the nurture of free beings, beginning so low down as to include insensate rocks and the very ether itself.

I have mentioned purposely this religious ideal in order to bring out in sharpest contrast that view of history which delights to ally it most closely with natural science, and to find the explanation of all human events in the structure and forces of the material environment. According to the materialistic school of historians there is no such thing as free will; each being is determined to be what he is by the totality of conditions.

I am not disparaging the study of man's environment, however, but only pointing out the extremes to which the reaction against the former somewhat abstract view has led. The old theory was

---

[†] The law of morality is to act in such a way that one's deed does not infringe on the freedom or self-activity of others; any such infringement would be self-contradiction, and would be self-destructive in the end.

made by men intoxicated with the great idea of individual freedom, and as a consequence it slighted the material factor of civilization. It was reluctant to admit the existence of such a factor. The reaction that has set in from the province of natural science proposes to ignore man's freedom and take account only of the determining circumstance, which surround individuals and groups of men. This contradiction is not, however, difficult to reconcile. Looking at the goal of human progress it is easy to see that man is on his way to conquer and reduce to his service the powers and products of Nature. The amount of human energy expended in compelling Nature to his use is far greater than that expended directly in attaining consciousness of himself and in realizing moral self-control. Man works for food, clothing, and shelter far more hours than for science, art, religion, and civil government.

He therefore spends most of his energy in reacting against his material environments, and is thus said to be enslaved by it. The materialists say that he is under necessity. But they ignore the obvious fact of self-activity. Man is acted upon, but he reacts on the external through his native energy. His reaction consists chiefly in turning out or dispossessing the control of Nature and in seizing control for his own uses. He turns Nature's forces against Nature's purposes and makes his environment acknowledge his sway.

Man's self-activity presupposes as its basis what Kant calls a transcendental freedom—a radiating center of pure self-activity not dependent at all on anything in time and space except for its manifestation. All Nature, all facts and events, belong to the secondary order of us, but not to the primary order of free causality; all things are for man's use, but man himself is a transcendental freedom that can dispense with the world and all that it contains by simply refraining from any act of manifestation. He can dispense with food and drink, letting his body starve; food and drink therefore do not determine him in any such sense as his will determines him. They can come only so far as to be secondary agencies in realizing his motives.

A direct efficient cause necessitates a change in something else, but a motive or purpose (called a "final cause") does not constrain an actor or doer; its presence in the mind is the product of one free act (namely, that of abstraction, which thinks of something else in the place of what is), and then its realization by the will is another free act, by which the soul affirms itself and encroaches on the independent existence of its environment by substituting its own purposes for those of Nature.

This factor of transcendental freedom is the soul of history, but of course it reveals itself or realizes itself only in modifying its environment to adapt it to human uses. In the frozen zone the Eskimo has fashioned himself a hut of snow and ice, using the product of cold to exclude the cold. The environment does not create the food, clothing, and shelter of the Eskimo. It is he, the self-active, who has reacted against it and forced various products out of their natural purposes into his own. Given his environment, and we can see and measure his amount of reaction against it—we can see how much he has conquered it. His conquest is the measure of his energy, and relatively the measure of the resistance to human energy.

But in proportion to man's inner development of ideas he is able to advance in the conquest of the environment and usurp the natural directive forces of the physical world.

With the reactive power of the Algonquin tribes the use of that environment was inconsiderable compared with that of the Anglo-Saxon. An ocean as an environment excluded the savage, but it was a good road to the European.

When man acts on Nature his products have two factors—the natural stuff or material and the modification or use forced on it by human will. The former factor is contributed by the environment, the second factor arises in "transcendental freedom."

Now it is evident that history has two researches to make, the first one an inventory of the environment, as complete as may be made of its things and forces; the second, an inventory of the people, including physical and intellectual traits and ideals.

The antecedents of the American settlers had already revealed in Europe what degree of reaction they possessed against environments of land, water, and climate. It had shown their ideals and their command of means to realize them. It had shown the growth of those ideals through the gradual assimilation of the purely spiritual ideas derived from the Hebrew Scriptures, the Greek literature, and the Roman political and social forms.

A civilization has its highest phase in the religious convictions of its people, revealed in its church, its literature, and its science; its second phase in the political form of the nation, including its legislative, executive, and judicial functions. The third phase of its civilization next in order from the highest is its industrial system and its method of utilizing the features of its material environment not merely for food, clothing, and shelter, but more especially for rapid and frequent intercommunication between its own citizens and with foreign peoples collecting and diffusing knowledge.

The geographical environment of the American continent has not materially modified the development of civilization already on its course of evolution when the emigrants were leaving their European homes for this country; we have developed further the ideas of Protestant Englishmen, Dutchmen, Germans, and French Huguenots of the seventeenth century, and we have taught their ideas to other immigrants that have come to live among us. We have gladly availed ourselves of the discoveries of science to carry forward the conquest of Nature and make it an indifferent matter where the citizen makes his home; whether North or South, East or West, he can command the productions of all sections and of all the world at a very cheap rate, thanks to the aid of steam on railroad and river.

In fact no civilization was ever before so indifferent to its natural environment, and so confident in its ability to create an environment of its choice.

The study of the environment has therefore become a sort of inventory of products of Nature which are to serve as raw material for human ingenuity to transmute into articles of use. Moreover, our civilization is continually lessening the effect of our immediate environment by making present all distant environments through the machinery of transportation.

History is a window of the soul, as I have often called it,* that looks out upon the deeds of the race. It shows man engaged in the work of revealing what is essential in his inward nature and what he makes real in his institutions—the family, civil society, the state, the Church.

* How to Study Geography (in this series), Editor's preface, p. vii.

The study of our own national history is first in order, but it can not be carried very far without involving us in the great European movements that led to the discovery and colonization of America. Nor can medieval or modern European history be understood except through an investigation of the three peoples—Greeks, Romans, and Hebrews—that furnish the three strands which combine to make modern civilization.

In the work of Dr. Hinsdale before us the reader will find the safe guidance of an author who honors and appreciates at their true value the two factors of history, the material and the spiritual. The teacher will derive essential assistance from the hints which crowd its pages, pointing out the discriminating marks that enable him to select the significant and to pass lightly over the unimportant.

W. T. HARRIS.
Washington, D.C., November 2, 1893.

4

Anonymous

"Preface," History and Biography of Washington County and the Town of Queensbury, New York *(New York: Gresham Publishing, 1894)*

The late 19th century witnessed intense growth of amateur history, often written, at least nominally, in service of the public spirit. Village, city, town, and county histories spoke of progress and improvement, and themes of liberal political order. Many such works were funded by local governments, but more often perhaps they were supported by private subscriptions or donations. As thousands of amateur historians told it, the history of the United States was a triumphant narrative about the protection of human rights with individuals cooperating to build a civilization out of the wilderness.

This selection from the history of one county in New York illustrates the then-dominant liberal view of history in American society. It is a statement of what historians at the time believed,

but it is also a philosophical statement of how they thought history should be written. Historians charted progress, and in the
local American context, that often meant recording useful facts
about county pioneers, narrating the participation of county
men in the Revolutionary War, and presenting detailed lists of
the acres of wilderness made into productive fields.

But written history also played a role in promoting progress. Themes of progress and liberty are clear in so many
similar county histories of the period, but perhaps nowhere
expressed so explicitly as in the preface to this selected volume.[15] The anonymous author insists on preserving the history of individuals and the society. History, the anonymous
author proclaims, is important for individuals and for the
community at various levels from the village to the nation.
This was history with a purpose of shaping a better society, a
forward-looking history of liberty.

OF A TRUTH it may be said that History, the highest form of
prose literature, is fast becoming one of the most popular and
important branches of human knowledge. It has rapidly risen in
our day from an empirical state to the rank of a science, and the
master minds of this century that have devoted their energies
to efforts in behalf of its advancement in accuracy, interest and
value, have transformed it from the princely eulogy and fairy tales
of olden times into a vast super-structure only less real than the
great drama of actual events it is intended to perpetuate in human
memory. This improvement has popularized History until it is no
longer the Pactolus of the learned, but has risen to be the guiding star of modern civilization. In it are reflected the principles

that govern the character and destiny of nations, and from it the statesman and reformer may construct a chart to guide all intelligent effort at reform in our old civilization, or in the upbuilding of the new. As in ancient times, so even at this hour, "Experience is a light for our footsteps," no less for the Nation or community than for the individual, and true History is human experience condensed and preserved.

Local history particularly has rapidly risen in importance since our Centennial year,[16] when the Congress of the United States, by joint resolution, recommended to each city, town and county in this country the duty of collecting for permanent preservation their local history and biography. In the first century of our National existence the annals of town and county, together with the individuality of the citizen, had been absorbed by the history of the State and the still more masterful theme of the life of the Nation. Since the opening of our second century it is becoming more generally understood that the history of a people resolves itself largely into the achievements of its leading men and women, and that in biography may be found that department of history most valuable for the intelligent study of National life and human advancement. Hence in the series of County Cyclopedia that bear the imprint of the publishers of this volume, much attention has been given to the collection and publication of biographical sketches of leading citizens, past and present. It is a fact that biography of this character must have prominent place in the local history of the future, and that the important and useful lessons it teaches will never fail to excite interest and give pleasure. It subserves the highest good by presenting examples worthy of emulation, and by perpetuating the memories of those who are worthy of remembrance.

From the time when this territory was yet a wilderness down to the present day, Washington county occupies an important position among her sister counties of the Empire State—a proud eminence based alike on her wonderful development, her industrial prosperity, and the prominent place she occupies in the history of the Revolution—the gigantic struggle for the rights of man, when a Nation was born in a day, and the dial hand on the clock of human progress moved forward in a greater advance than it had hitherto marked in five centuries.

That Washington county has kept well to the front in that general improvement which distinguishes these later times—in industrial development, art, science, literature, and everything that tends to ennoble life and make its possession priceless—is largely due to the energy, ability and character of the men who have found fitting notice on the pages of this volume—worthy descendants of the pilgrims and pioneers who first conquered this soil, and by brawn and brain reduced it to the uses of civilization.

5

Heinrich Rickert

Selection from Science and History:
A Critique of Positivist Epistemology
(Princeton, NJ: Van Nostrand, 1962
[original German 1899])

Heinrich Rickert (1863–1936) was a well-known neo-Kantian philosopher at the University of Freiburg, a student and colleague of Wilhelm Windelband. He was an influence on Maurice Mandelbaum and Austrian thinkers like Mises and Hayek. In Rickert's day, discussions about the nature of history in England were dominated by historians, but in Germany, philosophers often set the tone of the conversation.

Rickert must be regarded as a crucial figure in delineating the methodological autonomy of history. This is a view that believes history should be protected from the overreach of the hard sciences. History, according to Rickert and others who hold this view, is not just a weak, underdeveloped form of empirical observation with discoverable rules and patterns like any physical phenomenon. In short, Rickert argued that history had a method separate from the natural sciences, that it dealt with problems that the natural sciences could not yet solve.

In this selection, Rickert defines "historical method" as that which is interested in the "nonrepeatable event in its particularity and individuality." Rickert writes with a long philosophical wind-up, addressing concerns that are sometimes more relevant to his contemporary German colleagues than to American readers today. But when he comes to the method of history, his point becomes clear: human values are the determining force of history; strictly speaking, we can only ascribe meaning to that which is shaped by humans. Culture is the creation of human values.

The Principal Lines of Demarcation

Since the sciences can be distinguished from one another with respect to both *subject matter* and *method*, their classification is to be undertaken on both a *material* and a *formal* basis. Nor is it by any means self-evident, as many seem to believe, that these two principles of division coincide. Indeed, their careful separation is a primary prerequisite of their *logical* clarification.

Although it is generally acknowledged today that there are two essentially distinct groups of sciences, it is still almost universally the custom in philosophy to base the difference between them on the *material* distinction between *nature* and *spirit*. By the ambiguous word "nature" is usually understood corporeal existence, and by the even more ambiguous word "spirit," psychical existence. *Psychical* life, with its peculiarly characteristic content, is contrasted with the *physical* world, and from this antithesis is then derived the *formal* distinction between the two methods to be respectively employed by those of the human "spirit" (*Geisteswissenschaften*) and those which have "nature" for their subject matter.

One of the consequences that follows from this is that alongside *mechanics*, which is taken as the most fundamental and most general of the physical sciences, is placed a corresponding general science of mental life, viz., *psychology*, conceived as the most fundamental of the disciplines dealing with manifestations of the human "spirit," and further progress in the latter field is accordingly expected by way of the method of *psychology* in particular. As a result, history has come to be regarded as a kind of applied psychology—an interpretation that is hardly in keeping with the present state of that science.

However widely apart their different views may diverge in details, philosophers are nevertheless in essential agreement that the primary determining factor in the classification of the various sciences is in the peculiar nature of *psychical* existence. Indeed, this is taken for granted as perfectly self-evident even where, as with Dilthey, for example, in consequence of a strongly pronounced historical sense, the inadequacy of the *hitherto* prevailing psychology as a foundation for the historical sciences is fully understood. The demand is then made for a new "psychology" that is yet to be developed.

In contrast to the prevailing opinion among philosophers, it is becoming increasingly apparent to those actually engaged in empirical research that those disciplines which cannot be logically included among the natural sciences are characterized very unsatisfactorily indeed when they are referred to as sciences that deal with manifestations of the human "spirit" (*Geisteswissenschaften*). I believe, in fact, that the attempts at classification undertaken on the basis of the antithesis between nature and spirit—where the former is understood as signifying corporeal existence, and the latter, psychical existence—are incapable of understanding the *actually existing* distinction among the empirical sciences, which, after all, constitute the essential point at issue here. By way of preliminary orientation, I shall first try to show briefly the difference between what has come to be the generally accepted and established position in regard to this question and my own view of it.

It certainly cannot be denied that those empirical disciplines which cannot be logically included among the natural sciences do deal *predominantly* with psychical existence, and it is therefore not strictly a departure from the truth to refer to them as *Geisteswissenschaften*, i.e., sciences dealing with manifestations of the human "mind" or "spirit."

However—and this is all that is of importance here—such a way of describing them misses entirely the distinctive feature *essential* for methodology. For the concept difference between distinct kinds of scientific *interest*, which corresponds to the *material* difference between their objects, whereby those engaged in specialized research in one group of sciences consider themselves more closely united to one another than to those working in the other group. Nor can such an approach prove in any way more serviceable in establishing a logical (i.e., formal) antithesis between two *methods* of specialized research that are distinct from each other.

It is certainly no mere coincidence that those engaged in the natural sciences have been the chief collaborators of the philosophers in the field of psychology in recent years, while historians and the representatives of the other sciences which claim the domain of the human "spirit" for their subject matter generally do not concern themselves with modern psychology at all. On the contrary, the reasons for this are inherent in the very nature of the case, and a change in the situation is not probable nor perhaps even desirable. The importance of psychology for some of those sciences which are described as having the domain of the human "spirit" for their subject matter is, I think, very much overestimated not only by psychologists but also by writers on epistemology and logic. At all events, neither the contemporary science of psychology nor any general science of actual mental life that is yet to be developed can have the *fundamental* significance for the other half of the *globus intellectualis* of specialized research that mechanics has for the natural sciences. Indeed, the application of the *method* nowadays customary in psychology to the historical sciences must necessarily prove misleading, as it has in fact already done where theories of "social psychology" have taken the place of historical descriptions.

But still more important is the fact that a single principle of division and classification, such as the antithesis between nature and spirit, is by no means sufficient methodologically to do justice to the *diversity* of the various sciences, because the problems involved are much more complicated than is generally assumed. In my opinion, in the classification of the various specialized branches of science, instead of the *one* distinction between nature and spirit, methodology has to make use of two pairs of fundamental concepts.

Two groups of objects that differ from each other, as mind and matter do, with respect to the nature of their actual existence can never serve as a basis for differentiating between one group of empirical sciences and another because, at least in that part of reality which is directly accessible, there is *nothing* that could be exempted as a matter of principle from an investigation of the kind specifically conducted by the natural sciences. Understood in this sense, the proposition that there can be only *one* empirical science is altogether valid, since there is only one empirical reality. Reality as a whole, i.e., as the sum total of all corporeal and psychical existence, can and, in fact, must be viewed as entirely uniform, or "monistically," to use the current jargon, and accordingly, the various sciences can and must use one and the same method in dealing with each of its parts. If this is done, however, a common bond of interest will closely unite the sciences that investigate material events and those that investigate mental life.

Hence, the division of the various sciences into distinct groups on the basis of the *material* difference in the nature of their respective objects is legitimate only in so far as a number of things and events having a particular *meaning* or importance for us—and in which, therefore, we see something more than mere "nature"— stand out from reality as a whole. In their case the otherwise completely valid representation given by the natural sciences does not in itself *alone* suffice. We have to ask with respect to them quite different questions as well—questions referring primarily to those phenomena which fall within what can best be described as the domain of *culture*. In like manner, the divergence of *interests* separating those engaged in specialized research into two groups may best be expressed by a system of classification that distinguishes between natural and cultural sciences on the basis of the particular importance of cultural phenomena. For this reason it seems to me to be more appropriate to call the disciplines antithetic to the natural sciences *cultural* sciences than, as is customary, sciences dealing with manifestations of the human spirit. Thus, we have to determine what culture means in contrast to nature.

But we cannot stop here. Besides the material principle of classification there must also be a *formal* one; and in this regard the problem proves to be more complicated than it appears in the customary view, which, incidentally, owes its apparent simplicity only to the ambiguity of the word "nature."

It is obvious that the fundamental, formal differences in the methods of the various sciences can no more be deduced from any material characteristics of those aspects of reality which we designate as culture than from the distinction between nature and spirit. Consequently, we cannot speak forthwith of a "method" peculiar to the cultural sciences in the same way as we are wont to speak of the method of the natural sciences and we consider ourselves entitled to speak of the method of psychology. At the same time, however, it must be observed that even when we speak of "the method of the natural sciences" this expression has a *logical* meaning only if the word "natural" in it is understood as referring not just to the physical world, but to all that is included in the previously mentioned Kantian or *formal* signification of the term. In any event, therefore, the method of the natural sciences is *not* coterminous with "the method of the physical sciences," as it would have to be in order for it to serve as the appropriate antithesis to the *psychological* method if the latter is conceived as that of the sciences dealing with manifestations of the human "spirit."

On the contrary, only a concept that is likewise logical can constitute the opposite of the *logical* concept of nature as the existence of things as far as it is determined according to universal laws. But this, I believe, is the concept of *history* in the broadest formal sense of the word, i.e., the concept of the *nonrepeatable event* in its particularity and individuality which stands in formal opposition to the concept of universal law. Hence, in classifying the various sciences, we must speak of a distinction between *method of the natural sciences* and the *method of history*.

The classification we have undertaken here is based on *formal criteria* and therefore by no means coincides with that which was undertaken on the basis of *material* criteria as seems to be the case in the customary division of the sciences into those dealing with "nature" and those having the domain of the human "spirit" for their subject matter. Accordingly, the formal distinction between nature and history cannot be regarded as in any sense a *substitute for* the erroneous conception of a material distinction between nature and *spirit*; the latter can be replaced and supplanted only by distinction between nature and *culture*.

However, I certainly do believe it possible to show that a *connection* between our two principles of classification exists in so far as the necessary approach to all *cultural* phenomena is precisely by way of the *historical* method, the concept of which can at the same time be understood on the basis of a formal concept of culture that is to be developed later. Of course, the method of the natural sciences extends far into the domain of cultural phenomena as well, and it certainly cannot be said that history is the *only* science that deals with this domain. Conversely, in certain respects one can even speak of an historical approach within the natural sciences.

Hence, logical consideration must also be given to resulting *intermediate fields.* These are the twilight zones occupied by investigations in which the method of the natural sciences and the subject matter of the cultural sciences, on the one hand, and the method of history and the subject matter of the natural sciences, on the other, are found in close combination.

However, the fact that in these twilight zones the line dividing the natural sciences from the cultural sciences is crossed in actual practice certainly does not mean that the essential difference between these two fields of specialized research is thereby *annulled.*

On the contrary, with the aid of our concepts we can derive the basic *principles of division* needed in the empirical sciences by sharply marking off the concept of the *historical sciences which deal with cultural phenomena** both in material and in formal respects from the concept of the natural sciences. We can then demonstrate further that in spite of all transitional and intermediate forms, the method of the natural sciences is used *principally* in the investigation of nature, and the method of history *principally* in the investigation of cultural phenomena.

---

* [*Historischen Kulturwissenschaften.* This expression, which also appears as the title of chapter 10 and recurs at several places in the text, denotes those sciences which are classified as "cultural" on material grounds and as "historical" in virtue of the logical principle governing the formation of their concepts. They are, in other words, in individualizing sciences whose subject matter falls within the cultural domain and is therefore relevant to values. As such, they stand at the opposite pole, both formally and materially, from the natural sciences, which are defined as generalizing disciplines whose subject matter is indifferent to value. These are treated in chapter 6. Chapter 11 is devoted to those forms of knowledge which fall in the intermediate field between these two extremes: on the one hand, individualizing sciences, "historical" in their method, whose subject matter is "nature" or reality considered as indifferent to value; and on the other, generalizing sciences oriented to cultural values.—EDITOR]

It is my purpose in the following pages to expound more fully both the *material* distinction between nature and culture (in the sense already stated) and the *formal* distinction between the method of the natural sciences and that of history. I hope thereby to substantiate the thesis advanced here and to justify my departure from the customary manner of classifying the various sciences. However, I wish to emphasize once again that I must confine myself in this book by and large to the schematic exposition of the *principal* lines of demarcation between the sciences and can do no more than touch briefly on the more detailed arguments. It is not the intention of this essay to provide a complete *system* of epistemology that embraces *all* sciences or all branches of science. We completely disregard the method of *philosophy* here, and, for reasons which will soon become apparent, mathematics in its logical structure is likewise outside the purview of our investigation. We are concerned only with the empirical disciplines dealing with the *real* existence of the world of objects accessible to *sensory* perception. Only in their case it is valid to draw a distinction between the two mutually antithetic *basic forms* in which they carry their investigations and which warrant their classification and division into natural sciences and cultural sciences.

Nature and Culture

A strictly systematic investigation which put logical problems in the forefront would have to start from reflection on the *formal* differences between the methods of the various sciences. Thus, it would have to understand the concept of cultural science on the basis of that of *historical science*. However, the various branches of science are first distinguished by differences in their *subject matter*, and further progress in the *division of labor* among them is also determined primarily by the material distinction between nature and culture. Therefore, so as not to remove myself further from the actual interests of specialized research than otherwise necessary, I shall begin with the difference in subject matter and shall add to this a discussion of the formal differences in method. Finally, I propose to show the relations between the formal and the material principles of classification.

The words "nature" and "culture" are not unequivocal, and the concept of nature in particular is never more precisely defined than when it is confronted by its opposite. We shall best avoid the appearance of arbitrariness here if we first keep to its *originary* meaning. Products of nature are those which grow freely from the earth. The products of culture in its primary sense (e.g., agricultural) are brought forth only after man has ploughed and sown, i.e., when he has *cultivated* the earth. Accordingly, nature is the embodiment of whatever comes to pass of itself, of what is "born" and left to its "growth." Culture, on the other hand, comprises whatever is either produced by man acting according to valued ends or, if it is already in existence, whatever is at least *fostered* intentionally for the sake of the *values* attaching to it.

We may extend this antithesis as far as we like, but it is always necessarily connected with two facts, viz., that every cultural phenomenon embodies some *value* recognized by man, for the sake of which either it is brought to pass or, if it has already come to pass, it is encouraged; and that, on the other hand, whatever comes to pass and develops of itself *can* be considered without regard to values and indeed *must* be so considered if it really is nothing but an aspect of nature in the sense defined above.

Thus, values always attach to cultural objects. Therefore, we shall call them *goods*, in order to distinguish them as *valuable entities* from the values as such, which, considered in themselves are not real at all and can be disregarded. Science does not conceive of the objects of nature as goods. On the contrary, it views them as devoid of value and without relevance to it. If we abstract every value from our conception of a cultural object, we can say that it thereby becomes the same as a mere object of nature or that it can be scientifically treated as such. The presence or absence of *relevance to values* can thus serve as a reliable criterion for distinguishing between the two kinds of scientific *objects*. Indeed, in the interest of methodology, this is the *only* criterion we can employ here, because apart from the value attaching to it every real cultural phenomena must also be capable of being regarded as connected with nature and even as a part of nature. It will be shown later to what extent relevance to values is the determining factor in the *logical* structure of the *historical* sciences that deal with cultural phenomena.

To be sure, the material distinction between the different kinds of scientific objects can also be formulated differently, so that the implicit concept of value does not at once become clearly evident. We wish at least to touch briefly on this point since it involves a concept that has recently come to occupy a central position in the methodological inquiries, namely, that of *understanding (Verstehen).*

No doubt this idea can be of great importance in methodology. But the word "understanding" is very ambiguous, and the concept that it denotes therefore requires precise definition. The crucial question in drawing the distinction between the cultural and the natural sciences is what the *opposite* of understanding is conceived to be. We must distinguish it from *perceiving* and in so doing conceive the latter idea so broadly that the entire world accessible to the senses (i.e., all immediately given physical and psychical events) will be considered as the object of perception. But even then, in the interest of logical clarity, we cannot rest content with the acts of the *subject* who does the understanding. On the contrary, from the methodological point of view it is the *objects* which are understood that are essential. If the entire world of phenomena directly accessible to the senses is designated as the object of perception, then only nonsensorial *meanings* or *complexes of meaning* remain as objects of understanding, if this word is to retain any precise signification. They alone are *directly* understood, and when they are encountered, they require of science a kind of treatment different in its essential principles from that accorded to the objects of physical and psychical reality or the world of phenomena accessible merely to sensory perception.

But with this distinction between perceivable and understandable objects we have again approached our previous antithesis between nature and culture. Because understandable meanings and complexes of meaning are found only together with perceivable objects, we can also say: the objects of science are, on the one hand, those which, like cultural phenomena, have an importance or a meaning and which we wish to understand for the sake of this importance and this meaning; and, on the other hand, those which, like the phenomena of nature, are regarded as completely devoid of importance and meaning and which therefore remain incapable of being understood. Unquestionably, when the distinction is formulated in this way, it is important for epistemology and especially for the method of history.

Indeed, it may be thought to be even more comprehensive than the previously mentioned distinction between nature and culture and to be therefore capable of raising the latter to a sphere of greater generality. Interpreted thus, nature would be devoid of meaning; natural phenomena would have a merely perceived existence which would be incapable of being understood, while the phenomena of culture would comprise all objects whose existence is meaningful and understandable. And this is, in fact, the case.

Nevertheless, it is advisable, in marking off the separate domains of the various branches of knowledge and in attempting to draw a dividing line between the investigation of nature and the *empirical* sciences dealing with cultural phenomena, that we place the idea of *value* in the foreground, thus making it clear that there must be some reference to value if empirically real objects are to have meaning or importance for us, and that, conversely, if these objects were without relevance to any value, there would be nothing about them that we could "understand," in the strict sense of the word, as meaningful or important. We may even say that meaning and importance are first specifically constituted as such by virtue of a value and that therefore the understanding of meaning and importance *without* regard to values remains scientifically *indeterminate*.

At all events, in the distinction between nature as devoid of value and culture as affected with value we already have the *essential* principle of division for the classification of the sciences, and we could show that the relevance which the distinction between meaningless and meaningful objects (i.e., between those that are not understandable and those that are understandable) has for the logical structure of the methods of the various sciences cannot be demonstrated until the methodological significance of the relevance of objects to values has first become clear.

Accordingly, in this introductory presentation we shall stop at the separation between nature, conceived as devoid of value, and culture, conceived as affected with value, without going on to a consideration of the distinction between merely perceivable objects, devoid of meaning and not understandable, on the one hand, and meaningful, understandable objects, on the other.

We shall merely add a few words concerning the *character* of the value, which transforms realities into cultural goods and thereby sets them off from the phenomena of nature as distinctive objects in their own right.

In regard to values considered in themselves, one cannot ask whether they are *real*, but only whether they are *valid*. A cultural value is either actually accepted as valid by all men, or its validity—and thus the more than purely individual importance of the objects to which it attaches—is at least postulated by some civilized human being. Furthermore, civilization, or culture in the highest sense, must be concerned not with the values attaching to the objects of mere desire, but with excellences which, if we reflect at all on the validity of values, we feel ourselves more or less "obligated" to esteem and cultivate for the sake of the society in which we live or for some other concomitant reason. However, we must not think of these exclusively in terms of "moral necessity." It suffices that, in general, the value be connected with the idea of a norm or of some good that ought to be actualized. This is what distinguishes cultural objects from those that are, to be sure, valued and striven after by all men, but only instinctively, as well as from those that owe their valuation not, indeed, to mere instinct, but still only to flights of individual fancy or caprice.

It follows clearly that this antithesis between nature and culture, in so far as it refers to a difference between two groups of real *objects*, is the actual basis for the classification and division of the various sciences.

Religion, church, law, the state, custom, science, language, literature, art, economy, and the technical means necessary for their preservation are—at any rate at a certain stage in their evolution—cultural objects or *goods* precisely in the sense that either the value attaching to them is acknowledged by all members of a community or its acknowledgment is *expected* of them.

Hence we need only broaden our conception of culture to the point where we also take into consideration its *first rudiments* and the *stages of its decline*, as well as events that promote or hinder culture, for us to see that it embraces all the objects of theology, jurisprudence, history, philology, economics, etc., i.e., the subject matter of every one of the sciences dealing with manifestations of the human "spirit" (*Geisteswissenschaften*) with the exception of psychology. Consequently, the term "cultural science" is a thoroughly *appropriate* designation for those disciplines that cannot logically be included among the natural sciences.

The fact that farm equipment, machinery and chemical aids are also comprehended in the concept of culture is certainly not, as Wundt has supposed, an objection against using the term "cultural science." On the contrary, it shows that the various disciplines that cannot logically be counted among the natural sciences are more suitably characterized by this expression than by calling them, as Wundt recommends, sciences having the domain of the human "spirit" for their subject matter (*Geisteswissenschaften*). Technical devices are, to be sure, generally produced with the help of the natural sciences. Nevertheless, they themselves do not belong among the *objects* of inquiry constituting the subject matter of these sciences, nor can they very well be placed in the domain of the sciences that are described as dealing with manifestations of the human "spirit." Their only place is in a cultural science that would describe their historical development, and there is no need to prove how important they *could* be as well in contributing to culture in the "spiritual" sense, i.e., to the meaningful cultivation and enrichment of the inner life of man.

In the case of a few disciplines, like *geography* and *ethnography*, there can indeed be some question where they belong. However, a decision on this depends only upon the *point of view* they take toward the objects that constitute their subject matter, i.e., whether they regard them merely as parts of nature or relate them to cultural life. The earth's surface, in itself simply a product of nature, acquires, as the scenes of all cultural evolution, an interest beyond that of a merely natural object; and primitive people can, on the one hand, be studied by the methods of the natural sciences simply in regard to their specifically "racial" traits, or, on the other hand, they can be investigated also with a view to determining the extent to which they exhibit the "rudiments" of culture. Indeed, the fact that the same subject matter can be approached and treated from these two different sides only serves to substantiate our contention that the problem of classifying the sciences and determining the domain in which a specific subject matter belongs has nothing to do with distinctions like nature and spirit, in the sense of body and soul or the physical and the psychical. Accordingly, we need not hesitate to use the term *cultural science*, in the sense defined above, to designate the various disciplines that cannot logically be included among the natural sciences.

6

Charles George Crump

Selection from The Logic of History
(London: Society for Promoting
Christian Knowledge, 1919)

Charles George Crump (1862–1935) of Dorset, England, lived
in Italy with his parents from age 10, before returning to England to enter Oxford University, where he received a degree
in jurisprudence in 1883. He then spent three years in the civil
service in India, again returning to England, now for good, as he
spent much of the rest of his working life in the Public Records
Office.[17]

Crump was an archivist, novelist, and historian of the Middle
Ages and the classics. His book *The Legacy of the Middle Ages*
is certainly his most widely disseminated work, with World-
Cat noting 96 editions being held in 1,955 member libraries.
His two works on historical methods—*The Logic of History* (10
editions, 147 libraries) and *History and Historical Research* (18
editions, 316 libraries)—are also widely held, especially considering the narrowness of the historical methods genre.[18]

His books do not appear to have been widely reviewed in his day, and they now appear to be almost entirely forgotten and neglected. Although his works on historical method are dated, they have the advantage of being clearly written and based on experience in the archives.

Like other liberal writers on history, Crump addresses human action, free will, and determinism. He presents something of a sociology of knowledge, arguing not that history should be free of a scientific logic, but that all historical facts do not lie ready for the picking but are created or perhaps shaped by their acquisition. Crump understands historical knowledge as tentative and historical problems as having many possible answers. His curious description of history as an "inverse" science in which we work from the known to the unknown should be better known.

In a second short selection from the same book, Crump identifies the individual as the true focus of historical accounts. He questions whether modern historians can sympathize with individuals in the ancient past, and he concludes that yes, our basic concerns today are the same human concerns that have occupied our minds for millennia. In this selection, Crump joins the chorus of liberal historians who proclaim that progress and improvement have been chief characteristics of the modern age.

I. History as a Science

The historian who would claim for his study a place among the sciences must be prepared to meet certain criticisms, and to acknowledge certain difficulties. The common conception of a science involves the notion of accurate formulae, known as natural laws, giving accurate results derivable from these principles; and this suggests the criticism that as human action is infinitely variable, no certain results can be obtained in a study founded upon it. This theory would therefore confine history to narrative and refuse any attempt to discover any principles behind the drama. The student of natural sciences knows better than to make such a criticism. He is aware of the limitations of his invariable laws, and of the defects of his methods; and if he were to endeavour to exclude history from the sciences, he would probably base his exclusion upon the statement that the laws of human conduct are so imperfectly known that the methods employed in discussing them must be widely different from those that he is accustomed to employ. And yet Economics, Psychology, and Anthropology have one by one crept into the guarded circle; and it is difficult to insist that History may not follow them, and that historians may not look to their logic and try to establish their general principles as eagerly and as accurately as any other students. In any case, historians have always taken this line, and will take it, as necessary for any fruitful investigation.

It may be thought that at the outset of this enquiry it is needful to discuss the question of free-will. In reality, it matters very little whether the historian adopts free-will or determinism as his philosophy. His subject is human action, and the most enthusiastic adherent of free-will must admit that human action is not entirely free, that it is constrained by the action of other individuals, by the inherent limitations of the agent, and by natural and logical boundaries. On the other hand, the sternest determinist will allow that motives often evade human scrutiny. Both, therefore, allow that part of human actions falls outside their principles. In the part that the voluntaryist abandons, the historian may find room for the action of his laws; nor need the part yielded by the determinist be left to the dominion of incalculable chance. Even where the action of the individual is incalculable, the action of the crowd may have a common direction and a common aim. Statistical methods may be applied to reveal the existence of these or their absence, and thus, even in the arbitrary part of human action, guiding principles may be discoverable.

Buckle, indeed, went further than this. He is the protagonist of all those historians and politicians who appeal to known laws of history to support their own theories and to repel those of their opponents. Unaware, like the men of his time, of the limitations of natural laws in such studies as chemistry or physics, he sought to extend to history the certainty which he attributed to other sciences. His work is ingenious, brilliant and perverse. But he never understood that before we argue from the past, we must discover it; and that before we claim for history the rights of a science, we must rigidly determine the nature of its logic and know with what sort of science we have to deal.

History, viewed as a science, can only be regarded as an inverse science; its followers are continually employed in reasoning from what they know and see before them to what they have never known and never can see. As in all inverse sciences its problems are capable of many solutions, and the selection of the right answer from the many possible answers is at once the difficulty and the delight of the historian. The conception of an inverse science seems to be one that many minds seize with difficulty; and yet it is one that the child meets with in the earliest stages of its education. The first arithmetical process that we learn is addition, a direct process, which can always be carried out; the second is subtraction, the inverse process, which cannot always be carried out, because it is inverse; and though by the introduction of the new conception of negative quantities we evade this impossibility, we do not really escape from it. Any child can readily learn to solve the direct problem of finding the sum of several numbers; $7+3+2+1=13$. But no one can solve the inverse problem and tell us what four numbers added together will make 13. The only answer that the most expert arithmetician can supply is that the possible number of solutions is indefinitely large. Offer him another condition, for instance, that the numbers are all integral and positive, and he will reduce the possible number of solutions to a smaller and manageable extent. He will even, if pressed, tell you how many conditions he requires to be able to reduce the number of solutions to one; and he will warn you that, by fixing too many conditions, you may render the problem insoluble. But the original problem, the pure inverse problem, always remains one to which no certain answer can be given.

So it is with the historian. From a set of facts presented to his consciousness he is compelled to work backwards to preceding sets of facts, which is purely hypothetical. The number of possible solutions is indefinite; the selection of the most acceptable one is the peculiar task to which he dooms himself. He must remember always that history is an hypothesis to account for the existence of facts as they are.

When writers of history refer to this view of their study, they usually speak of it as arguing backwards from the known to the unknown. But curiously enough, this phrase is limited in use; the writer who is speculating upon the early history of land, or on early legal institutions, will use it and speak of its use as a new mode of investigation. If he is candid, he will explain the limits of the method and its peculiar perils. He may even admit that the student who uses it may sometimes find himself assuming a condition of things as known in order to deduce from it a preceding condition that he hopes may have existed; but he is not likely to point out that all historians of necessity pursue the same course, and that the man who takes a story on the authority of another investigator is arguing from the known to the unknown just as much as the man who breaks new ground for himself. And what is more, in using existing authorities the student is liable to exactly the same errors as he is when exploring new paths. In short, tradition, whether embodied in writing, or transmitted as oral statement, is only an existing fact, which may be used as a basis for investigation. Its peculiarities require special criticism, and its limitations will soon be obvious to those who rely too much upon its help. It is not needful here to discuss theory of testimony, but it is needful to insist on the fact that even if we base our history upon tradition, we are still only framing an hypothesis to account for the existence of things as they are; and that herein lies the peculiar difficulty of our task. It may be said that this difficulty is common to all scientific studies. It is no doubt true that the business of constructing a theory to include any set of facts is a matter of lucky guessing, and that many guesses are always possible. But in the case of most of the accepted sciences, the student has one great advantage over the historian. The phenomena with which he deals can be repeated at will; the circumstances under which they occur can be varied in as many ways as the investigator can devise. But no historian has yet discovered how to experiment with history. It is tempting indeed to imagine an historical laboratory, in which, under the care of skilled investigators, experiments should be tried upon different forms of societies and knowledge gained and theories tested. One might study the actual effect of prolonged war upon national character, and endeavour to settle, by repeated experiment, whether it improves men and women by inspiring them to bear hardship, or lowers the vitality of the race by killing off first the bravest and best among them. But all this is at present beyond the historian's power; and perhaps should be beyond his wishes, even in moments of scientific exaltation. He must, however reluctantly, leave experiments to chemists, physiologists and professors of physics, and fall back upon what methods remain to him.

From one science he can obtain especial assistance. The limitations of the historian apply equally to the geologist; indeed, in one respect the geologist is in even worse case, for geology is a younger science than history. When the seas were parted from the continents, no man stood by to watch; and no man saw how the earth's surface was folded into the mountain chains that build up her aspect. Earth as she is, is the subject-matter of geology; how she came to be what she is, is the object of his researches. His observation of the actual processes of change, the tradition of his study, scarcely extends over more than two centuries. And yet in that short space of time, geologists have framed, discarded and recalled many theories. For the present purpose, the noteworthy point is the slow recurrence towards a theory of catastrophes after the almost complete triumph of the doctrine that all geological changes could be accounted for by causes now in action; and an increased tendency to deal historically rather than descriptively with the whole subject. The result of the two tendencies is to produce a remarkable parallelism between the language of historians and geologists. The following paragraph from a geological book will show the likeness of the two lines of thought.

"The Difficulties of Geological Restoration.

"These arise chiefly from two causes—the imperfection of our knowledge, and the imperfection of the geological record. The first is being gradually removed by the industry of geologists; but there are still many parts of the British Islands about the geological structure of which we really know very little, and there are many others about which more detailed information is much to be desired. . . . The imperfection of the geological record is another great source of difficulty and one which will never be altogether overcome. The rocks which remain to us as the records of any one period are but a remnant of the deposits which were formed during that period, and yet before we can attempt to restore the geography of that time, we must replace in imagination the rocks that are lost so as to form a conception of the space over which they originally extended."

The quotation need not be prolonged further; there is no historical investigator who has not said the same thing in words but slightly differing. It need not surprise us to discover this; both geology and history are inverse studies; and both have to determine whether they will take for their guide the principle of uniformity, or will allow themselves to have recourse to catastrophes in case of need.

When the geologist talks of uniformity, the historian is apt to use the word development. This term is a useful servant when it is not employed as a screen for ignorance. But too often when we say that one state of things has developed out of another, we ought simply to state that a change of some kind can be discovered, and that we know neither the nature nor the method of the change. If the change is a large one, our dislike to admit ignorance may lead us to postulate a catastrophe, another term frequently used in a loose manner. Sometimes it means a change, the magnitude of which is inconveniently large for its duration; sometimes it means a change thrust upon a country by violence from without; sometimes, and most correctly, it means the turn of the scale, the final stage of the conquest of old conditions by the new forces, which have long been held at bay by the inertia of existing facts. The only accurate use of the term catastrophe is the last one; and before we use it we are bound to examine the growth of the new forces and the reason of their victory. Often this is an obscure, even an impossible, task; the whole truth eludes us. But it is always possible to prefer ignorance to blundering; and it is better to admit that we do not know the origin of the Reformation than to adopt the catastrophic view of the school-girl, who declared that Luther began the Reformation by burning the Pope's cow.

The controversy between the school of uniformity and the catastrophic school is an unreal one, and is chiefly concerned with the choice of the terms we shall use to conceal our ignorance of the progress of events. From one point of view, all change is uniform, from another, all change is discontinuous. Either method of statement, either line of thought, is valid for the discovery and expression of truth. The historian who discards one or the other of them limits himself to no good purpose.

The familiar story of the Norman Conquest will serve as well as any other as an illustration. The forces which brought William and his followers to England had been at work for many years. The resistance of the English had been weakened by the long tragedy of the Danish war and the failure of Canute's attempt at conquest. From this point of view, the Norman invasion and its success are nothing but the final result of uniform and intelligible processes slowly working to an inevitable result. The historians who talk of the incompetence of the English as the cause of William's victory would be better employed in pointing out that the Norman victory was won against a people exhausted by their long, and on the whole successful, resistance to the Danes.

. . .

IV. Ultimate Principles

It is not enough to collect materials and to learn to interpret them, unless a guiding principle can be discovered. In the end, all our conclusions must be based upon individuals and the character of individuals; and so we come to the question of permanence of human character. Can we reasonably assign to men in the past the same motives that we know to be active in our contemporaries? Can we assume that those motives produced in them the same results that we see produced among us to-day? If we cannot do this for individuals, can we do it for groups? Let us begin with the easier task, the character of a group or nation. The definition of the term "group" need not delay us; all we require is a set of men united by language, neighbourhood, and any other of the usual links that make up a community of similar persons. A difference in political or religious institutions need not necessarily imply a difference in character; at any rate it can often be allowed for in considering the main object of enquiry, namely, the group point of view.

Now, there are several matters upon which the group point of view has clearly changed completely in historical times, and there are others upon which it has changed in appearance and expression though perhaps not in reality; one such point is the question of slavery. No educated civilisation in the present day could base itself upon slavery; the cultivated and leisured classes of to-day have replaced slavery by industrialism. The possibility of slavery depended upon a wide difference in knowledge, in courage, in union, between the slave-owner and the slave. As this difference faded away, slavery faded with it. Industrialism lies too near us for it to be profitable to discuss here the conditions of its existence and its probable duration as a social form. Another of these changes was summed up by Sir Henry Maine in a famous phrase, when he said that the progress of society was "from status to contract." To-day a man is born into the world free; he inherits from his parents no legal or social condition, and even his nationality may be matter of doubt. His relations with his fellows are assumed by him of his free will by agreement not conferred upon him by accident of birth. This is the age, in fact, of contract; in the days of "status" a man received at birth his legal clothing and retained it all his life. Now it is undoubtedly true that, from a legal point of view, there is much to be said for this theory; in every body of law the proportion of the space given to the law of contract, as against the law of persons, has increased considerably; and whole classes of persons have disappeared from the lawyer's sight. If we leave on one side nationality, marriage, childhood, and a few other matters, there is not much left in the way of status that the law needs to investigate. But the lawyer's point of view and the group point of view are by no means the same; and the divergence between the two and their mutual influence are a curious matter for historical study. When Maine wrote men believed in the growth of freedom, and in free contract as part of freedom. There are signs that this view no longer prevails, and that a reaction against it has been going on for a long period. Just as the ideal of equality before the law overthrew the theory of status, the more modern ideal of equality before social and natural conditions tends to bring it back in a modified form. The conception of a naked individual, acquiring a social clothing by means of free contract, gives place to the conception of an individual for whom a social clothing must be provided by the society of which he is part. And so in late legislation there has been a tendency to enlarge the law of persons again. But there is this difference: the old status was a status which the individual could not cast off or acquire. The status of modern legislation can be abandoned or acquired within the limits of the will or power of the individual. To-day the new doctrine is finding opponents; whether they are the last upholders of a lost cause, or the leaders of a new reaction, will be known in the future. There are not a few other matters upon which a history of opinion might show a growth and alteration in this group point of view, and various attempts have been made to find a general expression for the changes. Here we are only bound to note the fact that the group point of view differs in different ages, and to insist that in historical investigation we must take this fact into account.

If we turn to individual minds the position is a different one. Here we have to deal, not with the steady slight pressure of many forces acting in one direction, and often only to be detected by the sum of their cumulative results, but with the isolated forces of single minds. Anyone who has ever played at table-turning will know the difficulty. The condition that the table should turn is that the large majority of the players should unconsciously push in one direction; if the unconscious pressure alters in direction, the table will move the other way. That is the group point of view, an unconscious majority pressing in one direction, quite irresistible while it lasts, and equally irresistible when it turns back on itself.

But the individual is another matter. Any yet, evade it as we may, it is to the individual that the historian must come at last, to his character, his motives, his desires, and his powers. If a change and growth be admitted in the group point of view, it follows, indeed, the same change and growth must be discoverable in the character of individuals. And yet it is more than doubtful whether any varieties of human character have disappeared during the ages of which we have knowledge, or whether any new types of character have come into existence. The motives that act on men have altered but little; their intellectual powers remain much as they were. The fundamental riddles of philosophy, religion, ethics, and art are the same, and the same answers are given to them. There is no question that has provoked attention in the past, that may not conceivably arise again in the future to demand an answer; and there is no reason to suppose that a new and final answer will ever be forthcoming. In one respect, and in only one, has the position of the individual man been altered. In the last three centuries he became with increasing rapidity the owner and controller of the store of energy accumulated in the earth. With this new mastery has come a new freedom and a new vigour. What his ancestors dreamed, the present race has achieved; and with this achievement came an impatience of delay—an intoxicated belief that modern man had only to desire in order to possess; and, finally, the disposition to use for any purpose, however evil, the power he had obtained. And yet it remains the truth, the consoling truth, that the essential individual remains much what he has always been.

7

Benedetto Croce

Selections from History as the Story of Liberty *(New York: Meridian Books, 1955 [original Italian 1938])*

Benedetto Croce (1866–1952) was an Italian philosopher, historian, and politician. He is perhaps best known for his work on aesthetics and literary criticism. In the first half of the 20th century, he was one of the most influential writers in Italy.

Croce wrote extensively on history, often as a critic of general trends in historiography and the philosophy of history. Most of those writings appeared in Italian in the years before World War I and were translated into English only decades later. *History as the Story of Liberty*—first published in English as *History as Thought and Action* in 1938—is a collection of Croce's essays on the philosophy of history and historical practice. The essay "History as the History of Liberty" might be his most famous. *History: Its Theory and Practice* (New York: Russell & Russell, 1960 [original Italian 1920]) is a work similar to his writings on historiography, demonstrating the thoroughly liberal character of his historical understanding.

Croce's prose is difficult to read (particularly so in translation, I assume), not just because of his long sentence structure and his now dated references, but because of his idiosyncratic or at least uncommon way of defining terms like "spirit." Regarding "history written on the so-called theory of historical materialism," Croce wrote, men appear "anti-human to the same degree as the theory which offends against the fullness and dignity of the spirit." Spirit, he said, was what distinguished histories from chronicles, uncritical collections of the great deeds of a people, or other narratives devoid of human motives.

Geist or "spirit" appears frequently in idealist philosophy, such as in Hegel's writings on history, and in the works of Heinrich Rickert. Unlike Hegel, Croce's "spirit" was not a transcendental, religious "spirit." By spirit, Croce meant mental activity, the workings of the mind. For this reason, Croce's views on history are often considered akin to those of R. G. Collingwood and Michael Oakeshott. All three were idealists who thought history had to be understood first and foremost as the ideas that inspired change. The proper subjects of history for all three liberal idealist historians were the minds of individuals.

This reader could draw on many possible liberal themes from Croce: his ridicule of Hegel and Marx, his rejection of utopian ends, his opposition to historical "laws" and Comtean positivism. To begin, this reader includes part of his essay "The Historical Meaning of Necessity," which is primarily concerned with the problem of cause and effect in historical explanations. Like other liberals, Croce distances the discipline of history from the methods of the natural sciences and likewise rejects a divine mover of history. In his words, it is critical to oppose "causal and transcendental necessity" to retain the liberty of individual actors.

Next is Croce's essay "History as the History of Liberty," reproduced in its entirety. Croce's line "liberty is the eternal creator of history and itself the subject of every history" is perhaps the closest approximation of liberal history that could fit on a bumper sticker.

IV. The Historical Meaning of Necessity

The following simple and fundamental truth can never be sufficiently insisted on; many minds lost in the shadows of naturalism and positivism find it hard to grasp: that "cause" (though it may seem superfluous we must here too insist that we mean the concept and not the word "cause" which belongs to ordinary conversation) the concept of cause must and should remain outside history because it was born in the realm of natural science and its place is there. No one has yet succeeded in practice in relating a fragment of history by matching certain causes with their effects. . . .

The other false notion of necessity is speciously presented as follows: there is a logic in history; there must be, for if there is logic in man there is also logic in history, and if the human mind thinks historically it obviously thinks logically. But the word "logic" in the above sentence means something very different from "logicalness" of a design or programme in accordance with which history begins, develops, and ends, and which it is the duty of the historian to unravel, so that he may find behind the apparent events a hidden mould giving a true and ultimate representation. Philosophers have frequently reasoned on this basis, deducing their design from the concept of an idea or of the Spirit or even of Matter; although Idea, Spirit, Matter were only different disguises for a transcendental God, who could think and impose his thought upon men and have it carried out. This is the naked and bare form to which the design must be reduced, and in that form contemplated: a form which Thomas Campanella[19] in his sonnets with no satirical or burlesque intention describes as a "book of words of the comedy of jesting" or as "a scenario" such as the theatrical managers of his day used to outline the action of the comedy, and to give each actor his part for the rehearsal. Abbé Galiani[20] found another simile for it in the vantage of card-cheats, who play with loaded or marked dice. However that may be, no one has yet written such a history; and the embarrassment of its partisans and adherents has already been shown in their method, by their very request, both contradictory and superfluous, that historical research should reveal a design beyond the range of evidence and documents, and therefore unattainable by those means. They made histories and christened them as such by using evidence sometimes as a symbol, sometimes as a superfluous ornament to decorate the display they made of their beliefs, tendencies, hopes and fears, in politics, religion or philosophy. On a par with causality, the transcendental God is a stranger to human history, which would not exist if that God did exist; for History is its own mystic Dionysus, its own suffering Christ, redeemer of sins.

110

Another false concept disappears from history together with this doubly false idea of necessity, from which it is derived; the concept of historical foresight. If the last act only in the divine programme was generally revealed (for example the coming of the Anti-Christ, the end of the world and the universal judgment day), yet the rest of the programme from the present backwards, was also—on that view—written in the book of Providence, and one small section might through grace be revealed to some pious man. Similarly with the causal concept the Chain of Cause and Effect proceeded and by calculation future links in it could be foreseen. In practice, however, it became confessedly impossible to predict anything, in the first case because of the inscrutability of the divine will, in the second because of the enormous complexity of the various causes concerned: so that the faithful naturalist behaved like the naturalistic author of the story of the Rougon Macquart family;[21] Zola in that novel worked out their family tree from the trunk to the branches and twiglets, submitting them to the cause of heredity, but then over the niche prepared for a child about to be born had nothing to ask but the ironic question left unanswered: "Quel sera-t-il?" Nevertheless the habit of prediction persists in the minds of many readers of history, and as a dignified duty on the part of many writers, and it gets satisfied in a succession of images which lack substance, except within the personal fears and tremors and hopes of those who collect these images.

The defenders of human liberty should boldly oppose both causal and transcendental necessity, so closely bound to each other in many harmful ways, but there is no need to go into battle, as they often do, against the logical necessity of historiography, which is indeed the very premiss of the liberty.

. . .

XII. History as the History of Liberty

Hegel's famous statement that history is the history of liberty was repeated without being altogether understood and then spread throughout Europe by Cousin, Michelet and other French writers.[22] But Hegel and his disciples used it with the significance which we have criticized above, of a history of the first birth of liberty, or its growth, of its maturity and of its stable permanence in the definite era in which it is incapable of further development. (The formula was: Orient, Classic World, Germanic World = one free, some free, all free.) The statement is adduced in this place with a different intention and content, not in order to assign to history the task of creating a liberty which did not exist in the past but will exist in the future, but to maintain that liberty is the eternal creator of history and itself the subject of every history. As such it is on the one hand the explanatory principle of the course of history, and on the other the moral ideal of humanity.

Jubilant announcements, resigned admissions or desperate lamentations that liberty has now deserted the world are frequently heard nowadays; the ideal of liberty is said to have set on the horizon of history, in a sunset without promise of sunrise. Those who talk or write or print this deserve the pardon pronounced by Jesus, for they know not what they say. If they knew or reflected they would be aware that to assert that liberty is dead is the same as saying that life is dead, that its mainspring is broken. And as for the ideal, they would be greatly embarrassed if invited to state the ideal which has taken, or ever could take, the place of the ideal of liberty. Then they would find that there is no other like it, none which makes the heart of man, in his human quality, so beat, none other which responds better to the very law of life which is history; and that this calls for an ideal in which liberty is accepted and respected and so placed as to produce ever greater achievements.

Certainly when we meet the legions of those who think or speak differently with these self-evident propositions, we are conscious that they may well be of the kind to raise laughter or derision about philosophers who seem to have tumbled on the earth from another world ignorant of what reality is, blind and deaf to its voice, to its cries, and to its hard features. Even if we omit to consider contemporary events and conditions in many countries, owing to which a liberal order which seemed to be the great and lasting achievement of the nineteenth century has crumbled, while in other countries the desire for this collapse is spreading, all history still gives evidence of an unquiet, uncertain and disordered liberty with brief intervals of unrest, rare and lightning moments of a happiness perceived rather than possessed, mere pauses in the tumult of oppressions, barbarian invasions, plunderings, secular and ecclesiastical tyrannies, wars between peoples, persecutions, exiles and gallows. With this prospect in view the statement that history is the history of liberty sounds like irony or, if it is seriously maintained, like stupidity.

But philosophy is not there just to be overwhelmed by the kind of reality which is apprehended by unbalanced and confused imaginings. Thus philosophy, when it inquires and interprets, knowing well that the man who enslaves another wakes in him awareness of himself and enlivens him to seek for liberty, observes with serenity how periods of increased or reduced liberty follow upon each other and how a liberal order, the more it is established and undisputed, the more surely decays into habit, and thereby its vigilant self-awareness and readiness for defence is weakened, which opens the way for a "recourse," as Vico[23] termed it, to all of those things which seemed to have vanished from the world, and which themselves, in their turn, open a new "course." Philosophy considers, for example, the democracies and the republics like those of Greece in the fourth century, or of Rome in the first, in which liberty was still preserved in the institutional forms but no longer in the soul or the customs of the people, and then lost even those forms, much as a man who has not known how to help himself but has in vain for a time received ministrations of good advice is finally abandoned to the hard school of life. Or philosophy looks at Italy, exhausted and defeated, entombed by barbarians in all her pompous Imperial array, rising again, as the poet said, "in her Tyrrhenian and Adriatic republics" like an agile sailor. Or philosophy contemplates the absolute monarchs who beat down the liberty of the barons and the clergy once they had become privileged, and superimposed on all men their own form of government, exercised by their own bureaucracy, and sustained by their own army, thus preparing a far greater and more useful participation of the people in political liberty. A Napoleon destroys a merely apparent and nominal liberty, he removes its appearance and its name, levels down the peoples under his rule and leaves those same people with a thirst for liberty and a new awareness of what it really was and a keenness to set up, as they did shortly afterwards in all Europe, institutions of liberty. Even in the darkest and crassest times liberty trembles in the lines of poets and affirms itself in the pages of thinkers and burns, solitary and magnificent, in some men who cannot be assimilated by the world around them, as Vittorio Alfieri[24] discovered in the eighteenth century grand-ducal Siena, where he found a friend, "freest of spirits," born "in hard prison," and abiding there "like a sleeping lion," for whom he wrote the dialogue in his *Virtue Unrecognized*. Yes, to the eye of philosophy, whether the age is propitious or unfavourable, liberty appears as abiding purely and invincibly and consciously only in a few spirits; but these alone are those which count historically, just as great philosophers, great poets, great men and every kind of great work have a real message only to the few, even though crowds may acclaim and deify them, ever ready to abandon them in order noisily to acclaim other idols and to exercise, under whatever slogan or flag, a natural disposition for courtisanship and servility. And on account of this, and through experience and meditation, the philosopher thinks and tells himself that if in liberal times one enjoys the welcome illusion of belonging to a great company, while in illiberal times one has the opposite and unwelcome illusion of being alone or almost alone, the first optimistic view was surely illusory, but maybe the second pessimistic view was illusory also. He sees this and he sees so many other things and he draws the conclusion that if history is not an idyll, neither is it a "tragedy of horrors" but a drama in which all the actions, all the actors, and all the members of the chorus are, in the Aristotelian sense, "middling," guilty-non-guilty, a mixture of good and bad, yet ruled always by a governing thought which is good and to which evil ends by acting as a stimulus and that this achievement is the work of liberty which always strives to re-establish and always does re-establish the social and political conditions of a more intense liberty. If anyone needs persuading that liberty cannot exist differently from the way it has lived and always will live in history, a perilous and fighting life, let him for a moment consider a world of liberty without obstacles, without menaces and without oppressions of any kind; immediately he will look away from this picture with horror as being something worse than death, an infinite boredom.

Having said this, what is then the anguish that men feel for liberty that has been lost, the invocations, the lost hopes, the words of love and anger which come from the hearts of men in certain moments and in certain ages of history? We have already said it in examining a similar case: these are not philosophical nor historical truths, nor are they errors or dreams; they are movements of moral conscience; they are history in the making.

8

Maurice Mandelbaum

Selection from The Problem of
Historical Knowledge: An Answer to
Relativism *(New York: Liveright Publishing
Corp., 1938)*

Maurice Mandelbaum (1908–1987), a philosophy professor
at Dartmouth University, was the founding father of the analytic philosophy of history. When Mandelbaum launched his
professional career in the 1930s, the "philosophy of history"
meant essentially what we would today call "speculative history," that is, grand theorizing about the ultimate cause and
course of history. Mandelbaum therefore called his new field
of interest "historiography," which of course today has multiple meanings: the history of history, the methods of history, or even the philosophy of history. All of these terms are
interwoven and confused because they are used differently
by different people over time.

At any rate, Mandelbaum was aware of the European, largely
German traditions of theorizing about history that dated to

the mid-19th century. He knew that the American historians were about a hundred years behind their German colleagues when it came to thinking about the nature of history.

In 1938, responding to new subjectivist epistemologies by American historians Charles Beard and Carl Becker, Mandelbaum wrote *The Problem of Historical Knowledge*, a defense of objective historical truths, which remains one of the best philosophical works on the topic. For the generation to follow, analytic philosophy of history remained focused on a few problems, primarily (a) epistemological problems, specifically the debate about subjective versus objective facts; (b) problems of causation—what it means for something to be the cause and another to be the effect; and (c) problems of the nature of historical knowledge, specifically the "covering laws," that is, is historical knowledge particular or general, does a specific historical event demonstrate deeper underlying laws or structure of history, like a particular experiment in the lab demonstrates deeper laws of physics?

In a 1989 article on Mandelbaum, Christopher Lloyd gives a worthy description of some important elements of Mandelbaum's views. According to Lloyd, Mandelbaum believed in the correspondence theory of truth:

> This says that the order of events that is found in nature and history really does characterize the mind-independent events of the world, which are not transformed by the mind in the act of knowing. Events have an existential relation of causal dependence on each other, and facts are statements about events, so the

relevance of facts to each other is not dependent on some epistemology, value system, interpretation, or theory. Rather, historical relevance, interpretation, and synthesis are based on the discoverable causality of the external world.[25]

By mind-independent, Lloyd means that the view that the world exists independently of one's mind; that the world is not the product of our imaginations, that it has real, physical existence. This view is essential for all who wish to stress the difference between history and the past. Such a distinction is sometimes lost on nonhistorians, and, indeed, on some historians. In Mandelbaum's thought, the past exists regardless of whether historians are around to analyze it. History, however, is the product of our minds' efforts to extract pattern and meaning from the past.

In this selection, Mandelbaum pays homage to Heinrich Rickert before criticizing his philosophy of history on multiple grounds. Readers will note that Mandelbaum was a true analytic philosopher, weighing arguments and counterarguments. At the same time—and unlike some other philosophers of history—he was not ignorant of historians' actual work and mental processes.

Rickert, more than any other thinker, stands at the center of all philosophic discussion concerning the problem of historical knowledge. *Die Grenzen der naturwissenschaftlichen Begriffsbildung* which he first published in 1902, and which has undergone alteration through five editions, is beyond dispute the classic work in the field. Together with Rickert's other discussions of the historical problem, it provides a theory which in scope, consistency, and logical subtlety far surpasses all other works with which we shall be dealing. For that reason it is in a sense unfair to Rickert to treat of him at this point. Yet if we are to understand the significance of Scheler and Troeltsch[26] it can only be through a contrast and comparison with Rickert, whose work, in its earliest form, provided the background for theirs. But we must be careful in considering Rickert here, not to discuss him merely as Scheler and Troeltsch first saw him, for each of the five editions of *Die Grenzen* has carried beyond the position which they—not without reason—ascribed to him. And yet Rickert's position, as he himself would insist, has not changed. If we draw the full logical consequences of his thought we shall see that in spite of his many polemical assertions and denials even his later statements are defenseless against most of the attacks which they launched against him.

Rickert, like Simmel,[27] starts from a thoroughgoing Kantian position, but unlike Simmel he attempts to show that the complete nature of a historical account is determined by values. In this we can see that he represents a step beyond Simmel, but a step taken in the same direction: for him not merely the form but the material of historical accounts depends upon non-existential factors. We must now consider closely, and in considerable detail, just how Rickert attempts to establish his view that values determine the complete nature of every historical account.

Rickert's earliest concern with the problem of historical knowledge arose out his attempt to undermine the then prevailing view that knowledge and "the scientific method" were identical. Following in the footsteps of Windelband's famous rectoral address,* Rickert drew a distinction between natural-scientific knowledge and historical knowledge. This distinction, which is drawn in the first sections of *Die Grenzen der naturwissenschaftlichen Begriffsbildung* may here be briefly discussed.

Rickert seeks to delimit the field of the natural-sciences not through an analysis of their subject matter but through a consideration of the formal elements involved in them. This procedure is paralleled in his treatment of historical knowledge, where he first inquires into the historian's purpose on the assumption that this purpose determines the form of historical accounts. This method of proceeding has its basis in Rickert's Kantian view that knowledge can never grasp actuality without transforming it, and that such transformation is always determined by the theoretical purpose (Erkenntniszweck) which lies behind the attempt to gain knowledge.

According to Rickert the characteristic form of natural-scientific knowledge lies in the use made of general concepts, or laws. The purpose of these concepts is to overcome the extensive and intensive multiplicity of things; to bring together and to simplify the infinite manifold of the external world. This the general concept does by virtue of its generality. It looks away from the individuality, the concreteness and the uniqueness of the manifold under consideration, concentrating on the recurring, or general, aspects of actuality.

---

* *Geschichte und Naturwissenschaft* (1894).

Historical knowledge, on the other hand, is characterized by an interest in the particular. It grasps both concreteness and individuality; its purpose is to discover not the general but the individual concepts of things. The specific function of history is to call attention to the uniqueness of certain objects. This difference between historical and natural-scientific knowledge is summarized by Rickert when he says: "Empirical reality becomes nature when we regard it with reference to the general (*das Allgemeine*), it becomes history when we regard it with reference to the particular and individual (*das Besondere und Individuelle*)."*

This distinction between the two forms of knowledge is basic to all of Rickert's discussion of history and for that reason he builds his argument slowly. Yet the point is clear enough, and well grounded: science is interested in the general, it strives for generalized systematic knowledge, and for it an individual thing is but the representative of a principle, an example that is used to establish a law; but history is interested in the particular, in what actually did occur, in the presentation of this or that unique happening. Rickert acknowledges that this formal distinction between the two types of knowledge is not absolute in the sense that all natural science is to be thought of as entirely devoid of historically represented things. His distinction is a logical one, and has formal validity only: there will be some crossing-over between the divisions, every object may be considered from either standpoint, and within each province there will be all degrees of

* *Die Grenzen*, p. 227.

generality and individuality. But as a formal distinction it is not open to attack.

Our problem, however, is not concerned with a further inquiry into the validity or the usefulness of such a distinction, but rather in tracing out the consequences of this distinction for Rickert's view of history. Starting from his contrast between the generality of scientific concepts and the individuality which characterizes history, Rickert seeks to determine what makes us contemplate an object as individual.[†] At once the criterion of indivisibility springs to mind. This criterion cannot, however, show us the meaning of historical individuality so long as it is interpreted as meaning physical divisibility. If we look, however, at the difference between the Kohinoor diamond and a lump of coal, we find the concept of indivisibility taking on new significance. Both the diamond and the coal are physically divisible, but they differ in their "historical" individuality. The diamond cannot be divided without losing some of its value and for the reason we look upon it as an individual: it is considered as an individual because we believe that it should not be divided. Obviously the reason why it should not be divided is the fact that it is a unique bearer of certain values, and therein lies its true individuality. Now this Rickert carries over into the realm of history proper, a historical individual being for him the unique bearer of certain values. Goethe or Napoleon is thus a historical personage in a sense in

---

[†] Concerning what follows, *Cf, Die Grenzen*, Ch. IV, Sect. 2 (Das historiche Individuum).

which the average man is not, and Goethe and Napoleon enter into historical works because it is seen that in them, uniquely, were realized certain values. In this way, starting from a contrast between the generality of the natural sciences and the particularity of history, Rickert finds that historical knowledge is based from the very foundations up on the acknowledgement of values.

Now Rickert is at this point careful to draw a distinction between the act of valuing (Wertung) and the act of relating an object to values (Wertbeziehung). That which makes an object a historical individual is not, according to Rickert, the fact that the historian personally values it, but rather that he sees its value-relevance, its relation to values. A person or a social movement only becomes a historical "individual" when we see that through him or it certain transcendent values enter into the realm of the actual. While the historian may personally value some friend, that friend only becomes an object for historical contemplation if he is so related to the universal cultural values of mankind as to be irreplaceable. For the historian the average man is to Goethe as a lump of coal is to the Kohinoor diamond.

This introduction of values into the historian's enterprise enables Rickert to offer a delimitation of history according to its subject matter. For if history is constrained by its theoretical purpose to deal with value-relevant objects, the field of historical inquiry can be readily defined. The only place at which values enter into actuality is through the valuations of human beings. Thus history must be essentially human in its scope. But if history is to be knowledge it must rise above the merely subjective and relate the objects of its contemplation to generally acknowledge values. These generally acknowledged individual values are identified by Rickert with "cultural" values (Kulturwerte), and history becomes, as a consequence, cultural knowledge (Kulturwissenschaft). The long and tortuous argument which led Rickert to this position cannot here be followed in detail. It may merely be noted that much of this argument was directed against a material delimitation of history which rested on the contrast between nature (Natur) and spirit (Geist). It is to the credit of Rickert that rather than fall in with the prevalent but vague notion of the "Geisteswissenschaften," he forged an alternative concept which, without sacrificing the value of that designation, stressed the important fact that history necessarily deals with socially significant events (Kultur).

But Rickert recognizes that this linkage of values and history does not carry him far enough, for he has up to this point merely demonstrated the relation of values to the historian's election of his subject matter. He wishes also to prove that the form of the historical account, the method in which the historian treats his subject matter, is determined by values. We must follow this argument in somewhat greater detail.

Rickert points out that in every historical account there is an element of selection, and it is his purpose to prove that what determines this selection process is the historian's orientation towards values. Now he takes it as an established fact that the historian selects the object of his account with reference to values. The portrayal of this object must also proceed with reference to these same values if the original choice is to have any meaning: it is inconceivable that a historian should determine what is "historical" through a consideration of values, and then proceed to leave these values totally out of account. In other words, if its relation to values makes an object "historical," the "historical" account of that object cannot fail to stress the object's relation to those same values. But Rickert does not wish to hold that the historian actually and directly relates the object of his attention to values, for this would run counter to all that we know of historical works. Furthermore, since the cultural values in question are, according to Rickert, purely formal in character (the state, art, law, morality, religion and the like), every historical work would necessarily be empty and formal. To avoid this reduction of history to the purely formal, and at the same time to hold that values determine the inner nature of a historical account presents Rickert with some difficulties. These he avoids by the introduction of the concept of concrete "value-structures" (*Sinngebilde*).* These value-structures are the manifestations of the formal values in particular situations; their nature is determined by the values, but in contradistinction to the latter they are individual and not general. It is with these concrete value-structures ("this particular state," instead of the value: "statehood") that the historian is concerned; his account is therefore neither empty nor formal. On the other hand, these value-structures can only be understood with reference to general values, for the particular state would not have its being were it not for the acknowledgement of the value of statehood. Thus Rickert is able to save his insistence on the relation of a historical account to universal values, and yet not give up the concreteness of history.

---

* Concerning what follows, *Cf., Die Probleme der Geschichts-philosophie*, Ch. I, Sect. 6, and *Die Grenzen*, Ch. IV, Sect. 9.

This introduction of the concept of concrete value-structure demands, however, that every historical account have as its central core human valuations as they appear in concrete cultural form (*Sinngebilde*). But here again actual historical accounts seem to deny Rickert's contention, and again, he must seek a reconciliation of his theory and those works. For while it is certain that valuations form part of the material with which the historian deals, it is equally certain that non-valuational, in fact non-human, elements, such as the contour of a battlefield, also have their place in a historical work. This fact Rickert seeks to explain by his distinction between the primary and the secondary historical objects. A primary historical object is one selected for consideration by the historian because of its relation to universal values; a secondary historical object, however, is not a unique bearer of universal values, but it enters into a historical account only because the historian must take cognizance of it in order to understand some primary object. Thus Goethe would be a primary historical object, while Goethe's father would be a historical object of the secondary type. Or, to take another example, the battle of Thermopylae would be a primary historical object, while the contour of that battlefield would be a secondary historical object. From these examples it can be seen that the relation holding between a secondary and a primary historical object is a causal relation. This Rickert recognizes. But we may well ask how, on Rickert's view, causal explanation can be related to value explanation. This question leads us into the very heart of his theory of a historical account.

Rickert recognizes that every historical event is temporal, that no non-enduring "event" is the subject of a historical account.

Further, he admits that every historical object, like every other phase of actuality, is heterogeneous rather than simple. Therefore, if value-relevance is to be the determining factor in the nature of a historical account, it must show itself through the whole of the historical individual, that is, through all its changing aspects. This can only be the case when each of the aspects of a historical object contributes to its value. And Rickert in fact insists that it is this which determines the selection of the elements which make up a historical object: the historian, relating the whole individual to a value, selects as aspects or elements of the individual those factors which determine its unique value. In this, as Rickert admits, every historical object when viewed as a series of events has the characteristic stamp of "teleology" on it. This teleological concept in which each part seems to lead purposefully into the next is nothing but the "developmental" view of a historical object. This Rickert recognizes, and he claims that every historical narrative is the account of a development. But our question remains to be answered: how is it that Rickert can hold to some measure of causal explanation and yet embrace the view that the elements of a historical object are those of its aspects which are relevant to the values embodied in the object as a whole?

To this question Rickert gives no clear answer. He holds that history must show not merely *what* was, but also why it was, that is, what caused it.* The historian, according to Rickert, must place the object of his contemplation in its proper context, and

---

* *Cf., Die Grenzen*, p. 373. Concerning what follows. *Cf., Die Grenzen*, pp. 393 ff., and *Die Probleme der Geschichtsphilosophie*, p. 81.

since every object, no matter what its nature, is at once an effect and a cause, the causal analysis of historical objects seems to be demanded. But what, in fact, is Rickert's view? After quoting with approval Schopenhauer's dictum that causality is no hack that one can stop when one will, Rickert holds that causal explanation forms part of a historical account in either of two ways. Firstly, one can trace the causes of a primary historical object back to secondary historical objects. Secondly, one can trace the causal relations existing between secondary historical objects just as far as one chooses, the limits being set either by caprice or by the amount of material demanded to cement together the elements of the historical account so that it can be re-experienced (nacherlebt) by the reader. As Rickert himself admits, this answer in its second aspect is of no theoretical significance. Yet it serves to illustrate the inner weakness of Rickert's entire theory.

It is certain that the historian must do more than trace a teleological manifestation of cultural values. But when he does more he is involved in causal explanation. Now Rickert is on safe ground when he admits that this causal explanation demands the introduction of secondary historical objects; for so long as the primary historical objects are selected for consideration on the basis of their value-relevance and the secondary historical objects are selected solely on the basis of their existential-relevance to these primary objects, the value-oriented nature of historical accounts remains unbroken. But Rickert apparently recognizes that no history is written in this manner, for if it were there would be no semblance of continuity in it. A historical account of, let us say, "the

Industrial Revolution" would, according to this view, have as its elements a series of descriptions of the inventions and techniques which were relevant to that concrete value-structure (*Sinngebild*) known as the Industrial Revolution. The causes of each of these elements would then be traced back into the realm of secondary historical objects (the circumstances of this or that man's life, the labor market in this or that town, etc.) until the historical work would become a combination of an ideal, value-oriented, teleological development on the one hand, and a collection of rather curious, isolated causal information on the other. Thus Rickert goes on to say that the historian must trace the causal connections between these secondary historical objects, since this alone would make of the work a truly historical account. But he holds that this tracing of causal connections (far from being an irresistible vehicle) halts wherever we choose to have it halt.

Let us now summarize what we have found concerning Rickert's view of a historical account. Rickert holds that theoretical purpose which determines the form of historical knowledge is an interest in the particular individual. The selection of which individuals are to be treated by the historian is determined by the recognition that in certain individuals general cultural values are uniquely embodied. These individuals are the primary historical objects. The historian builds his account of them with reference to the values which they embody, portraying in his account the successive stages by which the values are realized. But Rickert recognizes that the historian goes beyond such a portrayal in almost every historical work, examining causes as well as developmental consequences, analyzing as well as synthesizing. Thus he holds that the historian also traces the primary historical objects back to their actual causes. Recognizing that this would break the continuity of a historical account, Rickert acknowledges the facts that the historian also traces causal connections between the secondary historical objects, thus linking them to each other as well as to the primary historical individuals. However, he holds that the latter type of causal portrayal does not constitute a problem for the theory of historical knowledge.

His account of historical knowledge may perhaps become somewhat clearer to the reader if, before going on to a criticism of this view, we here list the general philosophical presuppositions which lie behind it. The first of these is that the facts of the past may be objectively known, whether those facts be valuations or non-valuational events. The second presupposition is that the knowledge of these facts does not in itself constitute "historical" knowledge; in order to have historical knowledge we must give these facts a particular form, dictated by our theoretical purpose. Third, that historical knowledge is similar in this respect to all knowledge whatsoever, since the true object of knowledge is never actual at all, but is always a transcendent value. Fourth, that the transcendent values are universal, demanding acknowledgement by all, everywhere. Fifth, that the only "objectivity" to be found in knowledge is the Kantian objectivity of universality and necessity: no knowledge ever reproduces actuality. Sixth, that causal explanation leads to an infinite regress, and if history is to be valid knowledge, its objectivity (necessity) must therefore depend upon some principle other than causal explanation.

Bearing these general presuppositions in mind, and remembering what has been said concerning the account of historical knowledge which Rickert gives, it will be well to conclude with a rather extensive criticism of Rickert's theory. Our criticism will fall under two headings: first, that Rickert has not actually provided an escape from historical relativism; second, that in spite of its scope and subtlety Rickert's account of historical knowledge is in itself untenable. Rickert's answer to relativism rests on two points in his theory: first, on the distinction between an act of valuing (Wertung) and the relating of an object to values (Wertbeziehung); second, on the claim that the values which determine the nature of historical accounts are of universal validity. Now the distinction between an act of valuing and the relating of an object to values is a valid distinction. Furthermore it enables Rickert to stress a fact which relativists sometimes seem to overlook, that the historian does not always choose his subject because he likes or dislikes it. It is true that it often appears as if, from the very outset, the historian values his material in terms of his own interests. But it is also true that every historian avows a theoretic interest in his material; the presence of this theoretic interest obliges his personal attitudes to give way before the demands of the material itself (Wertbeziehung). Only after he has portrayed the nature of the historical events with which he deals is the historian in a position to pass moral judgment upon past actions. But this he does as an ethical personality, and not as a historian.

This distinction drawn between valuation and value-relevance does not carry Rickert far enough. For at best it shows that the historian seeks to be objective; it certainly does not establish the objectivity of his judgments. Rickert's claim that the values involved are universally valid seeks to advance the argument for objectivity. It will be seen that if every historical judgment is constituted by the acknowledgement of a value which is valid for all people at all times, the relativist will not be able to hold his ground. To be sure, the relativist would claim that there are no such universal values; but Rickert has attempted to establish their reality by a long and careful argument. Therefore in considering Rickert's answer to relativism, it is necessary to grant him his contention that all values are universally valid, and to see whether, even on this assumption, he has provided for objectivity.

Now by the objectivity of a judgment Rickert does mean that the judgment mirrors that aspect of actuality with which it deals, for, according to his view, all knowledge is a transformation of actuality through concepts. What objectivity means in his system is the universal necessity of a judgment; that all persons in all times, when confronted by a given aspect of actuality will be forced (through the acknowledgement of transcendent values) to judge thus and not otherwise. If a historical judgment is objective in this sense, Rickert will have answered the relativist. Let us see how the matter stands.

Rickert has admitted that the historian does not deal directly with the transcendent values, but with the value-structures (*Sinngebilde*) through which these values are evidenced in actuality. The objectivity of a historical judgment becomes therefore a question as to whether the presence of universal values in a particular value-structure can force all beholders to judge identically of that value-structure (i.e., of that particular state, or of that particular religion). Now the particular value-structure must be more than a concretion of the universal formal values, for in so far as the historian deals with it, it belongs at least partially to the sphere of actuality.* Rickert holds that the elements in it which were actual (both what happened and what was actually valued by the person or persons in question) can be objectively known as facts. Because this factual information and the universal values are both objectively given to the historian, it seems as if the value-structures would also of necessity be objectively given. But this the relativist can and would deny.

The relativist would hold that a particular value-structure (this state, this literary ideal, and the like) is to be known neither through a set of facts which went to form part of its being, nor through the "universal" formal values which might be found represented in it, nor yet through both of these together. And his argument here would be plain. The historical object, being a particular value-structure, belongs to a realm which is an in-between realm; it is neither a mere actuality nor a pure value, but a result of both. To "understand" it the historian must be in a position to experience the intimate connection of these two diverse elements which went to form it. But the infinite and heterogeneous character of actuality makes such a re-experiencing of the past impossible. Therefore the historian must substitute for past actuality the contents of his own given present. This necessarily means that the value-structure which he experiences is not

* Cf., Die Grenzen, p. 537.

identical with the value-structure which he seeks to describe; it is, rather, a product of the "universal" values and his own given present. This is the ultimate basis of Troeltsch's insistence of on an intuitive re-experiencing, an insistence which Rickert has failed to understand.[†]

But Rickert might answer such a relativistic contention by saying the historian does not seek to re-experience the past or reproduce it in any sense. He might hold that the historian's judgments are no less universally necessary because they contain an admixture of his own present actuality. But this answer would overlook Rickert's own acceptance of the fact that actuality is a sphere of heterogeneity, a fact which makes it theoretically possible, if not logically imperative, to hold that the actuality presented to different historians is different in kind. This being the case, the value-structures which are the resultants of actuality and the universal values will change from historian to historian. And we see, in fact, that Rickert's whole case for objectivity rests on his appeal to universal values, even though the historian is concerned with value-structures which are not produced out of these values alone. The only real escape from relativism which Rickert could give would be an insistence on the ability of the historian to know all the facts which, in conjunction with the universal values, gave rise to particular value-structures. But his view that actuality presents an infinite manifold excludes any such solution: the facts of the

[†] *Cf., Die Grenzen,* p. xxix; p. 435, n. 1. Also, Kaufmann: *Geschichtsphilosophie der Gegenwart,* p. 26f.

past are themselves "selected." In this the last avenue for escaping relativism has been closed.*

We may now turn to our second set of criticisms of Rickert: that, in itself, his theory provides a false account of the nature of historical knowledge.

The inadequacy of Rickert's theory as a whole is to be found in the dualisms which beset it. The chief of these dualisms, and the one which we shall consider first, is the distinction which Rickert draws between factual knowledge of the past and true historical knowledge. His whole view of history rests on the assumption that objective factual judgments are possible, and that a historical account builds on these even though it then goes beyond them. However, Rickert's epistemology is of a sort that makes objective factual judgments concerning the past impossible. To this we must now turn.†

In regard to the validity of factual judgments concerning the occurrences of the past, he sees no special problem. He holds that factual judgments present no greater difficulties to historical writing than they do the natural sciences. This is certainly theoretically true, but we must ascertain whether Rick-

---

* It is significant to compare earlier and later editions of *Die Grenzen*. In the earlier editions relativism was in fact avoided by the appeal to the universal values. But this led to the frequent, and not unjustified, criticism that Rickert's view of history was formal and empty. To meet this criticism, emphasis was placed on the concrete value-structures. But this threw Rickert back towards that relativism which we have described.

† The following epistemological considerations are based chiefly on *Der Gegenstand der Erkenntnis*.

ert's view can account for the validity of any factual judgments whatsoever. His theory of the knowledge relationship maintains a dualism between what is known and the material of knowledge. This dualism is similar to the Kantian dualism of the given and the known, but is not identical with it, since givenness (Tatsächlichkeit) is itself a category according to Rickert. What we have is a dualism between the unformed and directly experienced (erlebt) sphere of actuality, and the sphere of the known, which is actuality brought under concepts. Now the act of knowing, or bringing actuality under concepts, is held to take place through a judgment, and a judgment is an affirmation or denial which is to be understood as the acknowledgement of a value or the denial of a disvalue. Bringing actuality under concepts, therefore, is an act which is value-oriented. The form of knowledge is determined by values, and the known itself is therefore to be understood only through its value determination. This is tantamount to saying, as Rickert himself would be the first to admit, that the relationships expressed in a true judgment are not derived from the material of knowledge (actuality) but from the form in which the subject is forced to express them. We could ask why, if this is the case, the concepts of science serve the practical purpose of aiding adjustment (as Rickert admits); for if the relationships expressed by those concepts were not paralleled by relationships in the sphere of actuality, it would be hard to see how adjustment could be aided by employing them. This problem, however, is left totally out of account by Rickert, due to his insistence on dealing with the form and not with the content of the knowledge. For him, as he says, actuality contains no problems worthy of philosophical discussion; the subject-matter of critical philosophy is the realm of the known. But such a treatment of knowledge leaves out of account the possibility that actuality may itself contain formal relationships which the factual judgment expresses. The reason for the neglect of this possibility is to be found in the dialectal structure of *Der Gegenstand der Erkenntnis*. There he accepts the immanental copy-theory (that ideas are copies of impressions) in its destructive aspect, treating its rejection of all forms of realism as beyond question; but the crumbling of this copy-theory in his own hands was not followed by a re-examination of the possibility of realism, but by a theory of his own. However, unless the destructive side of the immanental copy-theory (its denial of realism) is free from all definitions and postulates which characterize its positive side, this procedure of Rickert's is tantamount to lifting one's immaterial soul by one's bootstraps.

The whole emphasis on form in Rickert's analysis tends to eclipse an equally important subject for reflection: the source of the concrete content of our judgments. In holding that this source can never be known in itself (since all knowledge consists in a transformation), Rickert may have thought to escape the problem. But if he is incapable of dealing with actuality in itself, it is still possible to direct attention to those aspects of factual judgment which are not derived from the formal values. We may therefore say that Rickert's account of the factual judgment is in no wise complete, since it fails to deal with that which is of utmost importance for any account of history, namely, the relation of the content of a judgment to its referent, a portion of the flow of actuality.

But here we can go even further, and show that Rickert's account of the factual judgment is inadequate not only on the side of *what* the judgment expresses but also on the side of *why* the judgment expresses it. Rickert holds that we are to seek the *why* of a judgment in value-acknowledgements, and not in the presented material. But if this were the case, it would be hard to explain why we might not judge "this rose is red" without having a rose before us. To introduce the concept of logical validity affords no escape from the problem, because the criterion of logical validity concerns only the form and not the content of the judgment. On Rickert's view there would be no possibility of distinguishing between a true and false judgment; every judgment in so far as it is formally valid and is made "with good will," would be the product of a value acknowledgement, that is, it would be made under a transcendent and universal obligation. But then false judgments would cease to exist. It is here in particular that the formalism of Rickert's epistemology appears to be so vacuous.

This difficulty which inheres in Rickert's account of all factual judgments manifests itself even more clearly with respect to the historian's judgment of past facts. For it is evident that no pure value-acknowledgement can furnish the criterion for the truth or falsity of a judgment unless some portion of the realm of actuality is also presented.

But the historian who deals with the past does not have the possibility of getting into contact with the actuality which is relevant to a specific factual judgment concerning the past. He must therefore accept the accounts of past facts which have been handed down to him. Yet it is true that the historian also criticizes the accounts which are offered concerning past facts; through the "criticism of sources" he is often able to show that a supposed fact is untrue. Such criticism must remain forever unexplained by Rickert's theory of factual judgments.

Thus Rickert's theory of factual judgments is to be condemned from two points of view. On the one hand it fails to consider the possibility that a factual judgment may be expressive of actual relations which are independent of the act of knowing; on the other hand it fails to show how false judgments of fact are possible, and how such false judgments once made can actually be criticized. This being the case we may say that Rickert's theory of historical knowledge, assuming as it does the possibility of valid factual judgments, rests upon an insecure basis.

To this first criticism of Rickert's view of historical knowledge we may now add a second. We have already alluded to the fact that he attempts to combine causal explanation and value-relevance. These two aspects which he finds in all historical accounts are not, however, in any case compatible. For it will be remembered that he uses causal explanation not only to explain the relation of primary historical objects to secondary ones, but also to link the secondary historical objects to each other. Value-relevance, on the other hand, was used merely to link primary historical objects together. The incompatibility of these two methods of historical "understanding" lies in the fact that there is no reason to assume that the causal linkage of secondary historical objects will parallel the teleological linkage of the primary ones.* For example, the historian dealing with the judicial interpretations of the Constitution will be forced to take into account certain economic factors which will be causally related to the cases coming before the courts. But there is no guarantee that the chain of economic events necessary to explain these cases will parallel the chain of judicial interpretations; the two sets of factors may diverge. Thus if the historian is really attempting to include the causal chain of secondary factors in his account, he stands in danger of having his material draw him off in two opposite directions. Only the assumption that all causation is some "valuetropic" would enable the historian to follow both the causal and the teleological lines of understanding.† But, as Rickert would admit, such a metaphysical assumption lies beyond the province of the historian. It is apparently due to this discrepancy that he holds that the causal explanation of secondary historical objects proceeds merely as far as the historian chooses to have it proceed. As we have seen, this is to allow a theory of historical knowledge to break down at one of its most crucial points.

Our third, and final, criticism of Rickert's view consists in showing that the relation of past facts to values presupposes a full grasp

---

* No incompatibility exists between value-relevance and a causal explanation of primary historical objects by secondary ones. It is only the causal sequence of secondary historical objects which may run contrary to teleological views of the historical process. Frischeisen-Köhler tends to overlook this fact when he criticizes Rickert from substantially the same point of view as is here taken. (*Cf., Wirklichkeit und Wissenschaft*, p. 166f.)

† In an interesting attempt to defend and elaborate Rickert's position in regard to historical causation Sergius Hessen admits this fact. (*Cf., Individuelle Kausalität*, p. 52.)

of the historical material, and not merely a knowledge of isolated events, as Rickert would have us believe. Consider Rickert's view of the historian's activity: according to it, he selects the primary historical object which he is to describe because of its relevance to certain universal cultural values; he then selects as elements in his account those aspects of his object which are relevant to its manifestation of this value. Now if all historians were content to choose the objects of their consideration such events as are unambiguously associated with certain cultural values, Rickert's view could adequately account for their historical works. A historian might, for example, say, "I shall deal only with objects in which the value of statehood resides," and then trace out the particular and concrete manifestations of statehood at various times.

But let us suppose that our historian chooses to write a history of trade-unionism. With respect to what values, political or economic, should his account be built? The relevance of a phenomenon such as the rise of trade-unionism for either political or economic value can only be known after we already know the history of that movement. Or, let us take another example. If a man sets out to write a history of the frontier, with reference to what values should he select the elements of his account? If the work is really to be a history of the frontier (and not a study of its influence on American government, American religion, or the like) he must describe the successive migrations into new territory, the modes of life that developed in each locality, and the like. Only after he has done all this will he be able to see whether or not the elements in his account are relevant to political, moral, religious, legal, or artistic values; whether, in short, they are relevant to one or all of the universal cultural values.

By these examples we have sought to show that the relating of a fact to values presupposes a comparatively full knowledge of the fact in its actual historical context. It has been our purpose to do this, for if this is true then Rickert is mistaken in holding that it is the *value-relevance* of facts that explains their presence in a historical account. He assumes throughout (it is implicit in the very notion of a teleological development of value) that there is one particular form of value-relevance which runs through a whole historical account and determines its form. But a history of trade-unionism or a history of the American frontier could not originally be written on any such principle.

It need hardly be said that to have treated Rickert's work as a whole in these few pages is to have done it an injustice. Yet the criticisms which we have levelled against his view of historical knowledge can stand on their own strength. To summarize them, we may say that he has provided neither a philosophically sound answer to relativism, nor has he advanced an independent theory which is free of defects. The major defects which we have found in his system are three: first, his inability to render an adequate account of judgments of historical fact; second, the incompatibility of causal explanation with value-reference; and, third, the dependence of all value-relevant judgments on prior historical knowledge. Yet in spite of these faults Rickert's theory will long remain classic, for no other thinker has envisioned the problems with the same painstaking concern, nor has any other brought to these methodological inquiries an equal subtlety and dialectical skill. It should therefore be a disappointment to the reader, and not merely a relief, that we now leave the rarefied theoretical air of Rickert's speculation and return to the less rigorous atmosphere which we shall find pervading the theories of Scheler and Troeltsch.

9

R. G. Collingwood

Selection from The Idea of History, *rev. ed.,
edited with an introduction by Jan van der
Dussen (Oxford: Oxford University Press,
1994 [originally published 1946])*

In the mid-20th century, R. G. Collingwood (1889–1943) attained fixed status in the canon of philosophy of history. He is typically considered an idealist as opposed to a positivist historian, with views similar to those of Croce and Michael Oakeshott. A historian and philosopher of history, Collingwood was also an archaeologist and expert on ancient Rome.

Although he called himself a liberal, it was conservatives in the 20th century who owed much to Collingwood and looked up to him as "nearly correct" in his view of history. Some of this admiration must be ascribed to the easy access to his work, which was well-known and available in most large university libraries.

Conservative thinkers like Gordon Clark and Russell Kirk— not trained in history and unfamiliar with the intricacies of the historiography of the philosophy of history—discovered Collingwood even when they didn't discover say Louis Mink or Maurice Mandelbaum, other figures at the center of the field. Because his works were well written and in English also meant Collingwood was more accessible in the United States than were his German or French peers, even when their works were translated. One can find Collingwood's influence as well in works by Owen Barfield and John Lukacs.

Collingwood famously described history as a reenactment of thought. What he meant is up for debate, but what is clear is that Collingwood denied materialist explanations of history and placed ideas front and center.

As this selection will show, Collingwood refused to let history aspire to take the form of the natural sciences, but instead claimed that historical study itself was the proper method for studying the mind. He draws a distinction between scientists, who perceive events and search for their causes, and historians, who seek the thought that led to an event. In essence, historical facts are thoughts that the historian claims to understand. Because historical facts can only be considered facts when they are understood (whether the understanding is correct or not makes no difference here), they cannot be used to then seek scientific laws as would perceptions that are nonhistorical or not motivated by action.

The thesis which I shall maintain is that the science of human nature was a false attempt—falsified by the analogy of natural science—to understand the mind itself, and that, whereas the right way of investigating nature is by the methods called scientific, the right way of investigating mind is by the methods of history. I shall contend that the work which was to be done by the science of human nature is actually done, and can only be done, by history: that history is what the science of human nature professed to be, and that Locke was right when he said (however little he understood what he was saying) that the right method for such an inquiry is the historical, plain method.

I must begin by attempting to delimit the proper sphere of historical knowledge as against those who, maintaining the historicity of all things, would resolve all knowledge into historical knowledge. Their argument runs in some such way at this.

The methods of historical research have, no doubt, been developed in application to the history of human affairs: but is that the limit of their applicability? They have already before now undergone important extensions: for example, at one time historians had worked out their methods of critical interpretation only as applied to written sources containing narrative material, and it was a new thing when they learnt to apply them to the unwritten data provided by archaeology. Might not a similar but even more revolutionary extension sweep into the historian's net the entire world of nature? In other words, are no natural processes really historical processes, and is not the being of nature an historical being?

Since the time of Heraclitus and Plato, it has been a commonplace that things natural, no less than things human, are in constant change, and that the entire world of nature is a world of "process" or "becoming." But this is not what is meant by the historicity of all things; for change and history are not at all the same. According to this old-established conception, the specific forms of natural things constitute a changeless repertory of fixed types, and the process of nature is a process by which instances of these forms (or quasi-instances of them, things approximating to the embodiment of them) come into existence and pass out of it again. Now in human affairs, as historical research had clearly demonstrated by the eighteenth century, there is no such fixed repertory of specific forms. Here, the process of becoming was already by that time recognized as involving not only the instances or quasi-instances of the forms, but the forms themselves. The political philosophy of Plato and Aristotle teaches in effect that city-states come and go, but the idea of the city-state remains for ever as the one social and political form towards whose realization human intellect, so far as it is really intelligent, strives. According to modern ideas, the city-state itself is as transitory a thing as Miletus or Sybaris. It is not an eternal ideal, it was merely the political ideal of the ancient Greeks. Other civilizations have had before them other political ideals, and human history shows a change not only in the individual cases in which these ideals are realized or partially realized, but in the ideals themselves. Specific types of human organization, the city-state, the feudal system, representative government, capitalistic industry, are characteristic of certain historical ages.

At first, this transience of specific forms was imagined to be a peculiarity of human life. When Hegel said that nature has no history, he meant that whereas the specific forms of human organization change as time goes on, the forms of natural organization do not. There is, he grants, a distinction of higher and lower in the specific forms of nature, and the higher forms are a development out of the lower; but this development is only a logical one, not a temporal, and in time all the "strata" of nature exist simultaneously. But this view of nature has been overthrown by the doctrine of evolution. Biology has decided that living organisms are not divided into kinds each permanently distinct from the rest, but have developed their present specific forms through a process of evolution in time. Nor is this conception limited to the field of biology. It appeared simultaneously, the two applications being closely connected through the study of fossils, in geology. To-day even the stars are divided into kinds which can be described as older and younger; and the specific forms of matter, no longer conceived in the Daltonian manner, as elements eternally distinct like the living species of pre-Darwinian biology, are regarded as subject to a similar change, so that the chemical constitution of our present world is only a phase in a process leading from a very different past to a very different future.

This evolutionary conception of nature, whose implications have been impressively worked out by philosophers from M. Bergson, Mr. Alexander, and Mr. Whitehead, might seem at first sight to have abolished the difference between natural process and historical process, and to have resolved nature into history. And if a further step in the same resolution were needed, it might seem to be provided by Mr. Whitehead's doctrine that the very possession of its attributes by a natural thing takes time. Just as Aristotle argued that a man cannot be happy at an instant, but that the possession of happiness takes a lifetime, so Mr. Whitehead argues that to be an atom of hydrogen takes time—the time necessary for establishing the peculiar rhythm of movements which distinguishes it from other atoms—so that there is no such thing as "nature at an instant."

These modern views of nature do, no doubt, "take time seriously." But just as history is not the same thing as change, so it is not the same thing as "timefulness," where that means evolution or an existence which takes time. Such views have certainly narrowed the gulf between nature and history of which early nineteenth-century thinkers were so conscious; they have made it impossible to state the distinction any longer in the way in which Hegel stated it; but in order to decide whether the gulf has been really closed and the distinction annulled, we must turn to the conception of history and see whether it coincides in essentials with this modern conception of nature.

If we put this question to the ordinary historian, he will answer it in the negative. According to him, all history properly so called is the history of human affairs. His special technique, depending as it does on the interpretation of documents in which human beings of the past have expressed or betrayed their thoughts, cannot be applied just as it stands to the study of natural processes; and the more this technique is elaborated in its details, the farther it is from being so applicable. There is a certain analogy between the archaeologist's interpretation of a stratified site and the geologist's interpretation of rock-horizons with their associated fossils; but the difference is no less clear than the similarity. The archaeologist's use of his stratified relics depends on his conceiving them as artifacts serving human purposes and thus expressing a particular way in which men have thought about their own life; and from his point of view the palaeontologist, arranging his fossils in a time-series, is not working as an historian, but only as a scientist thinking in a way which can at most be described as quasi-historical.

Upholders of the doctrine under examination would say that here the historian is making an arbitrary distinction between things that are really the same, and that his conception of history is an unphilosophically narrow one, restricted by the imperfect development of his technique; very much as some historians, because their equipment was inadequate to studying the history of art or science or economic life, have mistakenly restricted the field of historical thought to the history of politics. The question must therefore be raised, why do historians habitually identify history with the history of human affairs? In order to answer this question, it is not enough to consider the characteristics of historical methods as it actually exists, for the question at issue is whether, as it actually exists, it covers the whole field which properly belongs to it. We must ask what is the general nature of the problems which this method is designed to solve. When we have done so, it will appear that the special problem of the historian is one which does not arise in the case of natural science.

The historian, investigating any event in the past, makes a distinction between what may be called the outside and the inside of an event. By the outside of the event I mean everything belonging to it which can be described in terms of bodies and their movements: the passage of Caesar, accompanied by certain men, across a river called the Rubicon at one date, or the spilling of his blood on the floor of the senate-house at another. By the inside of the event I mean that in it which can only be described in terms of thought: Caesar's defiance of Republican law, or the clash of constitutional policy between himself and his assassins. The historian is never concerned with either of these to the exclusion of the other. He is investigating not mere events (where by a mere event I mean one which has only an outside and no inside) but actions, and an action is the unity of the outside and inside of an event. He is interested in the crossing of the Rubicon only in its relation to Republican law, and in the spilling of Caesar's blood only in its relation to a constitutional conflict. His work may begin by discovering the outside of an event, but it can never end there; he must always remember that the event was an action, and that his main task is to think himself into this action, to discern the thought of its agent.

In the case of nature, this distinction between the outside and the inside of an event does not arise. The events of nature are mere events, not the acts of agents whose thought the scientist endeavours to trace. It is true that the scientist, like the historian, has to go beyond the mere discovery of events; but the direction in which he moves is very different. Instead of conceiving the event as an action and attempting to rediscover the thought of its agent, penetrating from the outside of the event to its inside, the scientist goes beyond the event, observes its relation to others, and thus brings it under a general formula or law of nature. To the scientist, nature is always and merely a "phenomenon," not in the sense of being defective in reality, but in the sense of being a spectacle presented to his intelligent observation; whereas the events of history are never mere phenomena, never mere spectacles for contemplation, but things which the historian looks, not at, but through, to discern the thought within them.

In thus penetrating to the inside of events and detecting the thought which they express, the historian is doing something which the scientist need not and cannot do. In this way the task of the historian is more complex than that of the scientist. In another way it is simpler: historians need not and cannot (without ceasing to be an historian) emulate the scientist in searching for the causes or laws of events. For science, the event is discovered by perceiving it, and the further search for its cause is conducted by assigning it to its class and determining the relation between that class and others. For history, the object to be discovered is not the mere event, but the thought expressed in it. To discover that thought is already to understand it. After the historian has ascertained the facts, there is no further process of inquiring into their causes. When he knows what happened, he already knows why it happened.

This does not mean that words like "cause" are necessarily out of place in reference to history; it only means that they are used there in a special sense. When a scientist asks "Why did that piece of litmus paper turn pink?" he means "On what kinds of occasions do pieces of litmus paper turn pink?" When an historian asks "Why did Brutus stab Caesar?" he means "What did Brutus think, which made him decide to stab Caesar?" The cause of the event, for him, means the thought in the mind of the person by whose agency the event came about: and this is not something other than the event, it is the inside of the event itself.

The processes of nature can therefore be properly described as sequences of mere events, but those of history cannot. They are not processes of mere events but processes of actions, which have an inner side, consisting of processes of thought; and what the historian is looking for is these processes of thought. All history is the history of thought.

But how does the historian discern the thoughts which he is trying to discover? There is only one way in which it can be done: by re-thinking them in his own mind. The historian of philosophy, reading Plato, is trying to know what Plato thought when he expressed himself in certain words. The only way in which he can do this is by thinking it for himself. This, in fact, is what we mean when we speak of "understanding" the words. So the historian of politics or warfare, presented with an account of certain actions done by Julius Caesar, tries to understand these actions, that is, to discover what thoughts in Caesar's mind determined him to do them. This implies envisaging for himself the situation in which Caesar stood, and thinking for himself what Caesar thought about the situation and the possible ways of dealing with it. The history of thought, and therefore all history, is the re-enactment of past thought in the historian's own mind.

This re-enactment is only accomplished, in the case of Plato and Caesar respectively, so far as the historian brings to bear on the problem all the powers of his own mind and all his knowledge of philosophy and politics. It is not a passive surrender to the spell of another's mind; it is a labour of active and therefore critical thinking. The historian not only re-enacts past thought, he re-enacts it in the context of his own knowledge and therefore, in re-enacting it, criticizes it, forms his own judgement of its value, corrects whatever errors he can discern in it. This criticism of the thought whose history he traces is not something secondary to tracing the history of it. It is an indispensable condition of the historical knowledge itself. Nothing could be a completer error concerning the history of thought than to suppose that the historian as such merely ascertains "what so-and-so thought," leaving it to some one else to decide "whether it was true." All thinking is critical thinking; the thought which re-enacts past thoughts, therefore, criticizes them in re-enacting them.

It is now clear why historians habitually restrict the field of historical knowledge to human affairs. A natural process is a process of events, an historical process is a process of thoughts. Man is regarded as the only subject of historical process, because man is regarded as the only animal that thinks, or thinks enough, and clearly enough, to render his actions the expressions of his thoughts. The belief that man is the only animal that thinks at all is no doubt a superstition; but the belief that man thinks more, and more continuously and effectively, than any other animal, and is the only animal whose conduct is to any great extent determined by thought instead of by mere impulse and appetite, is probably well enough founded to justify the historian's rule of thumb.

It does not follow that all human actions are subject-matter for history; and indeed historians are agreed that they are not. But when they are asked how the distinction is to be made between historical and non-historical human actions, they are somewhat at a loss how to reply. From our present point of view we can offer an answer: so far as man's conduct is determined by what may be called his animal nature, his impulses and appetites, it is non-historical; the process of those activities is a natural process. Thus, the historian is not interested in the fact that men eat and sleep and make love and thus satisfy their natural appetites; but he is interested in the social customs which they create by their thought as a framework within which these appetites find satisfaction in ways sanctioned by convention and morality.

Consequently, although the conception of evolution has revolutionized our idea of nature by substituting for the old conception of natural process as a change within the limits of a fixed system of specific forms the new conception of that process as involving a change in these forms themselves, it has by no means identified the idea of natural process with that of historical process; and the fashion, current not long ago, of using the word "evolution" in an historical context, and talking of the evolution of parliament or the like, though natural in an age when the science of nature was regarded as the only true form of knowledge, and when other forms of knowledge, in order to justify their existence, felt bound to assimilate themselves to that model, was the result of confused thinking and a source of further confusions.

There is only one hypothesis on which natural processes could be regarded as ultimately historical in character: namely, that these processes are in reality processes of action determined by a thought which is their own inner side. This would imply that natural events are expressions of thoughts whether the thoughts of God, or of angelic or demonic finite intelligences, or of minds somewhat like our own inhabiting the organic and inorganic bodies of nature as our minds inhabit our bodies. Setting aside mere flights of metaphysical fancy, such an hypothesis could claim our serious attention only if it led to a better understanding of the natural world. In fact, however, the scientist can reasonably say of it "je n'ai pas eu besoin de cette hypothese," and the theologian will recoil from any suggestion that God's action in the natural world resembles the action of a finite human mind under the conditions of historical life. This at least is certain: that, so far as our scientific and historical knowledge goes, the processes of events which constitute the world of nature are altogether different in kind from the processes of thought which constitute the world of history.

. . .

History as knowledge of mind

History, then, is not, as it has so often been mis-described, a story of successive events or an account of change. Unlike the natural scientist, the historian is not concerned with events as such at all. He is only concerned with those events which are the outward expression of thoughts, and is only concerned with these in so far as they express thoughts. At bottom, he is concerned with thoughts alone; with their outward expression in events he is concerned only by the way, in so far as these reveal to him the thoughts of which he is in search.

In a sense, these thoughts are no doubt themselves events happening in time; but since the only way in which the historian can discern them is by re-thinking them for himself, there is another sense, and one very important to the historian, in which they are not in time at all. If the discovery of Pythagoras concerning the square on the hypotenuse is a thought which we to-day can think for ourselves, a thought that constitutes a permanent addition to mathematical knowledge, the discovery of Augustus, that a monarchy could be grafted upon the Republican constitution of Rome by developing the implications of *proconsulare imperium* and *tribunicia potestas*, is equally a thought which the student of Roman history can think for himself, a permanent addition to political ideas. If Mr. Whitehead is justified in calling the right-angled triangle an eternal object, the same phrase is applicable to the Roman constitution and the Augustan modification of it. This is an eternal object because it can be apprehended by historical thought at any time; time makes no difference to it in this respect, just as it makes no difference to the triangle. The peculiarity which makes it historical is not the fact of its happening in time, but the fact of its becoming known to us by our re-thinking the same thought which created the situation we are investigating, and thus coming to understand that situation.

Historical knowledge is the knowledge of what a mind has done in the past, and at the same time it is the redoing of this, the perpetuation of past acts in the present. Its object is therefore not a mere object, something outside the mind which knows it; it is an activity of thought, which can be known only in so far as the knowing mind re-enacts it and knows itself as so doing. To the historian, the activities whose history he is studying are not spectacles to be watched, but experiences to be lived through in his own mind; they are objective, or known to him, only because they are also subjective, or activities of his own.

It may thus be said that historical inquiry reveals to the historian the powers of his own mind. Since all he can know historically is thoughts that he can re-think for himself, the fact of his coming to know them shows him that his mind is able (or by the very effort of studying them has become able) to think in these ways. And conversely, whenever he finds certain historical matters unintelligible, he has discovered a limitation of his own mind; he has discovered that there are certain ways in which he is not, or no longer, or not yet, able to think. Certain historians, sometimes whole generations of historians, find in certain periods of history nothing intelligible, and call them dark ages; but such phrases tell us nothing about those ages themselves, though they tell us a great deal about the persons who use them, namely that they are unable to re-think the thoughts which were fundamental to their life. It has been said that *die Weltgeschichte ist das Weltgericht*; and it is true, but in a sense not always recognized. It is the historian himself who stands at the bar of judgement, and there reveals his own mind in its strength and weakness, its virtues and its vices.

But historical knowledge is not concerned only with a remote past. If it is by historical thinking that we re-think and so redis-cover the thought of Hammurabi or Solon, it is in the same way that we discover the thought of a friend who writes us a letter, or a stranger who crosses the street. Nor is it necessary that the histo-rian should be one person and the subject of his inquiry another. It is only by historical thinking that I can discover what I thought ten years ago, by reading what I then wrote, or what I thought five minutes ago, by reflecting on an action that I then did, which surprised me when I realized what I had done. In this sense, all knowledge of mind is historical. The only way in which I can know my own mind is by performing some mental act or other and then considering what the act is that I have performed. If I want to know what I think about a certain subject, I try to put my ideas about it in order, on paper or otherwise; and then, having thus arranged and formulated them, I can study the result as an historical document and see what my ideas were when I did that piece of thinking: if I am dissatisfied with them, I can do it over again. If I want to know what powers my mind possesses as yet unexplored, for example, whether I can write poetry, I must try to write some, and see whether it strikes me and others as being the real thing. If I want to know whether I am as good a man as I hope, or as bad as I fear, I must examine acts that I have done, and understand what they really were: or else go and do some fresh acts and then examine those. All these inquiries are historical. They proceed by studying accomplished facts, ideas that I have thought out and expressed, acts that I have done. On what I have only begun and am still doing, no judgement can as yet be passed.

The same historical method is the only one by which I can know the mind of another, or the corporate mind (whatever exactly that phrase means) of a community or an age. To study the mind of the Victorian age or the English political spirit is simply to study the history of Victorian thought or English political activity. Here we come back to Locke and his "historical, plain Method." Mind not only declares, but also enjoys or possesses, its nature, both as mind in general and as this particular sort of mind with these particular dispositions and faculties, by thinking and acting, doing individual actions which express individual thoughts. If historical thinking is the way in which these thoughts are detected as expressed in these actions, it would seem that Locke's phrase hits the truth, and that historical knowledge is the only knowledge that the human mind can have of itself. The so-called science of human nature or of the human mind resolves itself into history.

It will certainly be thought (if those who think in this way have had patience to follow me thus far) that in saying this I am claiming more for history than it can ever give. The false view of history as a story of successive events or a spectacle of changes has been so often and so authoritatively taught in late years, especially in this country, that the very meaning of the word has become debauched through assimilation of historical process to natural process. Against misunderstandings arising from this source I am bound to protest, even if I protest in vain. But there is one sense in which I should agree that the resolution of a science of mind into history means renouncing part of what a science of mind commonly claims, and, I think, claims falsely. The mental scientist, believing in the universal and therefore unalterable truth of his conclusions, thinks that the account he gives of mind holds good of all future stages in mind's history: he thinks that his science shows what mind will always be, not only what it has been in the past and is now. The historian has no gift of prophecy, and knows it; the historical study of mind, therefore, can neither foretell the future developments of human thought nor legislate them, except so far as they must proceed—though in what direction we cannot tell—from the present as their starting-point. Not the least of the errors contained in the science of human nature is its claim to establish a framework to which all future history must conform, to close the gates of the future and bind posterity within limits due not to the nature of things (limits of that kind are real, and are easily accepted) but to the supposed laws of the mind itself.

Another type of objection deserves longer consideration. It may be granted that mind is the proper and only object of historical knowledge, but it may still be contended that historical knowledge is not the only way in which mind can be known. There might be a distinction between two years of knowing mind. Historical thought studies mind as acting in certain determinate ways in certain determinate situations. Might there not be another way of studying mind, investigating its general characteristics in abstraction from any particular situation or particular action? If so, this would be a scientific, as opposed to an historical, knowledge of mind: not history, but mental science, psychology, or the philosophy of mind.

If such a science of mind is to be distinguished from history, how is the relation between the two to be conceived? It seems to me that two alternative views of this relation are possible.

One way of conceiving it would be to distinguish between what mind is and what it does: and to entrust the study of what it does, its particular actions, to history, and reserve the study of what it is for mental science. To use a familiar distinction, its functions depend on its structure, and behind its functions or particular activities as revealed in history there lies a structure which determines these functions, and must be studied not by history but by another kind of thought.

This conception, however, is very confused. In the case of a machine, we distinguish structure from function, and think of the latter as depending on the former. But we can do this only because the machine is equally perceptible to us in motion or at rest, and we can therefore study it in either state indifferently. But any study of mind is a study of its activities; if we try to think of a mind absolutely at rest, we are compelled to admit that if it existed all (which is more than doubtful) at least we should be quite unable to study it. Psychologists speak of mental mechanisms; but they are speaking not of structures but of functions. They do not profess ability to observe these so-called mechanisms when they are not functioning. And if we look closer at the original distinction we shall see that it does not mean quite what it seems to mean. In the case of a machine, what we call function is really only that part of the machine's total functioning which serves the purpose of its maker or use. Bicycles are made not in order that there may be bicycles, but in order that people may travel in a certain way. Relatively to that purpose, a bicycle is functioning only when some one is riding it. But a bicycle at rest in a shed is not ceasing to function: its parts are not inactive, they are holding themselves together in a particular order; and what we call possession of its structure is nothing but this function of holding itself thus together. In this sense, whatever is called structure is in reality a way of functioning. In any other sense, mind has no function at all; it has no value, to itself or to any one else, except to be a mind, to perform those activities which constitute it a mind. Hume was therefore right to maintain that there is no such thing as "spiritual substance," nothing that a mind is, distinct from and underlying what it does.

This idea of a mental science would be, to use Comte's famous distinction, "metaphysical," depending on the conception of similarities or uniformities among those facts themselves. According to this idea, the task of mental science would be to detect types or patterns of activity, repeated over and over again in history itself.

That such a science is possible is beyond question. But two observations must be made about it.

First, any estimate of the value of such a science, based on the analogy of natural science, is wholly misleading. The value of generalization in natural science depends on the fact that the data of physical science are given by perception, and perceiving is not understanding. The raw material of natural science is therefore "mere particulars," observed but not understood, and taken in their perceived particularity, unintelligible. It is therefore a genuine advance in knowledge to discover something intelligible in the relations between general types of them. What they are in themselves, as scientists are never tired of reminding us, remains unknown: but we can at least know something about the patterns of facts into which they enter.

A science which generalizes from historical facts is in a very different position. Here the facts, in order to serve as data, must first be historically known; and historical knowledge is not perception, it is the discerning of the thought which is the inner side of the event. The historian, when he is ready to hand over such a fact to the mental scientist as a datum for generalization, has already understood it in this way from within. If he has not done so, the fact is being used as a datum for generalization before it has been properly "ascertained." But if he has done so, nothing of value is left for generalization to do. If, by historical thinking, we already understand how and why Napoleon established his ascendancy in revolutionary France, nothing is added to our understanding of that process by the statement (however true) that similar things have happened elsewhere. It is only when the particular fact cannot be understood by itself that such statements are of value.

Hence the idea that such a science is valuable depends on a tacit and false assumption that the "historical data," "phenomena of consciousness," or the like upon which it is based are merely perceived and not historically known. To think that they can be thus merely perceived is to think of them not as mind but as nature; and consequently sciences of this type tend systematically to dementalize mind and convert it into nature. Modern examples are the pseudo-history of Spengler, where the individual historical facts which he calls "cultures" are frankly conceived as natural products, growing and perishing "with the same superb aimlessness as the flower of the field," and the many psychological theories now fashionable, which conceive virtues and vices, knowledge and illusion, in the same way.

Secondly, if we ask how far the generalizations of such a science hold good, we shall see that its claim to transcend the sphere of history is baseless. Types of behaviour do, no doubt, recur, so long as minds of the same kind are placed in the same kind of situations. The behaviour-patterns characteristic of a feudal baron were no doubt fairly constant so long as there were feudal barons living in a feudal society. But they will be sought in vain (except by an inquirer content with the loosest and most fanciful analogies) in a world whose social structure is of another kind. In order that behavior-patterns may be constant, there must be in existence a social order which recurrently produces situations of a certain kind. But social orders are historical facts, and subject to inevitable changes, fast or slow. A positive science of mind will, no doubt, be able to establish uniformities and recurrence, but it can have no guarantee that the laws it establishes will hold good beyond the historical period from which its facts are drawn. Such a science (as we have lately been taught with regard to what is called classical economics) can do no more than describe in a general way certain characteristics of the historical age in which it is constructed. If it tries to overcome this limitation by drawing on a wider field, relying on ancient history, modern anthropology, and so on, for a larger basis of facts, it will still never be more than a generalized description of certain phases in human history. It will never be a non-historical science of mind.

To regard such a positive mental science as rising above the sphere of history, and establishing the permanent and unchanging laws of human nature, is therefore possible only to a person who mistakes the transient conditions of a certain historical age for the permanent conditions of human life. It was easy for men of the eighteenth century to make this mistake, because their historical perspective was so short, and their knowledge of cultures other than their own so limited, that they could cheerfully identify the intellectual habits of a western European in their own day with the intellectual faculties bestowed by God upon Adam and all his progeny. Hume, in his account of human nature, never attempted to go beyond observing that in point of fact "we" think in certain ways, and left undiscussed the question what he meant by the word "we." Even Kant, in his attempt to go beyond the "question of fact" and settle the "question of right," only showed that we must think in these ways if we are to possess the kind of experience enjoyed by men of his own age and civilization. He was, of course, not aware of this. No one in his time had done enough work on the history of thought to know that both the science and the experience of an eighteenth-century European were highly peculiar historical facts, very different from those of other peoples and other times. Nor was it yet realized that, even apart from the evidence of history, men must have thought in very different ways when as yet they were hardly emerged from the ape. The idea of a science of human nature, as entertained in the eighteenth century, belonged to a time when it was still believed that the human species, like every other, was a special creation with unalterable characteristics.

. . .

Conclusions

It remains to draw a few conclusions from the thesis I have tried to maintain.

First, as regards history itself. The methods of modern historical inquiry have grown up under the shadow of their elder sister, the method of natural science; in some ways helped by its example, in other ways hindered. Throughout this essay it has been necessary to engage in a running fight with what may be called a positivistic conception, or rather misconception, of history, as the study of successive events lying in a dead past, events to be understood as the scientist understands natural events; by classifying them and establishing relations between the classes thus defined. This misconception is not only an endemic error in modern philosophical thought about history, it is also a constant peril to historical thought itself. So far as historians yield to it, they neglect their proper task of penetrating to the thought of the agents whose acts they are studying, and content themselves with determining the externals of these acts, the kind of things about them which can be studied statistically. Statistical research is for the historian a good servant but a bad master. It profits him nothing to make statistical generalizations, unless he can thereby detect the thought behind the facts about which he is generalizing. At the present day, historical thought is almost everywhere disentangling itself from the toils of the positivistic fallacy, and recognizing that in itself history is nothing but the re-enactment of past thought in the historian's mind; but much still needs to be done if the full fruits of this recognition are to be reaped. All kinds of historical fallacies are still current, due to confusion between historical process and natural process: not only the cruder fallacies of mistaking historical facts of culture and tradition for functions of biological facts like race and pedigree, but subtler fallacies affecting methods of research and the organization of historical inquiry, which it would take too long to enumerate here. It is not until these have been eradicated that we can see how far historical thought, attaining at last its proper shape and stature, is able to make good the claims long ago put forward on behalf of the science of human nature. . . .

10

F. A. Hayek

"The Historicism of the Scientistic Approach,"
in The Counter-Revolution of Science:
Studies on the Abuse of Reason
(Indianapolis: Liberty Fund, 1979 [originally
published 1952])

Friedrich August Hayek (1899–1992) was born and educated in Austria, but spent most of his academic career in London, Chicago, and Freiburg. He shared the 1974 Nobel Prize in Economics with Gunnar Myrdal, and is known for his many and varied contributions to economics and social and political theory.

Hayek's most recognized contribution to history is certainly his edited book *Capitalism and the Historians* (1954), which defended the view that the Industrial Revolution in England raised material standards of living and largely improved the lives of workers.

Hayek's chapter reproduced here should be read as his theoretical statement about history. The book in which this

appeared, *The Counter-Revolution of Science*, found an audience among social scientists but appears to have had little
reception among historians. In the book, Hayek explains that
natural science is concerned with the relation of things to
things, whereas social science is interested in the relation of
men to men, or men to things. After the growth of science
in the Scientific Revolution, Hayek observes a "counterrevo-
lution" in which science has extended beyond its legitimate
domain of inquiry. One of those realms in which the scientific
method overstepped its bounds was history.

Hayek begins by establishing two kinds of "historicism": first,
the early form that avoided generalizations and eschewed
theory; and second, a later type that sought to derive theory
and large generalizations from empirical, historical observation. Hayek is concerned that historicists of both types recognize no role for theory and, in fact, little understand what
theory even means. Theory and generalization are necessary
in history, Hayek argues, so that we can make sense of individual phenomena, the true subject of historical study. But it
is when we treat generalized concepts as objects of inquiry
that we are confused about the purpose of generalization.

The Historicism of the Scientistic Approach

To see the "historicism" to which we must now turn described
as a product of the scientistic approach may cause surprise since
it is usually represented as the opposite to the treatment of social
phenomena on the model of the natural sciences. But the view
for which this term is properly used (and which must not be confused with the true method of historical study) proves on closer

consideration to be a result of the same prejudices as the other typical scientistic misconceptions of social phenomena. If the suggestion that historicism is a form rather than the opposite of scientism has still somewhat the appearance of a paradox, this is so because the term is used in two different and in some respect opposite and yet frequently confused senses: for the older view which justly contrasted the specific task of the historian with that of the scientist and which denied the possibility of a theoretical science of history, and for the later view which, on the contrary, affirms that history is the only road which can lead to a theoretical science of social phenomena. However great is the contrast between these two views sometimes called "historicism" if we take them in their extreme forms, they have yet enough in common to have made possible a gradual and almost unperceived transition from the historical method of the historian to the scientistic historicism which attempts to make history a "science" and the only science of social phenomena.

The older historical school, whose growth has recently been so well described by the German historian Meinecke, though under the misleading name of *Historismus*, arose mainly in opposition to certain generalizing and "pragmatic" tendencies of some, particularly French, 18th century views. Its emphasis was on the singular or unique (*individuell*) character of all historical phenomena which could be understood only genetically as the joint result of many forces working through long stretches of time. Its strong opposition to the "pragmatic" interpretation, which regards social institutions as the product of conscious design, implies in fact the use of a "compositive" theory which explains how such institutions can arise as the unintended result of the separate actions of many individuals. It is significant that among the fathers of this view Edmund Burke is one of the most important and Adam Smith occupies an honorable place.

Yet, although this historical method implies theory, i.e., an understanding of the principles of structural coherence of the social wholes, the historians who employed it not only did not systematically develop such theories and were hardly aware that they used them; but their just dislike of any generalization about historical developments also tended to give their teaching an anti-theoretical bias which, although originally aimed only against the wrong kind of theory, yet created the impression that the main difference between the methods appropriate to the study of natural and to that of social phenomena was the same as that between theory and history. This opposition to theory of the largest body of students of social phenomena made it appear as if the difference between the theoretical and the historical treatment was a necessary consequence of the differences between the objects of the natural and the social sciences; and the belief that the search for general rules must be confined to the study of natural phenomena, while in the study of the social world the historical method must rule, became the foundation on which later historicism grew up. But while historicism retained the claim for the pre-eminence of historical research in this field, it almost reversed the attitude to history of the older historical school, and under the influence of the scientistic currents of the age came to represent history as the empirical study of society from which ultimately generalization would emerge. History was to be the source from which a new science of society would spring, a science which should at the same time be historical and yet produce what theoretical knowledge we could hope to gain about society.

We are here not concerned with the actual steps in that process of transition from the older historical school to the historicism of the younger. It may just be noticed that historicism in the sense in which the term is used here, was created not by historians but by students of the specialized social sciences, particularly economists, who hoped thereby to gain an empirical road to the theory of their subject. But to trace this development in detail and to show how the men responsible for it were actually guided by the scientistic views of their generation must be left to the later historical account.

The first point we must briefly consider is the nature of the distinction between the historical and the theoretical treatment of any subject which in fact makes it a contradiction in terms to demand that history should become a theoretical science or that theory should ever be "historical." If we understand that distinction, it will become clear that it has no necessary connection with the difference of the concrete objects with which the two methods of approach deal, and that for the understanding of any concrete phenomenon, be it in nature or in society, both kinds of knowledge are equally required.

That human history deals with events or situations which are unique or singular when we consider all aspects which are relevant for the answer of a particular question which we may ask about them, is, of course, not peculiar to human history. It is equally true of any attempt to explain a concrete phenomenon if we only take into account a sufficient number of aspects or, to put it differently, so long as we do not deliberately select only such aspects of reality as fall within the sphere of any one of the systems of connected propositions which we regard as distinct theoretical sciences. If I watch and record the process by which a plot in my garden that I leave untouched for months is gradually covered with weeds, I am describing a process which in all its detail is no less unique than any event in human history. If I want to explain any particular configuration of different plants which may appear at any stage of that process, I can do so only by giving an account of all the relevant influences which have affected different parts of my plot at different times. I shall have to consider what I can find out about the differences of the soil in different parts of the plot, about differences in the radiation of the sun, of moisture, of the air-currents, etc., etc.; and in order to explain the effects of all these factors I shall have to use, apart from the knowledge of all these particular facts, various parts of the theory of physics, of chemistry, biology, meteorology, and so on. The result of all this will be the explanation of a particular phenomenon, but not a theoretical science of how garden plots are covered with weeds.

In an instance like this the particular sequence of events, their causes and consequences, will probably not be of sufficient general interest to make it worth while to produce a written account of them or to develop their study into a distinct discipline. But there are large fields of natural knowledge, represented by recognized disciplines, which in their methodological character are no different from this. In geography, e.g., and at least in a large part of geology and astronomy, we are mainly concerned with particular situations, either of the earth or of the universe; we aim at explaining a unique situation by showing how it has been produced by the operation of many forces subject to the general laws studied by the theoretical sciences. In the specific sense of a body of general rules in which the term "science" is often used these disciplines are not "sciences," i.e., they are not theoretical sciences but endeavors to apply the laws found by the theoretical sciences to the explanation of particular "historical" situations.

The distinction between the search for generic principles and the explanation of concrete phenomena has thus no necessary connection with the distinction between the study of nature and the study of society. In both fields we need generalizations in order to explain concrete and unique events. Whenever we attempt to explain or understand a particular phenomenon we can do so only by recognizing it or its parts as members of certain classes of phenomena, and the explanation of the particular phenomenon presupposes the existence of general rules.

There are very good reasons, however, for a marked difference in emphasis, reasons why, generally speaking, in the natural sciences the search for general laws has the pride of place, with their application to particular events usually little discussed and of small general interest, while with social phenomena the explanation of the particular and unique situation is as important and often of much greater interest than any generalization. In most natural sciences the particular situation or event is generally one of a very large number of similar events, which as particular events are only of local and temporary interest and scarcely worth public discussion (except as evidence of the truth of the general rule).

The important thing for them is the general law applicable to all the recurrent events of a particular kind. In the social field, on the other hand, a particular or unique event is often of such general interest and at the same time so complex and so difficult to see in all its important aspects, that its explanation and discussion constitute a major task requiring the whole energy of a specialist. We study here particular events because they have contributed to create the particular environment in which we live or because they are part of that environment. The creation and dissolution of the Roman Empire or the Crusades, the French Revolution or the Growth of Modern Industry are such unique complexes of events, which have helped to produce the particular circumstances in which we live and whose explanation is therefore of great interest.

It is necessary, however, to consider briefly the logical nature of these singular or unique objects of study. Probably the majority of the numerous disputes and confusions which have arisen in this connection are due to the vagueness of the common notion of what can constitute one object of thought and particularly to the misconception that the totality (i.e., all possible aspects) of a particular situation can ever constitute one single object of thought. We can touch here only on a very few of the logical problems which this belief raises.

The first point which we must remember is that, strictly speaking, *all* thought must be to some degree abstract. We have seen before that all perception of reality, including the simplest sensations, involves a classification of the object according to some property or properties. The same complex of phenomena which we may be able to discover within given temporal and spatial limits may in this sense be considered under many different aspects; and the principles according to which we classify or group the events may differ from each other not merely in one but in several different ways. The various theoretical sciences deal only with those aspects of the phenomena which can be fitted into a single body of connected propositions. It is necessary to emphasize that this is no less true of the theoretical sciences of nature than of the theoretical sciences of society, since an alleged tendency of the natural sciences to deal with the "whole" or the totality of the real things is often quoted by writers inclined to historicism as a justification for doing the same in the social field. Any discipline of knowledge, whether theoretical or historical, however, can deal only with certain selected aspects of the real world; and in the theoretical sciences the principle of selection is the possibility of subsuming these aspects under a logically connected body of rules. The same thing may be for one science a pendulum, for another a lump of brass, and for a third a convex mirror. We have already seen that the fact that a pendulum possesses chemical and optical properties does not mean that in studying laws of pendulums we must study them by the methods of chemistry and optics—though when we apply these laws to a particular pendulum we may well have to take into account certain laws of chemistry or optics. Similarly, as has been pointed out, the fact that all social phenomena have physical properties does not mean that we must study them by the methods of the physical sciences.

The selection of the aspects of a complex of phenomena which can be explained by means of a connected body of rules is, however, not the only method of selection or abstraction which the scientist will have to use. Where investigation is directed, not at establishing rules of general applicability, but at answering a particular question raised by the events in the world about him, he will have to select those features that are relevant to the particular question. The important point, however, is that he still must select a limited number from the infinite variety of phenomena which he can find at the given time and place. We may, in such cases, sometimes speak as if he considered the "whole" situation as he finds it. But what we mean is not the inexhaustible totality of everything that can be observed within certain spatio-temporal limits, but certain features thought to be relevant to the question asked. If I ask why the weeds in my garden have grown in this particular pattern no single theoretical science will provide the answer. This, however, does not mean that to answer it we must know everything that can be known about the space-time interval in which the phenomenon occurred. While the question we ask designates the phenomena to be explained, it is only by means of the laws of the theoretical sciences that we are able to select the other phenomena which are relevant for its explanation. The object of scientific study is never the totality of all the phenomena observable at a given time and place, but always only certain selected aspects: and according to the question we ask the same spatio-temporal situation may contain any number of different objects of study. The human mind indeed can never grasp a "whole" in the sense of all the different aspects of a real situation.

The application of these considerations to the phenomena of human history leads to very important consequences. It means nothing less than that a historical process or period is never a single definite object of thought but becomes such only by the question we ask about it; and that, according to the question we ask, what we are accustomed to regard as a single historical event can become any number of different objects of thought.

It is confusion on this point which is mainly responsible for the doctrine now so much in vogue that all historical knowledge is necessarily relative, determined by our "standpoint" and bound to change with the lapse of time. This view is a natural consequence of the belief that the commonly used names for historical periods or complexes of events, such as "the Napoleonic Wars," or "France during the Revolution," or "the Commonwealth Period," stand for definitely given objects, unique individuals which are given to us in the same manner as the natural units in which biological specimens or planets present themselves. Those names of historical phenomena define in fact little more than a period and a place and there is scarcely a limit to the number of different questions which we can ask about events which occurred during the period and within the region to which they refer. It is only the question that we ask, however, which will define our object; and there are, of course, many reasons why at different times people will ask different questions about the same period. But this does not mean that history will at different times and on the basis of the same information give different answers to the same question. Only this, however, would entitle us to assert that historical knowledge is relative. The kernel of truth in the assertion about the relativity of historical knowledge is that historians will at different times be interested in different objects, but not that they will necessarily hold different views about the same object.

We must dwell a little longer on the nature of the "wholes" which the historian studies, though much of what we have to say is merely an application of what has been said before about the "wholes" which some authors regard as objects of theoretical generalizations. What we said then is just as true of the wholes which the historian studies. They are never given to him as wholes, but always reconstructed by him from their elements which alone can be directly perceived. Whether he speaks about the government that existed or the trade that was carried on, the army that moved, or the knowledge that was preserved or disseminated, he is never referring to a constant collection of physical attributes that can be directly observed, but always to a system of relationships between some of the observed elements which can be merely inferred. Words like "government" or "trade" or "army" or "knowledge" do not stand for single observable things but for structures of relationships which can be described only in terms of a schematic representation or "theory" of the persistent system of relationships between the ever-changing elements. These "wholes," in other words, do not exist for us apart from the theory by which we constitute them, apart from the mental technique by which we can reconstruct the connections between the observed elements and follow up the implications of this particular combination.

The place of theory in historical knowledge is thus in forming or constituting the wholes to which history refers; it is prior to these wholes which do not become visible except by following up the system of relations which connects the parts. The generalizations of theory, however, do not refer, and cannot refer, as has been mistakenly believed by the older historians (who for that reason opposed theory), to the concrete wholes, the particular constellations of the elements, with which history is concerned. The models of "wholes," of structural connections, which theory provides ready-made for the historian to use (though even these are not the given elements about which theory generalizes but the results of theoretical activity), are not identical with the "wholes" which the historian considers. The models provided by any one theoretical science of society consist necessarily of elements of one kind, elements which are selected because their connection can be explained by a coherent body of principles and not because they help to answer a particular question about concrete phenomena. For the latter purpose the historian will regularly have to use generalizations belonging to different theoretical spheres. His work, thus, as is true of all attempts to explain particular phenomena, presupposes theory; it is, as is all thinking about concrete phenomena, an application of generic concepts to the explanation of particular phenomena.

If the dependence of the historical study of social phenomena on theory is not always recognized, this is mainly due to the very simple nature of the majority of theoretical schemes which the historian will employ and which brings it about that there will be no dispute about the conclusions reached by their help, and little awareness that he has used theoretical reasoning at all. But this does not alter the fact that in their methodological character and validity the concepts of social phenomena which the historian has to employ are essentially of the same kind as the more elaborate models produced by the systematic social sciences. All the unique objects of history which he studies are in fact either constant patterns of relations, or repeatable processes in which the elements are of a generic character. When the historian speaks of a State or a battle, a town or a market, these words cover coherent structures of individual phenomena which we can comprehend only by understanding the intentions of the acting individuals. If the historian speaks of a certain system, say the feudal system, persisting over a period of time, he means that a certain pattern of relationships continued, a certain type of actions were regularly repeated, structures whose connection he can understand only by mental reproduction of the individual attitudes of which they were made up. The unique wholes which the historian studies, in short, are not given to him as individuals, as natural units of which he can find out by observation which features belong to them, but constructions made by the kind of technique that is systematically developed by the theoretical sciences of society. Whether he endeavors to give a genetic account of how a particular institution arose, or a descriptive account of how it functioned, he cannot do so except by a combination of generic considerations applying to the elements from which the unique situation is composed. Though in this work of reconstruction he cannot use any elements except those he empirically finds, not observation but only the "theoretical" work of reconstruction can tell him which among those that he can find are part of a connected whole.

Theoretical and historical work are thus logically distinct but complementary activities. If their task is rightly understood, there can be no conflict between them. And though they have distinct tasks, neither is of much use without the other. But this does not alter the fact that neither can theory be historical nor history theoretical. Though the general is of interest only because it explains the particular, and though the particular can be explained only in generic terms, the particular can never be the general and the general never the particular. The unfortunate misunderstandings that have arisen between historians and theorists are largely due to the name "historical school" which has been usurped by the mongrel view better described as historicism and which is indeed neither history nor theory.

The naïve view which regards the complexes which history studies as given wholes naturally leads to the belief that their observation can reveal "laws" of the development of these wholes. This belief is one of the most characteristic features of that scientistic history which under the name of historicism was trying to find an empirical basis for a theory of history or (using the term philosophy in its old sense equivalent to "theory") a "philosophy of history," and to establish necessary successions of definite "stages" or "phases," "systems" or "styles," following each other in historical development. This view on the one hand endeavors to find laws where in the nature of the case they cannot be found, in the succession of the unique and singular historical phenomena, and on the other hand denies the possibility of the kind of theory which alone can help us to understand unique wholes, the theory which shows the different ways in which the familiar elements can be combined to produce the unique combinations we find in the real world. The empiricist prejudice thus led to an inversion of the only procedure by which we can comprehend historical wholes, their reconstruction from the parts; it induced scholars to treat as if they were objective facts vague conceptions of wholes which were merely intuitively comprehended; and it finally produced the view that the elements which are the only thing that we can directly comprehend and from which we must reconstruct the wholes, on the contrary, could be understood only from the whole, which had to be known before we could understand the elements.

The belief that human history, which is the result of the interaction of innumerable human minds, must yet be subject to simple laws accessible to human minds is now so widely held that few people are at all aware what an astonishing claim it really implies. Instead of working patiently at the humble task of rebuilding from the directly known elements the complex and unique structures which we find in the world, and of tracing from the changes in the relations between the elements the changes in the wholes, the authors of these pseudo-theories of history pretend to be able to arrive by a kind of mental short cut at a direct insight into the laws of succession of the immediately apprehended wholes. However doubtful their status, these theories of development have achieved a hold on public imagination much greater than any of the results of genuine systematic study. "Philosophies" or "theories" of history (or "historical theories") have indeed become the characteristic feature, the "darling vice" of the 19th century. From Hegel and Comte, and particularly Marx, down to Sombart and Spengler these spurious theories came to be regarded as representative results of social science; and through the belief that one kind of "system" must as a matter of historical necessity be superseded by a new and different "system," they have even exercised a profound influence on social evolution. This they achieved mainly because they looked like the kind of laws which the natural sciences produced; and in an age when these sciences set the standard by which all intellectual effort was measured, the claim of these theories of history to be able to predict future developments was regarded as evidence of their pre-eminently scientific character. Though merely one among many characteristic 19th century products of this kind, Marxism more than any of the others has become the vehicle through which this result of scientism has gained so wide an influence that many of the opponents of Marxism equally with its adherents are thinking in its terms.

Apart from setting up a new ideal this development had, however, also the negative effect of discrediting the existing theory on which past understanding of social phenomena had been based. Since it was supposed that we could directly observe the changes in the whole of society or of any particular changed social phenomenon, and that everything within the whole must necessarily change with it, it was concluded that there could be no timeless generalizations about the elements from which these wholes were built up, no universal theories about the ways in which they might be combined into wholes. All social theory, it was said, was necessarily historical, *zeitgebunden*, true only of particular historical "phases" or "systems."

All concepts of individual phenomena, according to this strict historicism, are to be regarded as merely historical categories, valid only in a particular historical context. A price in the 12th century or a monopoly in the Egypt of 400 B.C., it is argued, is not the same "thing" as a price or a monopoly today, and any attempt to explain that price or the policy of that monopolist by the same theory which we would use to explain a price or a monopoly of today is therefore vain and bound to fail. This argument is based on a complete misapprehension of the function of theory. Of course, if we ask why a particular price was charged at a particular date, or why a monopolist then acted in a particular manner, this is a historical question which cannot be fully answered by any one theoretical discipline; to answer it we must take into account the particular circumstances of time and place. But this does not mean that we must not, in selecting the factors relevant to the explanation of the particular price, etc., use precisely the same theoretical reasoning as we would with regard to a price of today.

What this contention overlooks is that "price" or "monopoly" are not names for definite "things," fixed collections of physical attributes which we recognize by some of these attributes as members of the same class and whose further attributes we ascertain by observation; but that they are objects which can be defined only in terms of certain relations between human beings and which cannot possess any attributes except those which follow from the relations by which they are defined. They can be recognized by us as prices or monopolies only because, and in so far as, we can recognize these individual attitudes, and from these as elements compose the structural pattern which we call a price or monopoly. Of course the "whole" situation, or even the "whole" of the men who act, will greatly differ from place to place and from time to time. But it is solely our capacity to recognize the familiar elements from which the unique situation is made up which enables us to attach any meaning to the phenomena. Either we cannot thus recognize the meaning of the individual actions, they are nothing but physical facts to us, the handing over of certain material things, etc., or we must place them in the mental categories familiar to us but not definable in physical terms. If the first contention were true this would mean that we could not know the facts of the past at all, because in that case we could not understand the documents from which we derive all knowledge of them.

Consistently pursued historicism necessarily leads to the view that the human mind is itself variable and that not only are most or all manifestations of the human mind unintelligible to us apart from their historical setting, but that from our knowledge of how the whole situations succeed each other we can learn to recognize the laws according to which the human mind changes, and that it is the knowledge of these laws which alone puts us in a position to understand any particular manifestation of the human mind. Historicism, because of its refusal to recognize a compositive theory of universal applicability unable to see how different configurations of the same elements may produce altogether different complexes, and unable, for the same reason, to comprehend how the wholes can ever be anything but what the human mind consciously designed, was bound to seek the cause of the changes in the social structures in changes of the human mind itself—changes which it claims to understand and explain from changes in the directly apprehended wholes. From the extreme assertion of some sociologists that logic itself is variable, and the belief in the "pre-logical" character of the thinking of primitive people, to the more sophisticated contentions of the modern "sociology of knowledge," this approach has become one of the most characteristic features of modern sociology. It has raised the old question of the "constancy of the human mind" in a more radical form than has ever been done before.

This phrase is, of course, so vague that any dispute about it without giving it further precision is futile. That not only any human individual in its historically given complexity, but also certain types predominant in particular ages or localities, differ in significant respects from other individuals or types is, of course, beyond dispute. But this does not alter the fact that in order that we should be able to recognize or understand them at all as human beings or minds, there must be certain invariable features present. We cannot recognize "mind" in the abstract. When we speak of mind what we mean is that certain phenomena can be successfully interpreted on the analogy of our own mind, that the use of the familiar categories of our own thinking provides a satisfactory working explanation of what we observe. But this means that to recognize something as mind is to recognize it as something similar to our own mind, and that the possibility of recognizing mind is limited to what is similar to our own mind. To speak of a mind with a structure fundamentally different from our own, or to claim that we can observe changes in the basic structure of the human mind is not only to claim what is impossible: it is a meaningless statement. Whether the human mind is in this sense constant can never become a problem—because to recognize mind cannot mean anything but to recognize something as operating in the same way as our own thinking.

To recognize the existence of a mind always implies that we add something to what we perceive with our senses, that we interpret the phenomena in the light of our own mind, or find that

they fit into the ready pattern of our own thinking. This kind
of interpretation of human actions may not be always successful,
and, what is even more embarrassing, we may never be absolutely
certain that it is correct in any particular case; all we know is that
it works in the overwhelming number of cases. Yet it is the only
basis on which we ever understand what we call other people's
intentions, or the meaning of their actions; and certainly the only
basis of all our historical knowledge since this is all derived from
the understanding of signs or documents. As we pass from men
of our own kind to different types of beings we may, of course,
find that what we can thus understand becomes less and less.
And we cannot exclude the possibility that one day we may find
beings who, though perhaps physically resembling men, behave
in a way which is entirely unintelligible to us. With regard to
them we should indeed be reduced to the "objective" study which
the behaviorists want us to adopt towards men in general. But
there would be no sense in ascribing to these beings a mind different from our own. We should know nothing of them which
we could call mind, we should indeed know nothing about them
but physical facts. Any interpretation of their actions in terms of
such categories as intention or purpose, sensation or will, would
be meaningless. A mind about which we can intelligibly speak
must be like our own.

The whole idea of the variability of the human mind is a direct
result of the erroneous belief that mind is an object which we
observe as we observe physical facts. The sole difference between
mind and physical objects, however, which entitles us to speak
of mind at all, is precisely that wherever we speak of mind we

interpret what we observe in terms of categories which we know only because they are the categories in which our own mind operates. There is nothing paradoxical in the claim that all mind must run in terms of certain universal categories of thought, because where we speak of mind this means that we can successfully interpret what we observe by arranging it in these categories. And anything which can be comprehended through our understanding of other minds, anything which we recognize as specifically human, must be comprehensible in terms of these categories. Through the theory of the variability of the human mind, to which the consistent development of historicism leads, it cuts, in effect, the ground under its own feet: it is led to the self-contradictory position of generalizing about facts which, if the theory were true, could not be known. If the human mind were really variable so that, as the extreme adherents of historicism assert, we could not directly understand what people of other ages meant by a particular statement, history would be inaccessible to us. The wholes from which we are supposed to understand the elements would never become visible to us. And even if we disregard this fundamental difficulty created by the impossibility of understanding the documents from which we derive all historical knowledge, without first understanding the individual actions and intentions the historian could never combine them into wholes and never explicitly state what these wholes are. He would, as indeed is true of so many of the adherents of historicism, be reduced to talking about "wholes" which are intuitively comprehended, to making uncertain and vague generalizations about "styles" or "systems" whose character could not be precisely defined.

It follows indeed from the nature of the evidence on which all our historical knowledge is based that history can never carry us beyond the stage where we can understand the working of the minds of the acting people because they are similar to our own. Where we cease to understand, where we can no longer recognize categories of thought similar to those in terms of which we think, history ceases to be human history. And precisely at that point, and only at that point, do the general theories of the social sciences cease to be valid. Since history and social theory are based on the same knowledge of the working of the human mind, the same capacity to understand other people, their range and scope is necessarily co-terminous. Particular propositions of social theory may have no application at certain times, because the combination of elements to which they refer to do not occur. But they remain nevertheless true. There can be no different theories for different ages, though at some times certain parts and at others different parts of the same body of theory may be required to explain the observed facts, just as, e.g., generalizations about the effect of very low temperatures on vegetation may be irrelevant in the tropics but still true. Any true theoretical statement of the social sciences will cease to be valid only where history ceases to be human history. If we conceive of somebody observing and recording the doings of another race, unintelligible to him and to us, his records would in a sense be history, such as, e.g., the history of an ant-heap. Such history would have to be written in purely objective, physical terms. It would be the sort of history which corresponds to the positivist ideal, such as the proverbial observer from another planet might write of the human race. But such history could not help us to understand any of the events recorded by it in the sense in which we understand human history.

When we speak of man we necessarily imply the presence of certain familiar mental categories. It is not the lumps of flesh of a certain shape which we mean, nor any units performing definite functions which we could define in physical terms. The completely insane, none of whose actions we can understand, is not a man to us if he could not figure in human history except as the object of other people's acting and thinking. When we speak of man we refer to one whose actions we can understand. As old Democritus said

"Man is what is known to all."[28]

11

Pieter Geyl

*Selection from Pieter Geyl, Arnold J. Toynbee,
and Pitirim A. Sorokin,* The Pattern of the
Past: Can We Determine It? *(Boston: Beacon
Press, 1949)*

Pieter Geyl (1887–1966) briefly served as a newspaper cor-
respondent in England, and from 1919 to 1935, he held a
professorship in Dutch history at the University of London.
Thereafter, he taught at Utrecht University.

Liberal historians before Geyl had played a substantial role
in the historiography of the Netherlands. The best known was
probably Robert Fruin, who—like Gustav Droysen in Germany,
Benedetto Croce in Italy, and Paul Fredericq and Henri Pirenne
in Belgium—wrote the history of freedom but with the nation
as the main subject. Geyl was not interested in the history of
Dutch national freedom per se, but the history of freedom of
the Dutch and Flemish people, whom he argued should be
seen as a common culture split apart in the Eighty Years' War.

Geyl primarily wrote about Dutch history from the 16th through the 18th centuries. During World War II, he was arrested by the Nazis and sent to Buchenwald for more than a year. He was released before the end of the war and became a contributor to the left-liberal Dutch magazine *Vrij Nederland* (*Free Netherlands*), which had been founded during the German occupation of the Netherlands.

Later in his career, Geyl turned to criticism and historical methods. He was a frequent interlocutor with Arnold Toynbee, the British historian known for *A Study of History*, which came out in 12 volumes from 1934 to 1961. Ultimately, Geyl should receive some credit for turning academic audiences away from Toynbee's work. Despite Geyl's criticisms, Toynbee called Geyl a friend and praised him as a first-rate historian in an obituary.

If liberal historians might be criticized for not developing a single, consistent philosophy of history, they might also be praised for it. Liberal history—unlike Christian history or Marxist history, for example—tends to a have a direction, that is, "progress." But except for liberal Hegelians and some liberal Progressives, liberal historians do not propose an inevitable end game of history. For liberals, history is not a giant puzzle to be solved. They tend to be skeptical or agnostic about any underlying purpose of all of history. The result is that liberals have been better at criticizing grand theories of history than at building them. As a biographer noted, Geyl is a good example of this: "Theory of history as such leaves him cold and hostile; yet the theoretical side of his writing is very strong and almost omnipresent, in the form of criticism—criticism of sources, of conception, and, not least, of both the makers and writers of history."[29]

Here we have the dry bones of a system to which the author gives flesh and life. The idea inspiring him is that of Christianity. It is true that Toynbee at times recalls Spengler, and his view of history is in fact not unrelated to the *Untergang des Abendlandes*. He expressly rejects Spengler's identification of civilizations with animate beings, which are born, are young, grow older, and die; when they break down it is by their own act alone. Similarly, he speaks emphatically against Spengler's connecting civilization with race. But if he insists on the freedom of choice, on the spiritual factor unrelated to blood or to the perishable flesh, he too carries to great lengths the presentation of his civilization as well-rounded units. Above all, during the centuries-long process of disintegration following upon breakdown, he sees them subject to a regularity of decay hardly less rigid than Spengler's parallel with the biological process.

In any case, however much he may diverge from Spengler, his system is even more diametrically opposed to historical materialism. He may speak of laws, his mind may be stocked richly with scientific notions, from which his language is ever borrowing terms and images; in reality the sovereignty and the freedom of the spirit are his main concern, and his Bible texts are more than a mere decoration of his argument, for in them he finds his profoundest truths foreshadowed and confirmed. God become man in Christ is to him the veritable sense of history. Of the great constructors of systems, St. Augustine is most closely related to him in spirit, and Professor Toynbee himself, in the preface to his second series, written in that gloomy year 1939, brings respectful homage to the bishop who completed *De Civitate Dei* while the Vandals were besieging his episcopal town. Material advantage is nothing in Toynbee's view; it is obstacles which rouse the spirit to consciousness. Violence he detests, he is a searcher after "gentleness." He meets history with ethical appreciations. The spirit, the highly gifted individual, the small group, these are the sources of creative force. Power is an illusion, if not a boomerang. As a civilization grows, it etherealizes. What exactly does he mean by this? He expresses it in morphological, in biological, in philosophical, and finally also in religious terms. No doubt all the rest for him is comprehended in the phrase belonging to the last-named category, according to which etherealization means: "a conversion of the soul from the World, the Flesh, and the Devil, to the Kingdom of Heaven."

But of what use to us is his system? To what extent does it clear up our insight into history, help us in disentangling its mysteries, contain the solutions which, each in our own particularist or parochial sphere, we have so far looked for in vain? A system which is presented to us, not as springing from the author's mind or imagination or faith, but as carefully built up in the course of empirical research—for this, we are told all through the voluminous work, is its method: we are the spectators of an expedition in quest of the norms, the regularity, the laws, of the historical process, and before our eyes the traveler gathers his data, from which, so he maintains, each time assuming our assent, his conclusions impose themselves, a system thus presented ought to render to all of us these very services. But to me at least it does not do so. Splendid as the qualities of the work are, fascinating as I have found it, grateful as I shall ever remain to the author for profound remarks, striking parallels, wide prospects, and other concomitant beauties—the system seems to me useless.

My most essential criticism, the criticism which embraces all others, is connected with this claim that his whole argument is based on empirical methods, in which it seems to me the author is deceiving himself. Had he really examined history with an open mind, merely formulating the theses supplied him by the observed facts, phenomena, developments, he could never have printed that imposing announcement of the division into so many parts in the opening pages of his first volume, nor could he in his references, as early as 1934, indicate what he was going to say about various chief problems in part 9 or in part 13, in 1950 or in 1960. Not that this is the ground of my doubting the genuineness of his empirical method; that is to be found in my examination of the six volumes themselves. The learning is miraculous, the wealth of examples and parallels overwhelming. But alas! the wealth of human history is ever so much greater. On looking closely, after having rubbed his dazzled eyes, the reader will see that Toynbee does not after all serve up more than a tiny spoonful out of the great cauldron. But no! this is a misleading comparison. When you fish in a cauldron you cannot select, and to select is exactly what he is doing all the time: he selects the instances which will support his theses, or he presents them in the way that suits him, and he does so with an assurance which hardly leaves room for the suspicion, not only that one might quote innumerable others with which his theses would not bear company, but especially that those cases he does mention can be explained or described in a different way so as to disagree no less completely with his theses.

So to me the rules, the laws, the standard patterns, laid down by the author after he has expounded examples and arguments at length and with never-failing gusto, do not seem to possess more than a very limited validity. At times they are no more than truisms. In any case, all these formulas of regularity, these distinctions alleged to present themselves in a fixed order, and these schemes of parallel development do not seem to be of much practical use. Personally, at least, I do not know how to work with them, let alone (and this, strictly speaking, ought to be possible) to make them operate unerringly.

Take even the striking formula of challenge and response. This—or its application from the science of psychology to history—must be pronounced a find. It hits off happily a form of movement in human communal life. There is no question here of a law, there is merely an observation of a frequent occurrence. But it will deepen our insight when in coming across a case of this description, we are conscious of its belonging to one of the usual categories of life. However, Professor Toynbee cannot stop there. He thinks he can state as a general rule that the easier the environment the less is the incitement to civilization man finds in it. And indeed one can hardly imagine the Land of Cockaigne becoming the cradle of so active a thing as a civilization. But now this lover of systems begins to ask whether perhaps the stimulus to civilization becomes stronger as the environment is more arduous. He therefore applies "our now well-tried empirical method" and in fact is able to adduce a number of striking instances. Art and labor had to be expended in making the valley of the Yellow River habitable, and even then it remained exposed to devastating floods; in that of the Yangtse, where the soil is equally fertile, no such terrible inconvenience is to be feared; and yet Chinese civilization came to birth not on the Yangtse but on the Yellow River. There is also the well-known contrast between the fat land of Boeotia and stony Attica—and everybody knows to which of the two Hellenic civilization owes the greater debt. Twelve more such cases are expounded, and later, after having shown by a number of instances how blows, pressures and penalizations evoke similar reactions, Toynbee writes that one might incline to the view that "'the greater the challenge, the greater the stimulus' is a law which knows no limits to its validity. We have not stumbled upon any palpable limits at any point in our empirical survey so far."

To my ears this has a rather naive sound. But just as I am on the point of arguing that fourteen cases of "hard countries," and perhaps a few dozen of each of the other kinds of obstacles, do not really amount to very much, and that it is hardly permissible to speak of empiricism unless the readers can test this so-called "law" by the hundreds or thousands of other cases they can dig up out of history—the author surprises me by announcing with an air of triumph that under the heading of "hard countries" he has not even mentioned two of the most striking examples, Venice and Holland. "What challenge could be more extreme than the challenge presented by the sea to Holland and to Venice? What more extreme, again, than the challenge presented by the Alps to Switzerland? And what responses could be more magnificent than those which Holland, Venice, and Switzerland have made? The three hardest pieces of country in Western Europe have stimulated their inhabitants to attain the highest level of social achievement that has yet been attained by any of the peoples of Western Civilization."

"Oh land wrung from the waves!" Every Dutchman has heard innumerable times his people's sterling qualities explained from their age-long struggle with the water. And nobody will contest that here is one factor in the building up of our special type of society. He who has kept hold of the thread of Toynbee's argument, however, will reflect that our author is really engaged in a discussion of the *origins* of civilizations, and of civilizations in the sense in which he calls them pre-eminently "fields of historical study," those twenty-one civilizations of his. The civilization of Holland, however, is no more than a parochial part of the great Western civilization. Of the *originating* of a civilization in the hard conditions of the Dutch soil there can therefore be no question. I note in passing that Professor Toynbee repeatedly commits this error—an error against his own method. But even if we overlooked this and permitted him to adduce *national* instances, we would still have to remark that even within the Netherlands community the form peculiar to Holland (the Western seaboard province of which Toynbee is obviously thinking) cannot be regarded as original. If one looks a little more closely, one will observe that within the European and even within the Netherlands cultural area the rise of Holland was fairly late, and this no doubt as a result of these very conditions created by sea and rivers. If in the end it overcame these conditions, it was not without the assistance of the surrounding higher forms of civilization (even the Romans and their dyke-building has an important share in making the region habitable). But can even after that initial stage the continued struggle with the water be decisive in explaining the later prosperity and cultural fecundity of the country? Is it not indispensable to mention the excellence of the soil, once it had become possible to make use of it? and above all the situation, which promoted the rise of shipping and of a large international commerce? Was the case of Holland then wholly due to hard conditions after all? Is it right to isolate that factor from among the multifarious complexity of reality and to suppress the favoring factors? And, we cannot refrain from wondering, would it not be necessary to apply a similar argument to the majority of Professor Toynbee's few dozen cases?

It would carry me too far if I attempt this. It is well-known that demonstrating an error demands more time than committing it. Let me merely make this general remark, that each of the instances discussed by Professor Toynbee of "blows" which had an invigorating effect is necessarily related by him in an extremely simplified form. But in the presentation of history simplification means, if not falsification, at least emphasizing one particular side of a matter which in reality has an infinite number of facets. Every historical fact—he himself mentions the objection he knows very well will be raised against his method—is unique and therefore incomparable with other historical facts. His reply is that the facts, in some respects unique, and in so far incomparable, belong in other respects to a class and are in so far comparable. There is truth in this—else no general ideas about history could ever be formulated—, but isolating the comparable elements is ticklish work. In a certain sense no historical fact is detachable from its circumstances, and by eliminating the latter violence is done to history. There is hardly an incident or a phenomenon quoted by Toynbee to illustrate a particular thesis which does not give rise to qualifications in the reader's mind—if the reader is conversant with the matter! Most of the time our author is writing about Greek or Arabic or Hittite or Cretan or Japanese history, where one—where I at least—find it more difficult to check him.

Professor Toynbee himself, however, feels that he cannot raise the intensity of his "challenges" indefinitely. It is in fact very simple, one does not need to conduct a learned, allegedly empirical, historical investigation. If I give you a blow on the head it is very likely that your energy will be strongly roused and that you will strike back with vigor; but the blow may prove so powerful that you will not have anything to reply, that (to put it in the style of Toynbee) the source of your energy will dry up for ever. In the world of communities it is likely enough that things will pass off in a similar fashion. So we see Professor Toynbee soon meditating "an over-riding law to the effect that 'the most stimulating challenge is to be found in a mean between a deficiency of severity and an excess of it,'" after which we get another 130 pages of more—under a chapter heading "The Golden Mean"—with instances of succumbing under pressure all too heavy or blows all too hard. One cannot refrain from the liveliest admiration for the rich variety of his knowledge, for the ease with which, after having sounded the causes of the downfall of Irish civilization, he does the same for the Icelandic, only to proceed with unflagging vivacity to Arabic history; until at long last he ventures to conclude: "There are challenges of a salutary severity that stimulate the human subject of the ordeal to a creative response; but there are also challenges of an overwhelming severity to which the human subject succumbs." My observations with regard to the blow on your head has a less impressive sound, but does it not convey precisely the same meaning? Yet our author is not yet satisfied. He repeats the phrase coined at the outset of his argument, "a mean between a deficiency of severity and an excess of it," and this time introduces it with the magic words: "In scientific terminology. . . ."

So here have a "law," scientifically established, or at least scientifically formulated. But what next? When we try to apply it, we shall first of all discover that in every given historical situation it refers to only one element, one out of many, one which, when we are concerned with historical presentation, cannot be abstracted from the others. Moreover, is it not essential to define what is too much and what too little, to stipulate where the golden mean lies? As to that, the "law" has nothing to say. That has to be defined anew each time by observation.

12

Herbert Butterfield

Selection from Man on His Past: The Study of the History of Historical Scholarship *(Cambridge: Cambridge University Press, 1955*)*

Herbert Butterfield (1900–1979) was Regius Professor of History at the University of Cambridge. He also authored biographies of Lord Acton and Napoleon, as well as works on European history, historiography, and the relationship between history and Christianity. Butterfield was well-known for his book *The Whig Interpretation of History* (1931), which argued against the 19th-century English liberal view of history as inevitably progressing toward liberal government or a successful present. It was a repudiation of William Stubbs and Edward Augustus Freeman and other Victorian English historians who drew a straight line from the Anglo-Saxons to the Glorious Revolution. It is perhaps ironic, however then, that we can identify liberal themes in his own writing. Butterfield also professed an expressly Christian

---

* *Man on His Past* was originally published in 1955. The author uses the 1969 version here.

view of history and was a staunch defender of the view that history cannot inform our morals.

In this selection, Butterfield defends Leopold von Ranke as a man of ideas, not just a historian who wove narratives out of a collection of assembled facts. Like Ranke, Butterfield argues for the uniqueness of historical events and personages, while still defending the usefulness and inevitability of generalizations. This is an important consideration for those who would charge methodological individualist liberal historians with atomism. Butterfield viewed Ranke as a historian who always reserved room for individual action in the past.

It is at this point that Ranke takes up the whole problem of the nature of technical history; and the reason for his interest in the matter is worth noting. Like the Göttingen professors he had a campaign to conduct—they were all anxious to rescue what was called "universal history," and what we should call "general history" from the hands of the philosophers. In reality, the work of providing a rational account of man on earth would seem to have been taken over from the theologians by the general philosophers in the eighteenth century. The need to know how mankind had come from primitive conditions to its existing state would appear to have been felt before the historians were in a condition to supply what was wanted. Man's reflections on the matter marched ahead of his researches; and it was the *philosophes*—the "general thinkers" as we might call them—who attempted to map out the course of things in time. And this would appear to be the reason why the philosophy of history, as it was called, came to its climax before the study of history had reached its modern form. The Göttingen school resented the facile generalisations which the men of the Enlightenment produced without research, and imposed upon human history from the outside.* Ranke's objections were exactly the same but they came to a point in his hostility to Hegel's philosophy of history. Both quarreled primarily with over-simplifications in philosophic history and with a schematisation that did not issue out of the recorded facts. In particular they set themselves against the policy of constructing the story of mankind on the basis of an assumed or presupposed doctrine of progress.

Ranke, like the men of the Göttingen school, however, is far from desiring to attack generalisations or general history. On the contrary he holds that two things are necessary for an historian. The first is a joy in detail as such, and a desire to participate in it wherever it comes—a passion for human beings in themselves, in spite of their contradictions, and a love of events in their very uniqueness. He states the case in the strongest possible manner: nothing in the world, he says, can ever be regarded as existing merely for the sake of something else. Secondly, however, he tells us that "the historian must have an eye for generalities"— his treatment of the details must lead him to a view of the broader

---

* See, for example, F. Rühs, *Geschichte Schwedens*, 1 (Halle, 1803), Vorrede, x. Cf. Rühs, *Entwurf einer Propadeutik des historischen Studiums* (Berlin, 1811), 252–3, on "Pragmatismus"; and ibid. 30: "In more recent times there have been two kinds of attempts to handle history philosophically; the first can be described as the French way, and it consists essentially in a vague way of reasoning about the facts of history, which instead of being treated properly, according to their individual nature and in the relations to time and place, are subjected to a criticism based on current fashionable principles or rather opinions."

course of change which the world has undergone.* It is curious that he should ever have been charged with loving merely isolated facts; when in reality he insists on generalisations and demands only that they issue out of the facts—his great anxiety is that the facts should merge into larger shapes, and that, like the natural sciences, history should move to higher degrees of generalisations. History, he says, "never has the unity of a philosophical system"; but it is not at all devoid of *inneren Zusammenhang*—not at all without interconnectedness. Far from repudiating general history, he said that all his mind was constantly pressing towards just that, striving to discover the connections and the continuities; and, as Edward Armstrong once said of him, "he had much belief in the educational power of lectures covering a long period of history."† Even when he was researching into some detailed

---

* For this and the following paragraphs, see L. von Ranke, *Uber die Epochen der neueren Geschichte* (München und Leipzig, 1921), 15–21, together with the Introduction by Alfred Dove, ibid 1-6. Cf. Theodore H. von Laue, *Leopold Ranke, the Formative Years* (Princeton, N.J., 1950), 115–16: "Ranke deeply loved the great variety of which human life was capable, and he loved it for its own sake, 'as one enjoys a flower.' He considered each expression of life in history as an original creation of the human spirit, without judging it or comparing with others. His main aim was to understand it from within . . . as a contemporary understanding its freedom of choice at any given moment, but as a retrospective historian also seeing the underlying necessity. . . . And in order to perceive the mysterious throbbings of the 'idea,' he strained all of the faculties of his mind, reason, emotion and intuition. . . . Without [this] Ranke could not so successfully have dealt with Renaissance Italy, the Ottoman and Spanish empires, the Serbian revolution, and the Papacy, all subjects far removed from his own mental background."

† *History of the Latin and Teutonic Nations* (revised translation in Bohn's Standard Library, London, 1909), p. xiii.

episode, he was trying all the time to put that episode into its place in the whole story of the world's development. Like the Göttingen professors, he saw the map of the universal history as the final objective, and, far from repudiating the idea of it, he simply claimed that it should be in the hands of historians rather than philosophers. Both he and his predecessors seem to have assumed that, if the historian himself does not undertake the task, some H. G. Wells will carry it out, and will acquire undue power over the minds of men. For our general outlook on the world is determined partly by the picture that we have made of universal history; and even the research student, except when his eye is fastened to his microscope—and perhaps even then—but certainly when his mind wanders into realms of general discussion—can hardly escape having such a picture as his constant basis of reference.

Ranke, therefore, insists on having the best of both worlds; and he boldly confronts the paradoxes. He is prepared to believe that there has been a development in the science of history, but he refuses to allow that anybody is a greater historian than Thucydides. He is ready to admit that in the course of time an improved moral standard may gain wider currency amongst larger classes of society; but to him there is no progress in ethics beyond the morality of the New Testament. In our time more people may benefit from the stable conditions in which it is fairly easy to live a sober and respectable life. But the present day does not excel the world of over a thousand years ago in examples of spiritual depth or in the moral strength that grapples with great difficulties and temptations.

And Ranke would not accept the view of the philosophers, that human history was moving inevitably to a predetermined consummation in this world. If on the one hand such an end were imposed on mankind from the outside, he said, it would do violence to the principle of free will. If on the other hand, the inevitability came from something that is innate in human beings, this is a view that turns man into either God or nothing. In other words the free choices of free men must be regarded as having a real part in the making of the story; and this means that God has left open to the future a multiplicity of alternative possible developments. What we ourselves do here and now will make a difference to the course which the future is to take; but involved in this is a process, the laws of which are not only unknown to us, but are more secret and profound than we can understand. In a sense, says Ranke, every individual must be regarded as free; and we must assume that at any moment something original may emerge—something which comes from the primary source of historical action, inside human beings. At the same time, all the parts of history are interwoven—they condition one another and have their constant repercussions on one another. In this sense, freedom and necessity, he tells us, are rubbing shoulders at every moment. We may conclude from this that on the one hand history is a story in which one never knows what is going to happen next. On the other hand it is a study of developments which become apparent and explicable when the course of things is viewed retrospectively. In this latter aspect it belongs not so much to the narrator, but rather to the expositor and the analyst.

In a parallel manner, it is necessary to avoid the temptation to regard a generation or an individual as merely a means to an end or a stepping-stone to something else. Ranke will not allow a past generation to be "mediatised," as he calls it; as though it did not have any standing of its own in the eyes of eternity—as though only the last generation in the chain of progress was going to have the right to be considered for its own sake. If you imagine all the generations laid out before the eyes of God, it is not merely the last of them—it is every single one in the whole series—which has to be directly related to eternity. So Ranke does justice to free will and to necessity, to what is unique and can be generalised, to personality as something always valid in itself and to the kind of movements which are supra-personal. When he comes to the marginal points at which our decisions about life affect our views concerning the structure of history, Ranke's cross-references are to that religion which he said was the primary impulse behind his study of the past. There might be faults in the edifice which came to be superimposed; there might be secularisation at certain levels of his historical thinking; but the few ideas which he laid down as fundamental are things which distinguish history as understood in a Christian world, even when that world has become secularised.* It is possible to imagine a strange culture which would answer the deeper problems of life and personality in a different manner. In this case historical writing might be of a different texture; or history might cease to have significance.

---

* The religious basis of this section of Ranke's thought (which has been overlooked by many people) is duly recognised, for example, by Hans Liebeschütz, *Ranke* (Historical Association Pamphlets, 1954), pp. 4–5, 8–9.

Ludwig von Mises

Selection from Theory and History:
An Interpretation of Social and Economic
Evolution *(New Haven, CT: Yale University
Press, 1957)*

Born in Austria of Jewish parents, Ludwig von Mises (1882–
1973) was an economist who came of age in the era of Vienna's
intellectual flourishing. He worked for the Austrian government, served in the Austro-Hungarian Army during World War
I, and was a professor in Geneva, Switzerland, in 1934, before
migrating to the United States in 1940. He is often regarded as
the primary 20th-century defender of liberalism, and a major
influence on libertarianism, particularly in the United States.

A seminal but often forgotten work in liberal history, Mises's
Theory and History carries forward views on the autonomy
of history. It also presents a coherent attack on Marxism and
a version of historicism. Mises had written about history and
even the philosophy of history in earlier works, but this book

is his full statement on the matter. Its main contribution was to ground a theory of history in subjective value rather than subjective facts. It was axiomatically true, not just empirically observable, Mises argued, that all people have subjective values. Because, Mises elaborates, it was the actions of individuals that determined the course of history, individual minds and decisionmaking should be the true subject matter of historians. History, from this view, can never be determined; nothing determines ideas or is responsible for events. Rather, it is people who make decisions given environmental constraints. It is free individuals who are responsible for action.

As I wrote elsewhere: "Mises's version of liberty is not the liberty of the state or of politics, nor is it a kind of Hegelian liberty that acts on the stage of history through the rational unfolding of an ultimate plan. For Mises, liberty is inescapably the subject matter of history. We literally cannot choose not to write about liberty when we write history."[30]

This view was a defense of methodological individualism and empiricism, but it was not anti-theoretical. Indeed, Mises emphasized the importance of theory, especially economic theory, derived from a priori reasoning, as an essential tool for explaining historical cause and effect. History then could never be just arranging facts in chronological order and intuiting correct explanations. The explanations for cause and effect, Mises notes, ultimately come from a priori thought, not observation. Over time, our concepts of cause and effect become reinforced as we interpret events to align with them. The selection below is part of Chapter 8 of *Theory and History*.

Chapter 8. Philosophy of History
The Theme of History

HISTORY deals with human action, that is, the actions performed by individuals and groups of individuals. It describes the conditions under which people lived and the way they reacted to these conditions. Its subject are human judgments of value and the ends men aimed at guided by these judgments, the means men resorted to in order to attain the ends sought, and the outcome of their actions. History deals with man's conscious reaction to the state of his environment, both the natural environment and the social environment as determined by the actions of preceding generations as well as by those of his contemporaries. Every individual is born into a definite social and natural milieu. An individual is not simply man in general, whom history can regard in the abstract. An individual is at any instant of his life the product of all the experiences to which his ancestors were exposed plus those to which he himself has so far been exposed. An actual man lives as a member of his family, his race, his people, and his age; as a citizen of his country; as a member of a definite social group; as a practitioner of a certain vocation. He is imbued with definite religious, philosophical, metaphysical, and political ideas, which he sometimes enlarges or modifies by his own thinking. His actions are guided by ideologies that he has acquired through his environment.

However, these ideologies are not immutable. They are products of the human mind and they change when new thoughts are added to the old stock of ideas or are substituted for discarded ideas. In searching for the origin of new ideas history cannot go beyond establishing that they were produced by a man's thinking. The ultimate data of history beyond which no historical research can go are human ideas and actions. The historian can trace ideas back to other, previously developed ideas. He can describe the environmental conditions to which actions were designed to react. But he can never say more about a new idea and a new mode of acting than that they originated at a definite point of space and time in the mind of a man and were accepted by other men.

Attempts have been made to explain the birth of ideas out of "natural" factors. Ideas were described as the necessary product of the geographical environment, the physical structure of people's habitat. This doctrine manifestly contradicts the data available. Many ideas are the response elicited by the stimulus of a man's physical environment. But the content of these ideas is not determined by the environment. To the same physical environment various individuals and groups of individuals respond in a different way. Others have tried to explain the diversity of ideas and actions by biological factors. The species man is subdivided into racial groups with distinctive hereditary biological traits. Historical experience does not preclude the assumption that the members of some racial groups are better gifted for conceiving sound ideas than those of other races. However, what is to be explained is why a man's ideas differ from those of people of the same race. Why do brothers differ from one another?

It is moreover questionable whether cultural backwardness conclusively indicates a racial group's permanent inferiority. The evolutionary process that transformed the animal-like ancestors of man into modern men extended over many hundreds of thousands of years. Viewed in the perspective of this period, the fact that some races have not yet reached a cultural level other races passed several thousand years ago does not seem to matter very much. There are individuals whose physical and mental development proceeds more slowly than the average who yet in later life far excel most normally developing persons. It is not impossible that the same phenomenon may occur with whole races.

There is for history nothing beyond people's ideas and the ends they were aiming at motivated by these ideas. If the historian refers to the meaning of a fact, he always refers either to the interpretation acting men gave to the situation in which they had to live and to act, and to the outcome of their ensuing actions, or to the interpretation which other people gave to the result of these actions. The final causes to which history refers are always the ends individuals and groups of individuals are aiming at. History does not recognize in the course of events any other meaning and sense than those attributed to them by acting men, judging from the point of view of their own human concerns.

The Theme of the Philosophy of History

Philosophy of history looks upon mankind's history from a different point of view. It assumes that God or nature or some other superhuman entity providentially directs the course of events toward a definite goal different from the ends which acting men are aiming at. There is a meaning in the sequence of events which supersedes the intentions of men. The ways of Providence are not those of mortal men. The shortsighted individual deludes himself in believing that he chooses and acts according to his own concerns. In fact he unknowingly must act in such a way that finally the providential plan will be realized. The historical process has a definite purpose set by Providence without any regard to the human will. It is a progress toward a preordained end. The task of the philosophy of history is to judge every phase of history from the point of view of this purpose.

If the historian speaks of progress and retrogression, he refers to one of the ends men are consciously aiming at in their actions. In his terminology progress means the attainment of a state of affairs which acting men considered or consider more satisfactory than preceding states. In the terminology of a philosophy of history progress means advance on the way that leads to the ultimate goal set by Providence.

Every variety of the philosophy of history must answer two questions. First: What is the final end aimed at and the route by which it is to be reached? Second: By what means are people induced or forced to pursue this course? Only if both questions are fully answered is the system complete.

In answering the first question the philosopher refers to intuition. In order to corroborate his surmise, he may quote the opinions of older authors, that is, the intuitive speculations of other people. The ultimate source of the philosopher's knowledge is invariably a divination of the intentions of Providence, hitherto hidden to the non-initiated and revealed to the philosopher by dint of his intuitive power. To objections raised about the correctness of his guess the philosopher can only reply: An inner voice tells me that I am right and you are wrong.

Most philosophies of history not only indicate the final end of historical evolution but also disclose the way mankind is bound to wander in order to reach the goal. They enumerate and describe successive states or stages, intermediary stations on the way from the early beginnings to the final end. The systems of Hegel, Comte, and Marx belong to this class. Others ascribe to certain nations or races a definite mission entrusted to them by the plans of Providence. Such are the role of the Germans in the system of Fichte and the role of the Nordics and the Aryans in the constructions of modern racists.

With regard to the answer given to the second question, two classes of philosophies of history are to be distinguished.

The first group contends that Providence elects some mortal men as special instruments for the execution of its plan. In the charismatic leader superhuman powers are vested. He is the plenipotentiary of Providence whose office it is to guide the ignorant populace the right way. He may be a hereditary king, or a commoner who has spontaneously seized power and whom the blind and wicked rabble in their envy and hatred call a usurper. For the charismatic leader but one thing matters: the faithful performance of his mission no matter what the means he may be forced to resort to. He is above all laws and moral precepts. What he does is always right, and what his opponents do is always wrong. Such was the doctrine of Lenin, who in this point deviated from the doctrine of Marx.

It is obvious that the philosopher does not attribute the office of charismatic leadership to every man who claims that he has been called. He distinguishes between the legitimate leader and the fiendish impostor, between the God-sent prophet and the hellborn tempter. He calls only those heroes and seers legitimate leaders who make people walk toward the goal set by Providence. As the philosophies disagree with regard to this goal, so they disagree with regard to the distinction between the legitimate leader and the devil incarnate. They disagree in their judgments about Caesar and Brutus, Innocent III and Frederick II, Charles I and Cromwell, the Bourbons and the Napoleons. But their dissent goes even further. There are rivalries between various candidates for the supreme office which are caused only by personal ambition. No ideological convictions separated Caesar and Pompey, the house of Lancaster and that of York, Trotsky and Stalin. Their antagonism was due to the fact that they aimed at the same office, which of course only one man could get. Here the philosopher must choose among various pre-tenders. Having arrogated to himself the power to pronounce judgment in the name of Providence, the philosopher blesses one of the pretenders and condemns his rivals.

The second group suggested another solution of the problem. As they see it, Providence resorted to a cunning device. It implanted in every man's mind certain impulses the operation of which must necessarily result in the realization of its own plan. The individual thinks that he goes his own way and strives after his own ends. But unwittingly he contributes his share to the realization of the end Providence wants to attain. Such was the method of Kant. It was restated by Hegel and later adopted by many Hegelians, among them by Marx. It was Hegel who coined the phrase "cunning of reason" (*List der Vernunft*). There is no use arguing with doctrines derived from intuition. Every system of the philosophy of history is an arbitrary guess which can neither be proved nor disproved. There is no rational means available for either endorsing or rejecting a doctrine suggested by an inner voice.

14

Jacques Barzun and Henry F. Graff

Selections from The Modern Researcher *(New York: Harcourt, Brace & World, 1962 [originally published 1957])*

Born in France, Jacques Barzun (1907–2012) came to the United States as a child, later graduating from Columbia University and teaching history there for more than two decades. He then worked in various administrative positions at the University of Cambridge. Barzun was an eminent cultural historian who approached history with a wide scope. He was particularly interested in good teaching and good writing, and devoted some of his research to these topics. Also the author of the popular book *Teacher in America* (1952), Barzun was interested in pedagogy. He knew that history doesn't give you a formula for understanding the world, although it can help make you a better learner and thinker in general. In later

THE LIBERAL APPROACH TO THE PAST

years, Barzun put his effort into understanding and helping preserve the big historical picture of Western civilization.

Henry F. Graff (1921–present), Barzun's colleague in the history department at Columbia, has published on presidential history, democracy, and the history of the American nation. He has served as a historical consultant for various media programs. While Barzun has often been labeled a conservative, Graff may be counted as a modern liberal (in the contemporary usage of the term): he has written more positively about recent Democratic presidents and presidential candidates than Republican ones. Neither, however, is a dogmatic thinker, and together their work probably represents a mainline or consensus in American historiography at midcentury.

In the following selection, Barzun and Graff give the generally liberal position that knowledge of the past can give us only limited power to predict the future, and this is knowledge that we can apply only in the roughest and most tentative of ways. With thorough research, we might be able to make accurate guesses about particularly narrow concerns. We ought not to condemn historical information as useless for the present and for the future, but we ought to recognize its limitations. It is an improved imagination, not prediction of the future, that is the true goal of historical training.

Since History theoretically contains man's whole past and history describes large portions of it, we are not surprised to find Lamartine, the poet who was part historian and part statesman, saying that "History teaches everything including the future." To be sure, most professional historians categorically disclaim the title of prophet. Many of them deplore the distortions brought about by "present-mindedness," the habit of going to history with modern ideas and intentions. Yet some have not hesitated to admit their desire to influence events by "proving" the rightness or wrongness of a cause out of its historical antecedents. And the makers of great historical systems, as we shall see, have set out to discover the "laws" of history so that man might map the shape of things to come. Such men, of whom Marx was the least deterred by doubts, believed that History herself was speaking through their mouths.

The laws, needless to say, have not yet been found, though the detailed knowledge of a particular culture or country often enables students to distinguish the constant from the fleeting and thereby to "predict" the outcome of a given situation. Thus in October 1943 nine American historians were brought together in Washington under General Arnold and "asked to predict largely on the basis of what had already happened, the ability of the Nazi war machine and the German people to stand up under Allied pressure [*New York Times*, June 8, 1946]. The nine men read secret documents, heard the testimony of scores of witnesses, and within three months made their report. When it was later reviewed in the light of events it was found "a remarkably accurate forecast" [ibid.].

The application of history to a purpose so sharply defined is rare. The benefit more usually expected of it is an enrichment of the imagination that promotes a quick and shrewd understanding of the actions of men in society. Hence the value of historical training to the student of any aspect of man's life and to the worker in any branch of social intelligence. . . .

We must be content, therefore, with the vast amount of imperfect knowledge that critical history discusses and delivers to us. Since all human knowledge is imperfect, we should take from each discipline its characteristic truths and accept the imperfections inherent in the purpose to which the discipline addresses itself. If historical knowledge sometimes seems more imperfect than other kinds, this is due to the vividness with which it re-embodies and makes articulate what is gone. It arouses interests as passionate as those of the present and its literary embodiment requires no initiation: "any number can play." Those who read and study history most closely do not disdain to give it credence: that too is an attested fact, whereas thoroughgoing skepticism is often a pose. To the justly skeptical and comparing mind, history at its best is no more uncertain than the descriptive earth sciences whose assertions most people seem willing to take on faith. Large parts of man's history are thoroughly well known and beyond dispute. True, the interpretations and the meanings attached to the parts, clear or obscure, are and will continue open to debate. But who has settled the interpretation or meaning of human life? Taken all in all, history is genuine knowledge: it is all the past there is, and we should be lost without it. . . .

What validates any pattern . . . is that it permits *a* meaning to be attached to otherwise dumb, disconnected facts. What prompts the systematic historian is *the* desire to find the meaning of *all* the facts—the meaning of History. He starts from the assumption that nothing in the chaos of events known to have happened on earth for the last 10,000 years can be pointless. His faith is strong that somewhere and at some time the good and evil, the successes and failures, the pluses and minuses, must produce a kind of total which, when read off, will have significance to all men. In other words, universal history to him is not what it seems to us: a vast network of incomplete stories, upon which patterns slightly clearer than life's confusion are imposed for convenience only; rather it is *one* story, with a beginning, a middle, and an end.

When an absolute system is believed to be discoverable, the believer offers a demonstration: he shows that despite surface differences, underneath there is unity. He is then forced to explain how the governing force "underneath" produces the welter above, and he is thus brought to the view that some one powerful cause, acting by necessity, moves all parts of the great web of History. Systematic historians, in short, are committed to the doctrine of the Single Cause.

15

Henry Steele Commager

Selection from The Nature and the Study of History *(New York: Garland Publishing, 1984 [originally published 1965])*

Henry Steele Commager (1902–1998) was an American intellectual and cultural historian who taught at New York and Columbia Universities and Amherst College. A prolific writer, he was the author of textbooks, biographies, monographs, and countless op-eds and newspaper pieces. He often wrote for the general public.

Commager represents a moderate left-wing stream of liberalism. For example, he idealized Thomas Jefferson and Franklin Roosevelt, and in his politically charged pieces showed himself an opponent of McCarthyism, the Vietnam War, and conservative interpretations of the Constitution. He was an advocate for civil rights and a believer in the power of national history as a form of civic education.

Originally a disciple of the Progressive Vernon Louis Par-
rington, Commager later distanced himself from the Progressive school of history. In 1968, he attacked historian Charles
Beard's economic interpretation of the Constitution as insuf-
ficient for explaining the motives of the Framers. "The idea
that property considerations were paramount in the minds of
those assembled in Philadelphia is misleading and unsound,"
Commager wrote, "and is borne out neither by the evidence of
the debates in the Convention nor by the Constitution itself.
The Constitution was not essentially an economic document.
It was, and is, essentially a political document."[31] This shows,
for one, Commager's interests in ideas over forces in historical explanation. For Commager, the Constitution was more
about Federalism than private interests.

The following selection of Commager's work shows 19th-
century liberal historicism alive in mid-20th-century left-liberal
thought, reflecting the resistance of historicist ideas against
the Progressive historians' trend to adopt sociological explanations. Commager was also known to side with Herbert Butterfield in rejecting the view that historians ought to make moral
judgments of past actors. Above all, he held to the liberal value
of openness to debate and alternative views of history.

If we were to explain the past, if we were to predict the future,
we needed something at once more rigorous and more specific
than the windy doctrine of progress or the impersonal doctrine of
evolution. Mathematics, biology, chemistry, physics, these things
had provided laws which explained so much that had heretofore
been mysterious; surely history, too, could provide laws which

would explain the past and illuminate the future. So said Auguste Comte, in France, who worked out an elaborate scheme of the social sciences; so said Herbert Spencer in England, who created a science of society on the basis of biology whose *Outlines of Cosmic Philosophy* drew on the whole body of social and philosophical thought to find laws which regulate the moral world, and whose many histories proved that these laws had operated in America from the beginning. Other social sciences boasted laws— Malthus' law of population growth, Gresham's law in economics, Ferdinand LaSalle's law of wages, Henry Buckle's law of geography, which was "one glorious principle of universal and undeviating regularity"—why should not history, too, have her laws?

Laws in History

"Four out of five students who are living today," wrote Henry Adams some sixty years ago,

> have, in the course of their work, felt that they stood on the brink of a great generalization that would reduce history under a law as clear as the laws which govern the material world . . . He seemed to have it, as the Spanish say, in his ink stand. Scores of times he must have dropped his pen to think how one short step, one sudden inspiration, would show all human knowledge; how in these thickest forests of history, one corner turned, one faint trail struck, would bring him on the high road of science.

Alas, when Adams himself hit on a law—it was the law of entropy, or the degradation of energy—it did not clear a way through

thickest forests, but put up a permanent barrier to further historical research. Twenty years later Edward P. Cheyney sounded the
same note:

> I look forward [he said in his Presidential Address to the
> American Historical Association in 1923] to some future
> meeting of this Association when the search for the laws of
> History and their application will have become the princi-
> pal part of their procedure . . . The most conspicuous part
> on the program will be assigned to some gifted young his-
> torical thinker who, quite properly disregarding the earlier
> and crude efforts of his predecessors, will propound and
> demonstrate to the satisfaction of all his colleagues, some
> new and far-reaching laws or laws of history.

Alas, again, for human hopes; forty years later the sessions of
the Historical Association were given over almost exclusively to
"technical history" and philosophical speculations were looked
upon with disfavor. Professor Cheyney himself propounded
six "laws of history" and it may be useful to recite them, for
they reveal, as well as anything of their kind, some of the difficulties inherent in the formulation of such laws. They are:
1. The law of continuity; 2. The law of mutability; 3. The law
of interdependence; 4. The law of democracy; 5. The law of the
necessity for free consent; 6. The law of moral progress. Now it
can be said of these—as of almost every attempt to formulate laws
of history—that either they do not deal with history, but with life
in general, or that they are not laws but expressions of hope and

faith. Take, for example. Cheney's law of continuity. If this means that we have constructed an historical chronology and that in this chronology one event appears to follow another, then it is valid but meaningless. If it means that everything that happens grows out of some antecedent cause which we can discover, then it is not so. The voyages of Columbus and the discovery of America doubtless grew out of a complex of antecedent causes which yield a logical pattern, but can it be said that the destruction of the Aztec and the Inca empires grew out of recognizable causes and followed a pattern which the natives of Mexico and Peru would have regarded as logical? Scholars who trace the history of Negro slavery in America construct a neat and logical pattern which almost makes us think that slavery was inevitable, but is there a comparable logic which would persuade Africans kidnapped and transported to America that slavery was inevitable for them? One major trouble with the principle of continuity and causation is that it assumes a single line of continuity, a single chain of causes, instead of a hundred or a thousand.

Or consider Cheyney's law of mutability: that nothing is permanent in history. But that is not a law of history, it is a law of life, and poets and moralists had proclaimed it more than two thousand years before Cheyney took it over for history. What is important—and what the historian wants to know—is that some things appear to be more permanent than others. Which seem to be more permanent, and why? To this urgent question the law of mutability says nothing. It is as if we should submit, as a "law" of history, that all men are mortal and that all flesh is grass.

And what of Cheney's other laws—democracy, liberty, morality? Clearly these are formulations of a Victorian liberal. How many Chinese or Russian historians would subscribe to the "law" of democracy; how many American Negroes would subscribe to the "law" of liberty; how many German Jews would endorse the "law" of moral progress, or for that matter how many of the survivors of Hiroshima or Dresden?

Confronted by the seemingly insuperable difficulty of formulating laws or solving the problems of causation, some historians have thrown in the sponge, as it were, and taken refuge in the principle of fortuity. Thus H. A. L. Fisher, whose *History of Europe* is something of a classic, confessed in his preface to that work that:

> One intellectual excitement has been denied me. Men wiser and more learned than I have discovered in history a plot, a rhythm, a predetermined pattern. These harmonies are concealed from me. I can see only one emergency following upon another as wave follows upon wave; only one great fact with respect to which, since it is unique, there can be no generalizations; only one safe rule for the historian: that he should recognize in the development of human destinies the play of the contingent and unforeseen. (Preface to *A History of Europe*, Boston: Houghton Mifflin Company, 1935–36.)

In its most unsophisticated form this becomes the "Cleopatra's nose" theory of history first stated by no other than Blaise Pascal: "Had Cleopatra's nose been shorter, the whole face of the earth would have been different." Voltaire embraced the same theory, and so too did his friend Frederick the Great: "The older one becomes, the more clearly one sees that King Hazard fashions three-fourths of the events in this miserable world."

"The passion for tidiness," Arthur Schlesinger, Jr., has written, "is the historian's occupational disease." It is, indeed, though we should add in all fairness that it is a kind of historical necessity, as well. Organization always does some violence to the stream of thought or the chaos of conduct that is life—the organization of melody into music, the organization of color into painting, the organization of inspiration into poetry, and of ideas into philosophy, and the organization of facts into history. Granted that history is a record of disorderly conduct; it does not follow that it is to be reported in a disorderly fashion, and it is the mark of a great judge that he is able to bring order and coherence out of conflicting evidence and arguments. History is a jangle of accidents, blunders, surprises and absurdities, and so is our knowledge of it, but if we are to report it at all we must impose some order upon it. Literature is able to compensate for this necessity by falling back on the "stream of consciousness" technique, but history cannot do this.

The danger is that in tidying up history the historian will convey the impression (he may even convince himself!) that everything was tidy from the beginning. A battle, for example, is often a nightmare of blunder and confusion; then the historian comes along and tidies it all up, tells us just how the battle was planned, how the center struck at this moment and the left flank moved in next, how the artillery joined in, or the cavalry charged, and there is your victory all nicely explained. Or he looks back upon a diplomatic incident, or upon an election, and explains it all very neatly, leaving out all the contingencies, all the unforeseen events, all the hesitations and fears and confusions. He presents us with the logic of some historical *fait accompli*—the Monroe Doctrine, or the Open Door policy, or Truman's Point Four, and we can indeed see how logical it all was; then we learn—as we have recently learned of Point Four, that it was all a series of accidents, and that far from being a deliberate policy it came even to President Truman himself as a happy surprise.

But while we must avoid assuming that history is a kind of chess game with every gambit logical and planned, we must avoid, equally, the other extreme, that of ascribing everything to accident or luck; we must avoid giving too much prominence to untidiness and disorder. For disorder is, in a sense, itself orderly; it is at once a principle of life and a rule of life. Birth is a very disorderly business, but we forget the disorder (or assume that it is taken for granted) and celebrate the birthday. The whole of life is disorderly—our growing-up, our education, our falling in love, our jobs or careers, our relations with friends or enemies. Our societies are disorderly—physically disorderly in their cities, institutionally disorderly in their economies, their politics, their social relationships. Intelligence tries to bring order out of all of this, and thereby to decrease the disorder, or to master it. So, too, in history, the intelligence of the historian is directed to bringing some order out of the chaos of the past.

And there is, too, a further and consoling consideration, that though accidents often change the pace or the pattern of history, they rarely change it in any fundamental way. For the sophisticated historian remembers what is, after all, the common sense of the matter, that there are always enough accidents to go around, and that accidents tend to cancel out, just as the sophisticated spectator at a football game knows that there are enough fumbles to go around and that a particular fumble rarely changes the course of a game, or a season of games. It is immature and almost perverse to assign too much importance to what we denominate the accidents of history. The wind scattered the Spanish Armada and helped the English destroy it, but that was not the reason why Spain failed to conquer England; Spain had never conquered England, wind or no wind, nor had any other power. Washington surprised the Hessians at Trenton on Christmas of 1776, and the American cause looked up; but that was not the reason the Americans finally won their independence. Even had the Hessians repulsed Washington's ragged troops the Americans would, in all likelihood, have won sooner or later. A Federal soldier picked up Lee's plan of battle for Antietam and took it to McClellan; that was not the reason Lee lost the battle of Antietam or the Confederacy lost the war. Even had Lee won the battle of Antietam it is highly improbable that the Confederacy would have won the war. President Wilson suffered a fateful breakdown on his train outside Wichita, Kansas, in the midst of his crusade for the ratification of the League of Nations, and the League was defeated. But that is not the reason that the Senate rejected the League or that the Republicans won the election of 1920; these things would have come about in any event, regardless of the fate of President Wilson.

Yet in every one of these instances, and in a hundred others which we could readily conjure up, fortuity did play a part, and an important part. It changed things; it meant that some men who might have lived, died; it meant that some battle had to be fought over again; it meant that what we call the course of history was slowed up or speeded up or temporarily deflected.

May we not conclude that fortuity itself is predictable, and that the mature historian takes it into account in his explanations, just as the wise general or statesman takes it into account in his calculations? An earthquake, a drought, the discovery of a new continent, or of gold and silver mines, an epidemic, an assassination, all of these are in a sense fortuitous, yet all of them are in a sense normal, as well, for such as these recur in the history of every country and every century.

Perhaps the most useful lesson the student of history can learn is to avoid oversimplification, and to accept the notion of multiple causation or to resign himself to the fact that as yet we do not know enough to explain the causes of things. To yearn for a single, and usually simple, explanation of the chaotic materials of the past, to search for a single thread in that most tangled of tangled skeins, is a sign of immaturity. More, it is a practice which encourages dangerous intellectual habits, for it leads, almost inevitably, to a simplistic view of the present as well as of the past. Any historian who invites us to accept some single explanation of the great events of the past excites our distrust; all too often such men find the explanation of prodigious events in some fortuitous occurrence, in some lurid conspiracy, or in some naive observation of character. They tell us that for want of a nail a kingdom was lost; they explain the Reformation in terms of Luther's desire to marry, or the Spanish conquest of Mexico in terms of

Cortez' mistress, or the "loss" of China by reference to traitors in the United States Department of State! They are those men of maxims against whom George Eliot has warned us:

> All people of strong, broad sense have an instinctive repugnance to men of maxims; because such people early discover that the mysterious complexity of our life is not to be embraced by maxims, and that to lace ourselves up in formulas of that sort is to repress all the divine promptings and inspirations that spring from a growing insight and sympathy.

> And the man of maxims is the popular representative of the minds that are guided in their moral judgment solely by general rules, thinking that these will lead them to justice by ready-made patent method, without the trouble of exerting patience, discrimination, impartiality, without any care to assure themselves whether they have the insight that comes from a hardly-earned estimate of temptation, or from a life vivid and intense enough to have created a wide fellow-feeling with all that is human.

16

J. H. Hexter

Selections from The History Primer
(New York: Basic Books, 1971)

Born in Memphis, Tennessee, J. H. Hexter (1910–1996) was a historian of 16th- and 17th-century England and a quintessential liberal (so much so that the philosopher of history William H. Dray would call him a "neo-Whig"). Hexter's ideal historian was Frederic William Maitland. That Hexter was interested in liberty as a theme is evident in his choice of works, where he was concerned with political history, specifically the origins of the British Parliament and modern conceptions of freedom.

Hexter was a historical pluralist, in the sense that he felt multiple approaches to the past should be welcome, and would lead to greater understanding. At the same time, he was a sharp critic of both the analytic philosophy of history and of social scientific approaches. The former, he felt, did not ask questions that truly concerned the historical practice. The latter, he argued, limited historians' explanations and led to overgeneralizations. The worst of the overgeneralizers, whom he labeled "lumpers," were the Marxist historians. Hexter frequently engaged in debate with Marxist historians of England like Christopher Hill.

Hexter remained firmly within the tradition of seeing history as an autonomous discipline, with its own method. In his *History Primer*, he was interested in thinking through questions of methods, of how to do "good history."

The liberal approach to the past carried on in the 20th century, but it was in the shadow of Marxist and other social scientific approaches. As Hexter relates, many traditional liberals also struggled to reconcile their intuitive beliefs about history with the new waves of philosophical thinking about history. Hexter too often relied on the argument that historical thinking was mostly just "common sense" without recognizing enough the irony of what common sense actually is and who defines it. His "primer" was an attempt to recover historical methods for the historians, pushing aside much modern philosophical theorizing about historical narrative and the like. At nearly 300 pages, and written in too high a style, the book missed the audience of a typical primer: those just beginning to study a subject, those who are looking for a "first book."

When Hexter retired from Yale in 1980, he moved to Washington University in St. Louis, where in 1986 he founded the Center for the History of Freedom. After Hexter's retirement from the Center, his colleague Richard W. Davis, also a historian of England, continued the center. Davis edited a book, *The Origins of Modern Freedom in the West*, inspired by Hexter's interests.[32]

Argument over history, what it is, and what historians do or ought to do has taken a somewhat different course among historians than it has among philosophers. As we have seen, in recent years philosophers have mainly occupied themselves with the problem of explanation "why" in history. During roughly the same period historians have been trying to measure up the relative value and status of what they call analytical history against what they call narrative history. The "new wave" historians mainly pride themselves on what they describe as their analytical approach, and they tend to regard those whom they describe as narrative historians as fuddy-duddies. Paradoxically at the very same time analytical philosophers of several varieties discovered that historians tell stories which make things about the past more intelligible. They then tried to discover the structure of "narrative explanation" regarding it as the characteristic mode of explanation "why" in history. Since instead of engaging in dialogue with each other, philosophers and historians at least in the English-speaking world have long had the habit of simultaneous monologue, the noncommunication between them is neither surprising nor new. It does, however, confirm an occasional impression of mine that some leaders of fashion in history have a rather special gift for leaping aboard intellectually sinking ships and drawing their innocent followers along with them.

. . .

At some point it may occur simultaneously to a good many historians that their common commitment to analysis should have common consequences in practice and method, not merely in interstitial declamation. Indeed there are signs that a crisis of this sort may not be far off. For several years *History and Theory* has been publishing the pasquinades of philosophizing historians and historizing philosophers, and some historians have been reading them. A few years ago philosophers and historians lived together for several days in a common symposium during an assignation arranged by Professor Sidney Hook. The brief cohabitation produced a mutual rapport no greater than the more protracted but less intense intercourse under the covers of *History and Theory*. Nevertheless the danger now exists that sooner or later some eager beaver historian who likes to gnaw at timber along the section of the intellectual stream where history and philosophy converge will bring together the utterances of historians in support of historical analysis and analytic history. Then he or someone else will notice that they are not uttering the same or similar statements, that the objects of their discourse (historical analyses) lack formal common traits, and that therefore discussion of analysis hitherto has produced some noise but little communication.

. . .

Hexter's "positivist-idealist syndrome"

. . . And this brings us back to the syndrome which underlies the error. Its components, positivist and idealist, are interlocked in practice, but they can be separated for examination. The positivist component goes as follows:

1. History is a collection of statements of facts about the past.

2. All such statements are either true or false.

3. Unless the statement can be shown to be true, it is false, or if one does not know whether it is true or false, mere opinion.

4. What is false or mere opinion has no place in true history.

5. Much of what is alleged as true statement of fact in history turns out to be false or mere opinion.

6. Very little history is true.

The Platonic idealist component runs as follows:

1. Truth is one, certain, and eternal.

2. Therefore what is really true is immutable, beyond doubt, and uniquely correct.

3. What is not immutable, beyond doubt, and uniquely correct is false or not true; it is unreal, or mere matter of opinion.

4. Every statement about the past is subject to change and doubt, and none totally precludes alternative possibilities.

5. Therefore all history that is not simply false is a mere matter of opinion.

To this positivist-idealist syndrome of propositions, which results in a wrong, debilitating, inconsistent, and counterproductive way of thinking about history one alternative would go somewhat as follows:

1. Potentially history is a credible, coherent, and patterned construal of the record of the past.

2.   Properly conducted historical investigation and properly constructed historical discourse usually result not in "mere opinion," but in close approximations to the truth about their objects of inquiry.

3.   Sometimes the evidence available in the surviving records of the past will satisfactorily sustain two or more divergent yet credible conclusions about what went on in the past; and although an omniscient God could eliminate all divergencies, historians are not and are unlikely to become omniscient gods, so some divergent historical conclusions will be almost equally credible.

4.   The rhetoric of history frequently permits two or more divergent alternative structures of discourse, and the alternatives are sometimes irreducible in principle either (a) because they equally maximize the truth values that they achieve or (b) because each maximizes sets of incommensurate truth values that cannot be maximized simultaneously within any single structure of historical discourse.

5.   Proposition 4(a) should cause neither historians nor anyone else any discomfort or wonder, since the existence of several equally valid solutions to a problem is far from being unique to the rhetoric of history. It is a phenomenon familiar to everyone who got as far as quadratic equations in algebra, which have two equally correct solutions. It will also be familiar to anyone who considers the innumerable ways of bringing about chemical reactions of which water will be an

end-product. In neither the algebraic nor the chemical case does the duality or multiplicity of correct solutions imply that there are no rules or that what counts as a correct solution is merely a matter of opinion. What is true of algebra and chemistry is also true of the rhetoric of history.

6. On the other hand position 4(b) may present considerable difficulties since it may imply and be symptomatic of a fundamental difference between history and the natural sciences rooted in differences between the two aspects of reality that are their respective objects—"the past" and "nature." If this is so, it is of great importance, and it will be worth close scrutiny later.

17

Roy A. Childs Jr.

Selection from "Big Business and the Rise of American Statism," Reason magazine, February 1971 and March 1971 issues[33]

Roy A. Childs Jr. (1949–1992) studied at the State University of New York at Buffalo but chose a career in the libertarian movement rather than attending graduate school to become a teacher or researcher. He was influenced by Robert LeFevre and his Freedom School, and was an admiring critic of Ayn Rand and a follower of Murray Rothbard. He edited the *Libertarian Review* from 1977 to 1981, then worked for the Cato Institute and later served as editorial director of Laissez Faire Books. He frequently wrote reviews, often of the longer form, like those found in the *New York Review of Books*.[34]

In a discussion of the history of American business, Childs perpetuates a number of themes of liberal history, including (a) that there is no historical necessity, no inevitable cause and effect; (b) that sociological concepts do not exist independently, but are descriptions of combined individual action; and (c) that history does not provide us with a moral direction.

History, Childs states, is concerned with selection, and our theories and biases shape what we select as much as how we interpret it. For this reason, empirical observation is never sufficient for proper historical interpretation. Instead, we must also apply reason and logic as a priori categories of understanding.

This essay constitutes a part of "revisionism" in history, largely domestic history. The term revisionism originally came into use referring to historiography after World War I. A group of young historians, eager to uncover the realities behind the blanket of myths surrounding the origins of this crucial conflict, discovered as a result of their investigations that Germany and Austria were not, contrary to popular mythology, solely responsible for the outbreak of that crisis. Thus, reevaluating the history of the immediate past, these historians came to see the Treaty of Versailles, forced upon the losers of that war, as monstrously unjust, and maintained that the rigid enforcement of its terms would lead to further world conflict. They came to advocate a radical overhauling and revision of the Versailles Treaty—whence the term "revisionism."

Since then, revisionism has been applied to virtually any renegade school of thought in historiography that took issue with the "official government line" on important events in history. As it is used today, revisionism is a general concept subsuming a wide variety of schools, or integrating conceptions of man's past. For at the time when any set of events occurs, in any context, there is almost always a specific set of interpretations of events, a given historical paradigm, which spreads throughout a given culture to the relative exclusion of other interpretations.

Those schools of historiography that are responsible for refuting the popular myths, for *revising* the historical record in accordance with new evidence, are thus called revisionist in nature. In this preface, it is my intention to sketch briefly what I consider to be the nature and status of history as a field of investigation. I want especially to focus on the crucially important, yet neglected, relationship of philosophy to history. In the nineteenth century, practically every great philosopher made extensive use of history, particularly in fields such as social philosophy; and, every great historian was usually well acquainted with philosophy. Yet today historians and philosophers often seem to be completely cut off from one another. This is unfortunate, for history is vitally important to the philosopher, at the very least in illustrating his theories, in filling in the outlines of an abstract theory with concrete units and events. Similarly, philosophy is critically important to history in at least two interrelated ways: philosophy necessarily serves as a critic, and a guide, on two important levels—methodology, and evaluation. No one who deals with questions of responsibility, causality, or even the problem of "knowing" concrete events to which the human mind no longer has direct access through immediate awareness (as opposed to inference), can escape the importance of philosophy.

But the problem is more complicated than that. Today, certain philosophers tend to dismiss specific social theories, such as libertarianism and laissez-faire, almost out-of-hand, usually because of alleged historical figures regarding centralization of economic power, depressions, unemployment, imperialism, war and so forth. And certain historians (usually those operating from an *implicit* philosophic base such as Marxism), in an attempt to pump "relevance" into history, insist on drawing explicitly *non-historical* conclusions from purely historical data. Thus, such key revisionist authors as Gabriel Kolko and William Appleman Williams often mention in the course of their historical studies that such-and-such was "a necessary consequence of American capitalism." Aside from the enormous problems involved in the question of "necessity" *as such* in all fields, surely we face here more than a strictly historic judgment! At the barest minimum, such a statement would put the responsibility of proof on the shoulders of the proponent, who must marshal not only historical data, but economic theory and social philosophy as well—not to mention epistemology, which alone can provide him with a systematic methodology. Notice this intricate statement in Joyce and Gabriel Kolko's masterly *The Limits of Power*: "A society's goals, in the last analysis, reflect its objective needs—economic, strategic, and political—in the light of the requirements of its very specific structure of power." This is certainly *not* a strictly historical judgment. These questions immediately arise: What does it mean to talk of a "society's" goals? What are a "society's objective needs, and how does one determine them? What are the "requirements" of a specific structure of power, and what is meant here by the term "specific structure of power"? The point is not to fall back on agnosticism and skepticism, but to raise the question of whether or not such questions can be answered—or even *raised*—from within the context of history *alone*. If they cannot be, then we obviously fall into such fields as economics and philosophy. But philosophy *first*: it is only philosophy that, properly speaking, will give us the means of *answering* the very question of whether or not such-and-such a problem can be answered by historical inquiry alone.

Although I have stressed the dependence of history on philosophy, I do not mean to imply that history is merely tangential to philosophy. The philosopher, in my view, should, if nothing else, regard history as a testing ground, an experimental laboratory in which he conceptually can apply his theories (particularly social and political theories, and ethics) in an attempt to see if they make sense. A philosopher who preaches total state control of individual human actions and decisions, for instance, might profitably look at history for instances of what has happened as his ideal has been approached, approached as a limit case. If he finds destruction, chaos and the like, then the burden of explaining this within the confines of his assertions of the supposedly beneficial nature of state control comes into play. Similarly, if an advocate of laissez-faire holds that depressions are impossible or unlikely in a free market economy, then he must be prepared to explain the nature and genesis of historical depressions by another theory than the prevalent ones, and to call into play historical data which other schools either neglect or misinterpret. Finally, the philosopher can profitably regard historical evaluations and interpretations as *practice* for actually applying his theories in interpreting contemporary events.

Since space does not permit me to detail every major issue in the philosophy of history, I shall restrict myself to presenting some of the more interesting points which a developed philosophy of history should focus on. And within these limits, I shall summarize my own approaches to some key problem areas.

What is history? History is a selective recreation of the events of the past, according to a historian's premises regarding what is important and his judgment concerning the nature of causality in human action. This selectivity is a most important aspect of history, and it is this alone which prevents history from becoming a random chronicling of events. And since this selectivity is necessary to history, the only remaining question is whether or not such judgments will be made explicitly or implicitly, with full knowledge of what one considers to be important and why, or without such awareness. Selection presupposes a *means, method,* or *principle* of selection. The historian's view of the nature of causality in human action also is determined by a principle of selection. He can have a conscious theory, such as economic determinism, or attempt to function without one. But without one, the result of historical investigation is likely to appear disintegrated and patched together. In this case, the historian depends necessarily on philosophy, on economics and on psychology. If he is not aware of his selections and presuppositions, then the result is a bad historian, or at best a confused one. Charles A. Beard was more self-conscious than most about the problems of historical method, yet he still could write, at the apex of his career, an essay entitled "Written History as an Act of Faith." Of philosophical evasion and bankruptcy are bad historians born, as are professionals in so many other fields. A professional in any field has the unshakable responsibility to be aware of and name his primaries, those presuppositions which function as axiomatic in his field. If he intends to be taken seriously, then he should be prepared to defend them. Evasion on any level produces disastrous consequences for man; on the highest political and intellectual levels, evasion can result in such things as physical destruction, or in entire generations of scholars being misled in their scholarly pursuits.

A popular philosophical doctrine holds that the methodology of history is entirely different from the methodology of other sciences. Yet *fundamentally* the methodology of *all* sciences is the same—*logic*. The nature of the evidence relevant to one field may differ from that relevant to another, and this indeed accounts for the *apparent* differences of method. Yet truths in any field are in fact verified by a process of applying man's reason to objective evidence. By "reason" I mean simply the faculty of integrated awareness which is responsible for all of man's *knowledge* above the perceptual level; by "objective evidence" I mean reality as presented to the intellect—"objective" meaning that which is determined by the nature of the entities existing in reality, and "evidence" referring to that context or "segment" of reality which a consciousness has become aware of.

The nature of the objective evidence which is largely considered in history is simply *human testimony*, direct or indirect. History as a field deals with past human thought and actions. Since we have no direct awareness of the contents of anyone's consciousness but our own, we must rely on inference from what a person says, and what he does. Considered from a different perspective, history deals with the ends that men have held in the past, and the means that they have adopted to attain these ends. Since no two individuals are specifically alike in every particular characteristic, it is impossible to recreate the past in the form of a laboratory experiment and to observe the effects of single causal factors on human action. Thus, all that one can do is to collect evidence concerning the context of individual men, their ideas and their actions, using a theory or model of the nature of causality in human action that interprets or selectively reconstructs events of the past, omitting what one judges to be unimportant, and offering an explanation for what one does consider to be important, in light of the evidence available. Utopian "completeness" is neither possible nor necessary in knowledge—in history or anywhere else. All knowledge is contextual, but this does not in any way hinder knowledge from being *valid*.

Turning from this sketch of historical *method*, I shall indicate, briefly, the *value* of history. Traditionalists often seek to use history as a guide to action, spurning abstract guides to conduct provided by the science of ethics, and adopting conventions and traditions instead. Yet it should be noted at the outset that to use history in any reasonable way to find rules of conduct presupposes a rational ethic. One must use a rational ethic to differentiate "good" traditions from bad, and in fact to supersede history altogether in projecting what is *possible* to man. If something has happened in history, then one rationally can conclude that it *is* possible for man; if something has *not* happened in history, the reverse is not true—one *cannot* conclude that it is *not* possible for man. History can *illustrate* principles, but cannot verify or refute them. It is important to point out the submission of history to a rational ethic in this regard.

People distraught with the present often seek stability and refuge in the past, idealizing it beyond recognition. Such an attitude, however, will only lead to a life built on illusions, to despair that tomorrow things will only be worse, and a general feeling of impotence and inefficacy, with the result that those who accept such a view will *not* act to attain a better future.

But to act to change things for the better presupposes not only that one understands a rational ethic and its principles, but that one has some idea of "where one is," historically speaking. One has to answer the question: what is the present context of man? To answer this takes a knowledge of what ends men have sought up to now, in a broad cultural and political sense, and what means they have adopted to attain them. One then applies the principles of a rational philosophy to his actions; understanding his context, he acts to change things in a certain direction.

If either history or philosophy, specifically, ethics, is left out of this, an ideology is necessarily incomplete. On the one hand there is the error of those who, like William Appleman Williams, "are committed to the proposition that History is the most consequential way of learning who we are and what we should do." On the other hand, there is the fallacy of those who develop a social philosophy and attempt to apply it without any knowledge of what is going on in the world.

In response to Williams, it can be said that history *cannot* tell us "what we should do." At best, it can pinpoint problems which people historically have faced, and solutions which they have attempted to apply.

In response to the others, it should be stated that the application of the most consistent philosophy to real events requires a journalistic knowledge of the state of the world. This differentiates ideology from philosophy. Whereas philosophy abstracts from time, and hence from history, the fundamental truths about man and his relationship to reality, ideology is a consistent world view. It integrates philosophy with one's context, applies the principles of philosophy to the concrete realities of the world. Philosophy is concerned with the nature and validity of human knowledge, with validating and detailing the precepts of a rational ethic with *truth*. Ideology is concerned with applying philosophy to any given historical context—with *making truth relevant*, which comes from an integrated focus on man as he is in any historical context.

The transition from philosophy to ideology is largely accomplished by history. To use an analogy, philosophy discovers a rational ethic, but every given individual must apply its precepts to his own life by identifying the context he faces and making concrete choices by means of logic. The "major premise" in this version of the Aristotelian "practical syllogism" is the ethical premise itself. The "minor premise" is the concrete in anyone's life which the principles subsume. The "conclusion" is the action to be taken.

Similarly in the transition from philosophy to ideology, the major premise is the ethical-philosophic principle; the minor premises are the concrete details, or "existential premises" summarizing some aspect of the context of man in some historical period. The conclusion is the ideological stand to be taken.

It is important to emphasize the overwhelming necessity of having a valid existential premise in either the individual or the general case. In ideology, invalid historical or existential premises can make the stand taken totally inconsistent with the basic thrust of the philosophy which generated it initially. The result of errors may be that the ideological stand ends up on the wrong side of the fence.

Now a word on some of my own positions on basic issues. Believing that the universe consists of a number of distinct entities which are related to each other by both real and mental relations (having an objective foundation in fact), I hold that things necessarily act in accordance with their individual natures, producing results in accordance with such natures. Concepts and theories are therefore formed by integrating particulars according to common characteristics into new mental entities.

In history, I hold that events consist of the actions of *individuals* motivated toward certain ends and using certain means to attain them. But since individuals often have the same values and conceptions of appropriate means to attain their ends, they often work together. In fact, the whole function of institutions is to enable individual human actions to be systematically and consciously integrated in producing common ends. It is this fact which gives rise to all classifications and hence all "class analysis." "Classes" in social theory, or political theory, or historical investigation, must of necessity be groups of individuals having common characteristics. It is my view that man has free will, and that the concept and existence of free will is a necessary postulate if an obvious fact of man's nature is to be explained: his capacity for conceptual and propositional speech, and his ability to identify facts of reality. Determinism, in the strict sense, is contradictory. For if a man's mental processes—specifically, his attempts at reasoning—are not free, if they are determined by environment and heredity, then there is no means of claiming that theory x is true and y is false—since man can have no way of knowing that his mental processes might not be conditioned to force him to believe that x is logical, when in fact it is not.

This means that "classes" in history are not primarily economic, in the usual sense of the term, but rather, are *ethical*. Man is not born with values, or preferences except on a sensory level (pleasure or pain), and he does not merely absorb values from a culture like a sponge absorbs water. Rather, men must *choose* their values, by intention or default. And the realm of chosen values is the realm of ethics. This belief in ethical classes is the *root* of my disagreement with Marxism.

A related fallacy of Marxism, especially in relation to its effect in guiding historical investigation, is its simplistic conception of what constitutes a class "interest."

"Interests" are not primary, nor automatic. Apart from that category of things which actually benefit men (whether or not men are aware of them) "interests" can only be arrived at through a process of consciousness; *evaluation*. This means that, given an objective standard of the organism's life and well-being, a given man's values and conception of his own or his "class's" interests can be right or wrong. More importantly, *classes are derived from and validated by reference to concrete individuals, actions and values, not vice versa.* Classifications are derived from things, not vice versa.

This is important to focus on for a moment. For Marx, despite all his anti-Idealistic and anti-Hegelian rhetoric, is really an Idealist and Hegelian on the issue of classification. Whatever attempts he makes to get around this point, Marx is still asserting, at root, that a classification (a social class) precedes and determines the characteristic of those who are members or units of the classification. Marx is, in fact, very unclear on the nature of the exact process of causation which occurs in the interaction between those people who own the "means of production," their ideas ("interests") and actions, and those people relating to them. Since any such theory of causality in human action is vitally important in historical investigation, it is to be expected that Marxism corrupts historical investigation.

Interestingly enough, this is very relevant to the subject of this essay: the role of big business in promoting American statism. For if nothing else, this essay shows that the "class lines" in American history are different from what they were thought to be. Some of the men in larger businesses supported and even initiated acts of government regulation while others, particularly relatively smaller and more competent competitors, opposed such regulation. Thus we have a clear-cut case in American history that contradicts Marxian theory: the lines of battle and conflict were *not* drawn merely over the issue and criterion of individuals' relation to the means of production, but on much more complicated grounds. A better classification might be along the lines set down by Franz Oppenheimer: the state-benefited and the state-oppressed—those who gained their wealth by means of confiscation, robbery and restriction of other people's noncoercive activities, and those who gained their wealth by means of free trade in a free market, by the method of voluntary exchange. But even here the lines are not clear-cut, and we find cases of those who were honest producers sanctioning theft and parasitism, as well as cases of those who were parasites and benefiters from statism opposing controls—twin cases of hypocrisy and altruism.

Needless to add, many contemporary Marxists have responded to the challenge with ever new wings being added on to classical Marxist theory to "explain," in an ad hoc fashion, the events which do not fit into classic Marxist paradigms. Historically, *whenever* defenders of some classic paradigm, in any field, begin to confront problems which conflict with the basic theory, they begin increasingly to modify the particulars of the theory to conform to fact without ever questioning the basic paradigm itself. But sooner or later any such imitation of the path taken by the followers of Ptolemy must end in the same way: the paradigm will collapse and be replaced by a new paradigm which explains all the known facts in a much simpler manner, thus conforming to a fundamental rule of scientific methodology: Occam's razor.

The new paradigm, I think, will be the paradigm of libertarianism.

The purpose of this particular essay is simply to apply some of the principles of libertarianism to an interpretation of events in a very special and important period of human history. I have attempted to give a straightforward summary of New Left revisionist findings in one area of domestic history: the antitrust movement and Progressive Era. But I have done so not as a New Leftist, not as a historian proper, but as a *libertarian*, that is, a social philosopher of a specific school.

In doing this summary, I have two interrelated purposes: first, to show Objectivists and libertarians that certain of their beliefs in history are wrong and need to be revised under the impact of new evidence, and simultaneously to illustrate to them a specific means of approaching historical problems, to identify one cause of the growth of American statism and to indicate a new way of looking at history. Secondly, my purpose is to show New Left radicals that far from undermining the position of laissez-faire capitalism (as opposed to what they call state capitalism, a system of government controls which is not yet socialism in the classic sense), their historical discoveries actually *support* the case for a totally free market. Then, too, I wish to illustrate how a libertarian would respond to the problems raised by New Left historians. Finally, I wish implicitly to apply Occam's razor by showing that there is a simpler explanation of events than that so often colored with Marxist theory. Without exception, Marxist postulates are not necessary to explain the facts of reality.

Conflicting Schools of Thought

In historiography different schools of thought exist in much the same way and for the same reason as in many other fields. And in history, as in those other fields, different interpretations, no matter how far removed from reality, tend to go on forever, oblivious to new evidence and theories. In his book, *The Structure of Scientific Revolutions*, Thomas Kuhn shows in the physical sciences how an existing paradigm of scientific explanation tends to ignore new evidence and theories, being overthrown only when: (a) the puzzles and problems generated by a false paradigm pile up to an increasingly obvious extent, so that an ever-wider range of material cannot be integrated into the paradigm, and an ever-growing number of problems cannot be solved, and (b) there arises on the scene a new paradigm to replace the old.

In history, perhaps more than in most other fields, the criteria of truth have not been sufficiently developed, resulting in a great number of schools of thought that tend to rise and fall in influence more because of political and cultural factors than because of epistemological factors. The result also has been that in history there are a number of competing paradigms to explain different sets of events, all connected to specific political views. In this essay, I shall consider three of them: the Marxist view, the conservative view and the liberal view. I shall examine how these paradigms function with reference to one major area of American history—the Progressive Era—and with respect to one major issue: the roots of government regulation of the economy, particularly through the antitrust laws and the Federal Reserve System. Other incidents will also be mentioned, but this issue will be the focus.

Among these various schools, nearly everyone agrees on the putative facts of American history; disagreements arise over frameworks of interpretation and over evaluation.

The Marxists, liberals, and conservatives all agree that in the economic history of America in the nineteenth century, the facts were roughly as follows. After midcentury, industrialization proceeded apace in America, as a consequence of the laissez-faire policies pursued by the United States government, resulting in increasing centralization and concentration of economic power.

According to the liberal, in the nineteenth century there was an individualistic social system in the United States, which, when left unchecked, led inevitably to the "strong" using the forces of a free market to smash and subdue the "weak," by building gigantic, monopolistic industrial enterprises which dominated and controlled the life of the nation. Then, as this centralization proceeded to snowball, the "public" awoke to its impeding subjugation at the hands of these monopolistic businessmen. The public was stirred by the injustice of it all and demanded reform, whereupon altruistic and far-seeing politicians moved quickly to mash the monopolists with antitrust laws and other regulation of the economy, on behalf of the ever-suffering "little man" who was saved thereby from certain doom. Thus did the American government squash the greedy monopolists and restore competition, equality of opportunity and the like, which was perishing in the unregulated laissez-faire free market economy. Thus did the American state act to save both freedom *and* capitalism.

The Marxists also hold that there was in fact a trend toward centralization of the economy at the end of the last century, and that this was inherent in the nature of capitalism as an economic system. (Some modern, more sophisticated Marxists maintain, on the contrary, that historically the state was *always* involved in the so-called capitalistic economy.) Different Marxists see the movement towards state regulation of the economy in different ways. One group basically sees state regulation as a means of prolonging the collapse of the capitalistic system, a means which they see as inherently unstable. They see regulation as an attempt by the ruling class to deal with the "inner contradictions" of capitalism.

Another group, more sophisticated, sees the movement towards state regulation as a means of *hastening* the cartelization and monopolization of the economy under the hands of the ruling class.

The conservative holds, like the liberal, that there was *indeed* such a golden age of individualism, when the economy was almost completely free of government controls. But far from being evil, such a society was near-utopian in their eyes. But the government intervened and threw things out of kilter. The consequence was that the public began to clamor for regulation in order to rectify things that were either not injustices at all, or were injustices imposed by initial state actions. The antitrust laws and other acts of state interference, by this view, were the result. But far from seeing the key large industrialists and bankers as monopolistic monsters, the conservatives defend them as heroic innovators who were the victims of misguided or power-lusting progressives who used big businessmen as scapegoats and sacrifices on the altar of the "public good."

All three of the major schools of interpretation of this crucial era in American history hold two premises in common: (a) that the trend in economic organization at the end of the nineteenth century was *in fact* towards growing centralization of economic power, and (b) that this trend was an outcome of the processes of the free market. Only the Marxists, and then only a portion of them, take issue with the additional premise that the actions of state regulation were anti-big business in motivation, purpose and results. And both the conservatives and the liberals see a sharp break between the ideas and men involved in the

Progressive Movement and those of key big business and financial leaders. Marxists disagree with many of these views, but hold the premise that the regulatory movement itself was an outgrowth of the capitalistic economy.

The Marxists, of course, smuggle in specifically nonhistorical conclusions and premises, based on their wider ideological frame of reference, the most prominent being the idea of *necessity* applied to historical events.

Although there are many arguments and disputes between adherents of the various schools, none of the schools has disputed the fundamental *historical* premise that the dominant trend at the end of the last century was toward increasing centralization of the economy, or the fundamental *economic* premise that this alleged increase was the result of the operations of a laissez-faire free market system.

Yet there are certain flaws in all three interpretations, flaws that are both historical and theoretical, flaws that make any of the interpretations inadequate, necessitating a new explanation. Although it is not possible here to argue in depth against the three interpretations, brief reasons for their inadequacy can be given.

Aside from the enormous disputes in economics over questions such as whether or not the "capitalistic system" inherently leads toward concentration and centralization of economic power in the hands of a few, we can respond to the Marxists, as well as to others, by directing our attention to the premise that there was in fact economic centralization at the turn of the century. In confronting the liberals, once more we can begin by pointing to the fact that there has been much more centralization since the Progressive Era than before, and that the function, if not the alleged purpose, of the antitrust and other regulatory laws has been to increase, rather than decrease, such centralization. Since the conservatives already question, on grounds of economic theory, the premise that the concentration of economic power results inevitably from a free market system, we must question them as to why they believe that (a) a free market actually existed during the period in question, and (b) how, then, such centralization of economic power resulted from this supposed free market.

18

R. M. Hartwell

History and Ideology *(pamphlet published by the Institute for Humane Studies, Arlington, VA, 1974)*[35]

Ronald Max Hartwell (1921–2009), was an Australian-born economic historian who served as Professorial Fellow of Nuffield College, Oxford University, and briefly as the president of the Mont Pelerin Society. He gained some fame for arguing, contra the standard Marxist position, that the initial stages of the Industrial Revolution in England had not led to a lower standard of living for the working class. This view led to a protracted debate in the 1960s with Eric Hobsbawm and other Marxist historians who argued the contrary.[36]

In *History and Ideology*, Hartwell explains that he thought historical debates could be settled by presenting evidence, that "historical controversy was concerned primarily with truth and error." Here, he speaks of "historicism" of the type Karl Popper identified: not simply the belief that the past could yield knowledge of its own kind, but that it could provide or direct ultimate knowledge of the course of history. In Hartwell, we find the maturing of a liberal history without the 19th-century liberal overtones of inevitable progress and national advancement. Instead, history is very much contingent on individual actions; it is discoverable and understandable through evidence and open inquiry.

I WRITE about history and historical controversy not so much as a scholar but as a teacher, one whose profession for more than thirty years has been to teach the young, especially the gifted young. My subject for research and teaching is modern economic and social history, with special reference to the industrial revolution in England and in Europe. In teaching students about that "great discontinuity" which divided a Europe of slow economic growth and mass poverty, in which population and real incomes were rising very slowly or not at all, and were sometimes falling, from the modem Europe of economic growth and widespread wealth, in which population has grown at an almost terrifying speed and in which there has been, also, a sustained growth of real incomes, I was confronted, and still am, with a widely held aversion to the economic and political system which provided the institutional framework for modern economic growth and, more remarkable, with a belief that this growth was achieved at the expense of depressing, or at least of holding down, the standard of living of the working classes. The phenomena are linked, but it is the belief in "immiseration" which, as F. A. Hayek has pointed out, is the "one supreme myth which more than any other has served to discredit the economic system to which we owe our present-day civilization."

This myth, based on an extensive literature about the industrial revolution, was accepted by perhaps the majority of students and teachers in schools and universities and had become part of the conventional wisdom. This myth engendered attitudes which were explicitly anti-market economy and included belief in the necessity for, and desirability of, an increasing role for the state in economic and social life. This myth attributed all the ills of modern society, imagined and real, to industrialization; it argued that the only beneficiaries of modern economic growth were the rich and privileged; it estimated that the social cost of industrialization was greater than the private gain. But, it was obvious to me, the myth was based on history which was demonstrably false; it was based on an historical interpretation of the industrial revolution that was as perverse as it was incorrect. It was against the myth, and the attitudes it encouraged, that I argued with colleagues and students. And so, much of my teaching life has taken the form, not of imparting new information and of instructing in the methods of historical inquiry, but of therapeutic exercises in myth-breaking.

The actual mix of myth-making history was complex, but three sets of beliefs particularly interested me as an economic historian of industrialization. First, the belief that the industrial revolution in England had resulted not only in a deterioration in the standard of living of the mass of the workers for upwards of a century, but also in a permanent deterioration in their way of life; insofar as wealth had increased in the early period, it had resulted only in increasing inequality, with the rich getting richer and the poor poorer. Second, the belief that the subsequent, in-the-long-run improvement in the material condition of the working classes, which the critics of capitalism have found difficult to deny, was caused not by industrialization and economic growth, but by income redistribution, by working class industrial organizations which were able to force a large share of national income from reluctant capitalists, and through the development of the welfare state, which also was the direct result of the increasing political power of the working classes. Third, the belief that much of the increasing wealth of the industrial countries of Europe, which went mainly to the capitalists, came from non-Europeans; increasing European wealth, including that of the masses, was partly at the expense of the non-European masses and was achieved through a process of colonial exploitation known as imperialism. It is because of the prevalence of these beliefs, because of their widespread and uncritical acceptance, that I was driven to argument, both verbal and printed.

At first I assumed that historical argument could be settled simply by the refutation of error. I assumed, for example, that historical myths based on false facts would disappear by confronting "false" facts with "true" facts. I believed, indeed, that historical controversy was concerned primarily with truth and error. I soon realized, however, that much debate in history was not about "facts" but about "values," about how the world should be and not about how it actually was. Most of the important historical debate, I finally decided, was ideological dispute. And the particular debate in which I was a disputant turned out to be particularly ideological, with as many implications for the world in which I lived as for the historic world about which I was writing and arguing. The political implications, especially about liberalism and market economy, I found paradoxical and disturbing:

paradoxical, because of the dislike and rejection of a liberal economic system which had produced economic growth, which had lifted so many people above subsistence, and which had promoted social mobility to the advantage of the working classes; disturbing, because of the acceptance of interventionist and illiberal theories of politics and economics which enhanced the power of the state over the individual. The historical implications were also disturbing. The beliefs were undoubtedly founded in history; history was being used to "prove" the evils of capitalism and to preach the desirability of socialism. And, making these beliefs more difficult to reject, revelation was turned into prophecy; the problems of capitalism became part of the inevitable decline of capitalism and the inevitable advent of socialism. The lessons of history thus became the laws of history. To oppose the "supreme myth" of working class deterioration, therefore, it was necessary to oppose a theory of historical inevitability.

In writing history, the historian, with varying motives, attempts to reconstruct the past. History is widely read, partly out of interest and for entertainment, but more seriously to increase understanding of society and its problems. History, it is generally believed, is useful; there are lessons to be learnt from history; history answers real needs and is rooted in contemporary problems. But can history tell the reader how he should act? On this question there is basic disagreement between those who believe in the laws of history and, therefore, in historical inevitability, and those who believe that, although the scope of human choice is often limited, there are always choices to be made. "It is widely believed," Karl Popper has written, "that a truly scientific and philosophical attitude towards politics, and a deeper understanding of social life in general, must be based on a contemplation of history." In the study of history, in this view, "we may discover the secret, the essence of human destiny," and thus "the path on which mankind is destined to work." This is historicism, and historicists believe that history is governed by laws that can be discovered. In contrast, the empiricists among historians believe that history is relevant for the better understanding of contemporary problems, but not in a determinist sense. History is written and studied by empiricists under the motivation of real needs and interests, but history does not determine either their aims or their actions. To the empiricist, mankind is purposeful and relatively free in his choice of actions, and his history is meaningful in reference to his problems. To the historicist, history determines whatever purpose there is in life, identifies "the preordained movement of impersonal forces," and thus defines inevitable action.

Historical writing about the industrial revolution includes a large input of historicism, which treats industrialization as a phase in the history of capitalism. In the inevitable development and decline of capitalism, the immiseration of the working classes is a necessary prelude to the rise of labor movements and the welfare state. To combat the myth of working class deterioration, therefore, the uncommitted historian has not only to prove misuse and misinterpretation of the historical evidence, but has also to argue against historicism. Thus, controversy is necessary both for professional and ideological reasons. It would be misleading, however, to represent all historical controversy as dispute about historicism. Controversy also arises, for example, because of uncertainty about what is being debated, because of the conflicting and biased nature of historical evidence, and because of differences in expertise among historians. It is my purpose, however, to analyze the ideological reasons for controversy, including the methods by which historicists turn even non-ideological dispute to their advantage.

Historians often argue, frequently with vehemence and bad temper, denigrating each other's competence and character, as they have always done, especially when any historian challenges the deeply held beliefs and values of his contemporaries. For example, when Edward Gibbon combined his history with damaging criticism of the beliefs of "the majority of English readers," beliefs which not only explained the past but guided the present, his reward was sustained abuse:

> Let me frankly own that I was startled at the first discharge of ecclesiastical ordnance; but as soon as I found that this empty noise was mischievous only in the intention, my fear was converted into indignation; and every feeling of indignation or curiosity has long since subsided in pure and placid indifference.

As great an historian as Gibbon could afford to ignore his critics; his *Decline and Fall* was his best defense. Lesser historians might be equally startled, but not equally indifferent. It is difficult, for example, to ignore the barrage of pejorative adjectives and phrases used about historians who, since J. H. Clapham, have challenged the view that the working classes were getting worse off during the industrial revolution. For example, Clapham and others were accused in a recent article of being "committed" to an "*a priori* case" and to have had "a desire to prove preconceived notions"; to have used sources and evidence which were "suspect for their . . . bias," "irrelevant," "anachronistic," "feeble props," "negligible," and "highly untypical"; to have derived conclusions which were "brash," "unqualified," "implausible," "improbable," "frivolous," "careless," "cursory," "ill-informed," "inconclusive," "unsupported," "illegitimate," "futile," "purely rhetorical," "striking perversions of fact" and which were "not now based on reliable evidence."

An outburst in such unscholarly language is explicable only in terms of the tenderness of the nerves touched, of passionate commitment to a particular interpretation of the industrial revolution, and of the consequent need to abuse those who disagree with it. Much, if not most, contemporary historical controversy is, similarly, the consequence of the sceptical historian challenging doctrinal views of the past, and in turn being fiercely attacked by the historians who believe that history happened *in a certain way*. In particular, controversy about some of the major events of British history stems largely from the fact that the Marxists, or historians influenced by the Marxists, have a well-propagated interpretation of the event which all other historians must sooner or later come to terms with, implicitly or explicitly, in their teaching and writing of history. The Marxists, moreover, try to impose a conventional wisdom, or they assume one, and argue, as E. J. Hobsbawm does for the industrial revolution, for a "conventional view" and "the traditional case" with which the majority of historians and good men agree ("few would doubt," "common consent," "a predominance of informed opinion," "general agreement," etc.). The assumption of a traditional view with majority support, of course, seems to throw the burden of disagreement on the assumed minority and to put *them* at a disadvantage; as Hobsbawm argues, again, "the onus of proving the . . . traditional views are wrong, continues to rest squarely on [those who disagree]." However, were it not for a widespread acceptance of the Marxist interpretation of history, many of the controversies which bedevil the writing of history would be unnecessary. This is certainly true for the two great controversies of modern English history, that about the rise of the gentry and the civil war, and that about the social and economic consequences of the industrial revolution.

Disagreement about what happened in the past, however, is almost inevitable among historians. In his essay on Ranke in *Debates with Historians*, Pieter Geyl quoted Agatha Christie, perhaps an unlikely source of historical wisdom:

> Agatha Christie, in one of her witty books, *The Moving Finger*, introduces a girl fresh from school and lets her run on about what she thinks of it. "Such a lot of things seem to me such rot. History, for instance. Why, it's quite different out of different books!" To this her sensible elderly confidant replies: "That is its real interest."

Geyl went on to make two obvious but important points about history, that written history can only be "a part of that reality" it represents, and that such history "gets mixed up with . . . the personality of the historian." The historian, limited by his personality, values, and ability on the one hand, and by evidence which is necessarily incomplete on the other, must infer from the surviving "facts" about the "facts" of history which have not survived, and he must then construct a written history which purports to represent the reality of the past. Even from the surviving evidence, he must choose what is relevant for his purpose. Thus, the collection of historical data, the choice from these of relevant data, and inference from relevant data, make written history possible: the surviving facts of history do not speak for themselves; they have to be collected, selected, and organized to make sense of the past. But selection and organization are not mechanically determined; they depend on hypotheses invented by the historian to enable him to construct a meaningful written history from the surviving data. Writing history requires an intellectual effort which, unfortunately, allows the free play of doctrine and prejudice, and the use of *a priori* theories of historical change, as easily as the use of inductive and deductive reasoning and of scientific inference. Interpretation by the use of given formulae is easier than interpretation which requires the trial and error use of differing hypotheses to explain available evidence. As much construction and explanation in written history derive from uncritically accepted "historical laws" that predict the course of history, as from scientific inquiry, from the scrupulous investigation and interpretation of unique historical evidence. The consequence is that different historians write different histories about the same event. Ability and training combine with beliefs and values, and these in varying degrees determine the quality of the historian's reconstruction of the past. Differing histories of differing quality about the same event lead to controversy, and there then exists the methodological problem of disentangling the causes of controversy, of separating out the elements of incompetence and confusion from those of bias and ideology, and of finding out, as far as the evidence permits, what actually happened in the past.

While it is important always to criticize incompetence and error, it is more important to expose the ideological content of historical controversy, and especially of controversy about the great discontinuities of modern history. Great discontinuities, indeed, raise most explicitly the problems of explanation in history, problems of causation, process, and consequences, which invite generalization and theories about the nature of historical change. Because of their importance, discontinuities attract the positivists and historicists, who see in discontinuity dramatic confirmation of their theory of history, which is "to represent the historical process as a concatenation of events, one following upon the other inevitably, caused as they all are by a superhuman force or by impersonal forces working in society independently from the wishes or efforts of individuals." Such a view of history is attractive, especially when used to explain a large and complex event, because it provides a perspective from which past, present, and future can be judged and because it contains prescriptions for present behavior. The avowed aim in writing such history, indeed, is to influence the present. The Marxists, for example, are not only writing history, they are making history. Writing history in this fashion makes the historian an actor in history. Even so, the most frightening implication of historicism is to deny any significant role in history to the individual, who is powerlessly trapped in a preordained web of social processes, without hopes beyond those which the laws of history have already determined. And the larger the event being analyzed—for example, the industrial revolution—the more convincing is the theory of individual powerlessness, and the more acceptable the thesis of historical inevitability. Once convinced of both, the individual can passively subject himself to the forces of history. As Pieter Geyl has pointed out, "Where there is no choice, there is no anxiety; and a happy release from responsibility." And, in these circumstances, individual action can be "unimpeded by doubts of success or by moral scruples." Determinist theories of history, therefore, are prescriptions for unthinking behavior, for fanaticism or passive inaction; they deny any role to human values and motivation.

The importance of historical controversy to those who value freedom should now be obvious. There should be only one thing inevitable about the theory of historical inevitability: controversy. If there are lessons to be learnt from history, one is that only free societies can allow historical controversy; only in a free society can the myth of historicism be challenged. One measure of freedom in a society, indeed, is the degree to which there is no official history to prove how present conditions inevitably developed out of past conditions, and no effective use of history to justify the present by the use of the past. History in the unfree society is part of the essential framework of official ideology. In free societies history is part of an intellectual heritage, culturally enriching as well as usefully educating, but it is not a prescription for conduct, in spite of the very common habit of appealing to history for lessons. In free societies there is always historical controversy because there are always historians with determinist theories who, since they are the custodians of revealed truth, are impervious to criticism, yet must be opposed. Historical controversy, therefore, is necessary in a free society if that society is to retain freedom of ideas. Both to the historicists, who must attack those who question their theories, and to the nondoctrinaire historians, who must criticize the historicists, controversy is *an* imperative. But those who do question positivist assumptions and theories, and especially those who challenge the Marxists, find themselves not only in historical controversy but in a political debate in which their writing of history is used to locate them unfavorably in the spectrum of modern political beliefs, and hence to condemn them. Thus, controversy is not for the fainthearted; rational analysis and argument are likely to be met with abuse, misrepresentation, and irrelevancies. Also, since most historians are softer to the "left" than to the "right," those who argue against the left are received generally with less tolerance than those who argue for the left; the reactionary historian is seen as morally flawed, suspect both for his history and his politics. But as long as there are historians who will not surrender to doctrine and who continue to treat the writing of history as a serious academic discipline and not just as a medium for propaganda, there will be historical controversy.

In *Capitalism and the Historians*, F. A. Hayek pointed out the importance of history in shaping political beliefs, the importance of myths in shaping the content of written history, and the importance of one particular myth—the myth of immiseration—in creating a "widespread emotional aversion to 'capitalism.'" It is surprising that there is not more discussion about the pervasive and influential role of history in the formation of attitudes towards society and economy. History is no longer considered to be the appropriate training for men of affairs, but it is still universally taught in schools, widely taught in universities, and popular with the general public. At no other time in history, probably, were so many books on history being published and read as there are today. Indeed, casual empiricism might lead us to conclude that history had lost its serious role in education and had become part of the entertainment industry, just another service demanded by an increasingly affluent society. But history is no such innocent consumer good. History must be seen as a weapon in the armory of ideological conflict, a major influence in the formation of political and economic attitudes. History is, therefore, a potent force for good or for ill, and its role in education should be considered more carefully, especially by those who value freedom. There is no doubt that history, as taught in schools and universities, helps to form beliefs and attitudes, so that the present political and economic beliefs of adults are to an important extent based on knowledge of past political and economic experience, that is, on history. At the same time, the present beliefs of adults influence their interpretation of the past. Here is a closed circle of dependence: history forms opinions, and these opinions impose a pattern on the past in a mutually reinforcing process. And when the opinions are harmful to a free society, and the history is based on myths, the result is a vicious circle, an intellectual trap for the young and unwary from which the best escape lies in the breaking of the historical myths. That, unfortunately, is no easy solution. Those who teach know how powerful is the anti-intellectual combination of unquestioning doctrine reinforced by historical myth.

History, however, is not the only force at work in opinion-formation which is anti-liberal and anti-market economy in its influence; indeed, it is only one element in a battery of self-reinforcing prejudice. Similar attitudes, based often on the same myths, are propagated in other disciplines. Much of the study of literature, for example, has moved from analysis of the univer-sals of artistic expression to the sociology of literature, often in terms of the artist's reaction to "relevant" social problems. The worth of a writer is now often measured in terms of his reaction to the social problems of his day, social problems defined by the critic and not by the author. Economics, similarly, is often more concerned with the efficiency of government intervention, with how to make a mixed economy work better, than with critical analysis of the interventionist philosophy. Basic to much teach-ing of economics is the assumption that the market economy is not working because it cannot work, rather than the assumption, equally viable, that market economy does not work because it is not allowed to work. And what schools and universities propa-gate in formal education, many other institutions reinforce: much of the social teaching of the Christian churches is anti-market and interventionist in spirit; the mass media maintain a con-stant barrage of criticism of liberalism and, in particular, over-dramatize the ills of industrial society; creative art caters too often for irresponsible and destructive views of society; both trade unions and employer organizations constantly demand govern-ment intervention for vaguely specified, social reasons; and more transient groups like anti-pollutionists and consumer-protectors see only government-directed solutions for their problems. It is not surprising, therefore, that so many young people grow up to accept the need for government intervention to solve all society's ills, and to believe that conditions are as good as they are because of government intervention, or that conditions are as bad as they are because of lack of government intervention.

The apparent paradox of a society and economy which produces so many goods for so many people, many of whom believe that the system is both inefficient and immoral, derives a major impetus from the continuing influence of the myth of immiseration. This myth, which is basic to that dislike of capitalism which is so widespread in the high-income democracies, still persists. This myth is basic to the widely accepted discrediting of the economic system of private property and free enterprise; it is basic to the naive acceptance of alternative economic and political systems which allegedly achieve progress without cost to the working classes; it is basic to that frantic and fanatical attack on liberal democracy and its institutions which is made by so many of the young in the universities. The importance of this myth, indeed, cannot be exaggerated. Destroy it and much of the easy ideological attack on liberalism and market economy is weakened and is made more difficult to sustain.

The importance of historical controversy is now apparent, for it is mainly in historical controversy that the ideological content of history is made explicit and myths are discredited. But controversy means, in particular, conflict with the Marxists and with those who, often for moral reasons, support them. On the industrial revolution the strongest ideological group, and the most rigid of historicists, are the Marxist historians. They know why and how the industrial revolution occurred, and its consequences, and they are very active in popularizing their beliefs. What is so interesting is that so many intelligent historians can accept the Marxist interpretation of the industrial revolution, that so many non-Marxist historians can accept implicitly that the Marxist interpretation is the most important and relevant to discuss, that so much of the historical profession can accept naively the moral superiority of the Marxists over historians who see good in the industrial revolution, and that, in particular, the Marxist interpretation has so much emotional appeal to the young and gifted. It is partly because the Marxists have built on a long socialist tradition; the historical left in England were intellectually and morally superior to the Marxists, but they developed a basic antagonism to capitalism and the industrial revolution on which the Marxists could capitalize. It is interesting, also, that the profession of historians seems unaware of the political implications of the controversy about industrialization and looks on that controversy as serious discussion about the facts of history, when so much of it is ideological battling aimed more at changing the world today than at understanding the past. The Marxists write history for political purposes, and debate with them is about values rather than facts.

   This article on history and ideology has been concerned mainly with historical controversy, and particularly with controversy about the industrial revolution. In analyzing controversy, I have been both diagnostic and remedial: diagnostic, by revealing the ideological content of controversy and its anti-liberal implications; remedial, by challenging both the history and propaganda of the historicists. But remedy is not easy, and diagnosis is often seen, among historians, as bad manners. The historical profession rarely questions the assumed moral superiority of the critics of capitalism and the industrial revolution. Too often it is assumed that the historian who criticizes the "right" is a "liberal," while the historian who criticizes the "left," no matter how carefully, is a "reactionary polemicist." This double standard has resulted in overpoliteness in criticism of the left, and unprofessional tolerance of their unacceptable standards of scholarship. When an historian, whatever his political beliefs, is demonstrably wrong or dishonest or perverts history for propaganda, he should be exposed, and his incompetence and dishonesty documented. The critical scholar has always the grave responsibility of challenging historians when they are wrong, and of proving them wrong, for so many of those who write about the industrial revolution have the qualities which the Whig Macaulay, in a famous review, attributed to the Tory Southey: "two faculties which were never, we believe, vouchsafed in measure so copious to any human being, the faculty for believing without a reason, and the faculty of hating without a provocation."

19

Sheilagh Ogilvie

"Towards a Critical Classical Liberal History," Humane Studies Review *4, no. 2 (1987)*

Sheilagh Ogilvie (1958–present) is a Canadian-born professor of economic history at the University of Cambridge and a fellow of the British Academy. In her award-winning research, she has focused on early modern European economic growth and the lives of ordinary people. She has investigated the nature and impact of guilds in European history, the economics of serfdom, and the growth of the modern state, among other topics.

This article is a call for liberal historians to look to new techniques and approaches to history to help overturn some of the many myths and falsehoods perpetuated in written history.

Premodern people acted rationally (from their own perspective). The nation-state should not be expelled from historical accounts. Liberals have to show how the state has been a source of coercion, but, she notes, not the only source of coercion. The article, then, serves partly as a corrective to a kind of libertarian history that ascribes all sources of coercion to the state.

Ogilvie leans toward a comprehensive liberal history that uses a variety of tools and perspectives to analyze society. At the core of liberal history, she argues, is the individual. Her views are particularly pertinent for those who study the premodern world. The takeaway is this: historians err when they ascribe all historical change to geography or class or some force outside the actions of the individual, and while individuals have reasons to justify their actions, these reasons are seldom concomitant with those of modern people.

> Few men will deny that our views about the goodness or badness of different institutions are largely determined by what we believe to have been their effects in the past. There is scarcely a political ideal or concept which does not involve opinions about a whole series of past events. . . . Historical myths have perhaps played nearly as great a role in shaping opinion as historical facts. . . . The influence which the writers of history thus exercise on public opinion is probably more immediate and extensive than that of the political theorists who launch new ideas.*

Even more pernicious than the type of historical myth here castigated by Professor Hayek are unquestioned historical assumptions. Among the influences that have drawn the most dynamic

---

* F. A. Hayek, "History and Politics," *Studies in Philosophy, Politics, and Economics* (Chicago: University of Chicago Press, 1967), p. 201.

young historians in the last generation to the new methodologies and to Marxian-influenced social history have been their iconoclastic tendencies: the readiness "to criticize accepted views, to explore new vistas and to experiment with new conceptions."* Using new techniques and hitherto-neglected documentary sources, historians have been able to question and falsify basic historical assumptions (especially concerning the beliefs and behavior of the great illiterate mass of the common population in the past) that had previously been thought to be untestable, a matter only of literary interpretation or dogma.†

Unfortunately, few liberal historians have tuned to the new, rigorous social, economic, and demographic history, and thus, although some false assumptions about the past are being questioned, others (for instance, the pernicious effects of the transition to capitalism, the benefits of state and corporate intervention in the economy and in social behavior, and the irrational and harmful effect of individual decision-making) persist uncriticized. The new theories being put forward to replace the falsified assumptions, and benefiting from the iconoclastic glamor, tend to derive from Marxian theory, and are already establishing a socialist and coercive tradition among practitioners of the new rigorous history.

---

* F. A. Hayek, "The Intellectuals and Socialism," *Studies*, p. 193.

† These new techniques and sources are discussed and exemplified in Peter Laslett, *The World We Have Lost*, 2nd ed. (London: Methuen, 1971); and in Keith Wrightson, *English Society 1580–1680* (London: Hutchinson, 1982), esp. p. 11. Some of the French tendencies are illustrated in Marc Bloch, *French Rural History: An Essay on Its Basic Characteristics* (London: Routledge, 1966).

Genuinely liberal historians must equip themselves with the new historical techniques so that the iconoclastic results made possible by historical demography,[‡] microsimulation,[**] census analysis,[††] and *Annales*-school "*histoire totale*"[‡‡] and "*histoire de la longue durée*"[***] not be made the sole intellectual property of statists.

Three Directions

There are three main directions in which liberal principles can be creatively applied using the new historical techniques to debunk established assumptions. One is to question and provide an alternative to the traditional assumption (almost as rife among "conservatives" and nineteenth-century liberals as among *étatistes*) that the nation-state is the natural and inevitable unit of historical analysis.

Another is, in Professor Hayek's formulation, to have the courage to "defend capitalism from the capitalists."[†††] Classical liberal and

---

[‡] An excellent instance is John Hajnal's seminal essay, "European Marriage Patterns in Perspective," in *Population in History*, ed. D. V. Glass and D. E. C. Eversley (London: Transaction Publishers, 1965), pp. 101–13. Other controversial results are discussed in E. W. Wrigley, *Population in History* (London: Weidenfeld and Nicolson, 1969), and other basic texts of the Cambridge Group for the History of Population and Social Structure.

[**] See, for instance, Kenneth W. Wachter with Eugene A. Hammel and Peter Laslett, *Statistical Studies of Historical Social Structure* (New York: Academic Press, 1978).

[††] Peter Laslett and Richard Wall, eds., *Household and Family in Past Time* (Cambridge: Cambridge University Press, 1972); Richard Wall, Peter Laslett, and Jean Robin, eds., *Family Forms in Historic Europe* (Cambridge: Cambridge University Press, 1983).

[‡‡] Defended and demonstrated in Fernand Braudel, *The Mediterranean and the Mediterranean World in the Age of Philip II* (New York: Collins, 1972).

[***] Emmanuel LeRoy Ladurie, *Les Paysans de Languedoc* (Paris: S.E.V.P.E.N., 1966).

[†††] F. A. Hayek, "Intellectuals and Socialism," p. 192.

libertarian historians have excelled in identifying the ways in which markets are distorted and abusive privilege perpetuated by the state,[‡‡‡] but they must not stop here. They must also be willing to identify institutions other than the state that distort markets in goods and information, and that appear repeatedly in history as beneficiaries of state coercion: merchant cartels and occupational corporations are two such potent and little-discussed sources of entrenched privilege.

And finally, classical liberal historians must cease to accept the assumption of the *Kulturhistoriker* that rational behavior was invented only in the eighteenth century, and that the actions of people in the past are comprehensible only in terms of "peasant irrationality" and "pre-industrial mentalities."[*] Unless individuals can be trusted to have acted in their own interests, using the best knowledge available within the constraints of their situations, the assumption that is and historically always has been beneficial and necessary to establish coercive organs to protect them from harming themselves will continue to gather support from historical studies.

Questioning the Nation-State

I have argued that unquestioned historical assumptions are more dangerous than even historical "myths" about specific events. The

[‡‡‡] For instance, Douglass C. North and Robert Paul Thomas, *The Rise of the Western World: A New Economic History* (Cambridge: Cambridge University Press, 1973); or in the essays of F. A. Hayek, ed., *Capitalism and the Historians* (Chicago: University of Chicago Press, 1954).

[*] See Joyce Oldham Appleby, *Economic Thought and Ideology in Seventeenth-Century England* (Princeton, NJ: Princeton University Press, 1978), which was written to explain the "puzzle" of "how Adam Smith was able to assume that human beings possessed an innate commercial mentality," p. ix. But see also a myriad of precursors, among whom R. H. Tawney, *The Acquisitive Society* (London: Bell, 1921), p. 17 and *passim*.

assumption that "history" is the history of the development and interactions between nation states was, until recently, such an unquestioned assumption. It is ironic that it was most energetically promoted by precisely those nineteenth-century nationalist liberals, those "Whig" historians, whose reputation Hayek essayed to rescue from Herbert Butterfield's strictures.[†] After the flowering of liberal history at the hands of Hume, Robertson, Ferguson and Gibbon in the eighteenth century, the discipline was captured by the irrationalist German historicists, Ranke, Treitschke, Droysen, and their followers. Both the "Whig" historians criticized by Butterfield and the German historicists suffered from a deep-seated cultural determinism, a concentration on national units, and an exclusive attention to political and cultural elites.

It was only with the advent, since 1945, of the *Annales* school in France and the Cambridge school in Britain, both concerned to turn history into a science, that the vast, producing, taxpaying common population of the past has begun to be studied, instead of merely the state that ruled it. Both new schools insisted that the traditional

---

[†] F. A. Hayek, "History and Politics," pp. 202–3. This nineteenth-century assumption, which generalizes the mistake Hayek calls "monetary nationalism," is well described in the following definition of monetary nationalism: "The monetary realists between small adjoining areas are alleged to differ from those between larger regions or countries and this difference is supposed to justify or demand different monetary arrangements." F.A. Hayek, *Monetary Nationalism and International Stability* (London: Longmans, Green and Co., 1937), p. 4. See also F. A. Hayek's *Denationalization of Money: An Analysis of the Theory and Practice of Concurrent Currencies* (London: Institute of Economic Affairs, 1976) for a discussion of one of the many areas of human activity that would have to be fundamentally rethought if the libertarian historian were successful in bringing to the intellectual consciousness how pervasive (yet how unquestioned) the national state is, and how contingent on a unique historical path its development in fact was.

assumptions about "social history" underlying accounts of changes in intellectual currents and political events be tested rigorously, often with recourse to local and apparently dry and mundane documentary sources—parish registers, tithe and tax accounts, local court minutes—hitherto ignored by all but genealogists and antiquarians.* In the last two decades assumptions about the family and demographical behavior,† economic attitudes and actions,‡ popular culture and religion,** and the harmonious and egalitarian nature of pre-industrial communities,†† have all variously been submitted to the test of new records, of exploiting old records in new ways, or simply of exposing traditional notions to the light of criticism.

* The definitive treatise on the new methodology of record-analysis was Alan Macfarlane's *Reconstructing Historical Communities* (Cambridge: Cambridge University Press, 1977), although indications of it had already appeared much earlier, e.g., in T. H. Hollingsworth, *Historical Demography* (Cambridge: Cambridge University Press, 1969).

† Summarized (for their eras) in E. A. Wrigley, *Population in History* (London: Weidenfeld and Nicolson, 1969) and Jean-Louis Flandrin, *Familles: Parenté, maison, sexualité dans l'ancienne société* (Paris: Hachette, 1976).

‡ Foremost Alan Macfarlane's brilliant *The Origins of English Individualism: The Family, Property and Social Transition* (Oxford: Blackwell, 1978); but also Samuel Popkin, *The Rational Peasant: The Political Economy of Rural Society in Vietnam* (Berkeley: University of California Press, 1979); and, much in the same line, Carl Dahlman, *The Open Field System and Beyond* (Cambridge: Cambridge University Press, 1980).

** Keith Wrightson, *Poverty and Piety in an English Village* (New York: Academic Press, 1979); Carlo Ginzburg, *The Cheese and the Worms: The Cosmos of a Sixteenth-Century Miller* (Baltimore: Johns Hopkins University Press, 1980); Robert Mandrou, *De la Culture Populaire au 17e et 18e Siécle: La bibliotheque bleue de Troyes* (Paris, 1964): Michel Vovelle, *Piété Baroque et Déchristianisation en Provence au XVIIIe Siécle* (Paris: Imago, 1973); Brian Pullan, *The Jews of Europe and the Inquisition of Venice 1550–1670* (Oxford: Oxford University Press, 1983).

†† Alan Macfarlane, *The Origins of English Individualism* and Keith Wrightson, *English Society 1580–1680*. Both books emphasize continuity over change in viewing English society between medieval and modern times.

These two historical schools have captured the imagination of the younger generation of historians because of their willingness to be iconoclastic, and their insistence on studying hitherto neglected and "invisible" groups: the governed rather than the governors, the taxed rather than the taxmen, workers rather than capitalists, the illiterate rather than the elite, women and children rather than adult males, the vast rural population rather than the tiny minority in urban centers. These historical schools have also accomplished the necessary and desirable step of rejecting the national state as the unit of historical analysis and looking at these neglected groups across cultures. Demographic patterns and family structures have been compared between societies in the European past.‡‡ Theories have been advanced to explain contemporaneous social unrest in seventeenth-century European states, invoking the concept of a European "General Crisis of the seventeenth century."*** And an attempt has been made to explain that

‡‡ Laslett and Wall, *Household and Family in Past Time* set the stage for this sort of systematic cross-cultural comparison. It has since been overtaken by another such exercises.

*** People at the time were aware of the international nature of the crisis of the seventeenth century: from seventeenth-century diarists, through Hobbes to Voltaire, who remarked on the contemporaneous revolutions in European countries, as well as in Poland, Russia and China, in his *Essai sur les Moeurs et l'Esprit des Nations* (Paris, 1756). The nineteenth-century obsession with the nation-state caused these observations to be submerged and forgotten until the 1950s. The two basic essays, from diametrically opposite ends of the political spectrum, are E. Hobsbawm, "The Crisis of the Seventeenth Century," *Past and Present* 5–6 (1954), and H. R. Trevor-Roper, "The General Crisis of the Seventeenth Century," *Past and Present* 16 (1959). These and the other "general crisis" essays were collected in two volumes over the next two decades, a symptom of the growth of the supranational historical perspective: Trevor Aston, ed., *Crisis in Europe 1560–1660* (London: Routledge, 1965); and Geoffrey Parker and Lesley M. Smith, eds., *The General Crisis of the Seventeenth Century* (London: Routledge, 1978).

unique European phenomenon, industrialization, in terms of the rapid expansion of cottage industry for foreign markets ("proto-industrialization," it is called), all over Europe in the seventeenth and eighteenth centuries.[†††]

Thus, these two schools partly derive their attraction from their willingness to transcend national boundaries, a tendency very much in accord with the principles of classical liberalism, but which has been unaccountably neglected by classical liberal historians. This issue is important precisely because most modern political thinking accepts the nineteenth-century historians' assumption that national states are timeless and inevitable: the question is not whether to have national states, but how to organize them, or how to prevent them from blowing one another up. One of the first jobs of the classical liberal, therefore, in attempting to counter this unquestioning acceptance of the state, is to show that the national state is contingent rather than necessary, and to trace the steps by which it came into being and came to dominate all other forms of organization in early modern Europe.

History books have generally displayed one of two attitudes toward the state. Either they have adopted a "Whig" attitude, showing how government responded creatively and helpfully to "social" (or other) "problems," thereby adding yet another function

[†††] The basic texts for the theory of proto-industrialization are F. F. Mendels, "Proto-Industrialization: The First Phase of the Industrialization Process," *Journal of Economic History* 32 (1972) and Peter Kriedte, Hans Medick, and Juergen Schlumbohm, *Industrialization before Industrialization: Rural Industry in the Genesis of Capitalism* (Cambridge: Cambridge University Press, 1981), trans. Beate Shempp, first published as *Industrialisierung vor der Industrialisierung* (Göttingen: Vandenhoeck and Ruprecht, 1977).

to those previously exercised by it.* Or they have seen the state as a tool of a particular class, and have focused their historical attention on that group at the expense of the state itself.† The *Annales* and Cambridge schools have taken one step forward, in demonstrating conclusively that the nation-state is not the natural, the inevitable, or the best unit of historical analysis and explanation, any more than the actions and words of the governing groups (monarchs, counsellors, officials, elected representatives, military figures) provide the natural, the inevitable, or the best window onto the human past. No longer can the "social background" to political and intellectual changes be dealt with in a handful of quotations from the writings of literate contemporaries.‡ Historical generalizations are no longer immune from criticism, but are expected to conform to the same standards of rigor (for example, consistency and falsifiability) as statements in other sciences.

---

* This process, whereby successively more and more functions were taken over by the state, runs straight through European history, from the Reformation to antitrust laws. See, for instance, the seldom-noted statism which emerges in any standard account of the Reformation, e.g., A. G. Dickens, *The English Reformation* (London: Collins, 1964) or Kurt Aland, *Die Reformation Martin Luthers* (Güetersloh: Mohn, 1982).

† An example is the Hobsbawm article referred to in footnote *** ["The Crisis of the Seventeenth Century"]. The notion of the "capture theory" so beloved of Marxists has recently been argued against by Sam Peltzman, "Toward a More General Theory of Regulation," *Journal of Law and Economics* 19, no. 2 (1976): 211–40; by Gary S. Becker, "Comment," *ibid.*, pp. 245–48: and by Gary S. Becker, "A Theory of Competition among Pressure Groups for Political Influence," *Quarterly Journal of Economics* 98, no. 3 (1983): 371–400.

‡ Although eloquent and entertaining attempts are made by Lawrence Stone, *The Family, Sex and Marriage in England, 1500–1800* (London: Weidenfeld and Nicolson, 1977); Keith Thomas, *Religion and the Decline of Magic: Studies in Popular Beliefs in Sixteenth- and Seventeenth-Century England* (London: Oxford University Press, 1971; and Philippe Ariès, *L'Enfant et la Vie Familiale sous l'Ancien Régime* (Paris: Plon, 1973).

In the process of moving away from the purely literary, however, history has been steered in the direction of the less rigorous (and more ideological) social sciences. The process of demystifying the state and its personnel as the natural spokesmen for the human past has not been undertaken systematically.

Both the *Annales* and the Cambridge schools have tended to err in the opposite direction, often writing as if political and institutional structures are entirely passive to "underlying" social, economic, and ecological forces. The best-known to emanate from the *Annales* group, Fernand Braudel's panoramic *Mediterranean*, was in fact written to show how utterly constrained the political actors (including Philip II himself) were by their geographic, social, and economic circumstances. A geographical entity (the Mediterranean) is chosen as the unit of analysis, rather than a political state. The book is in three parts: "*Structures*," "*Conjonctures*" (situations and conjonctures) and "*Evenements*" (events). The political narrative of the final part is designed to show that, given the "*structures*" and "*conjonctures*" of the first two parts, nothing was left to human choice. As Braudel puts it in his introduction, political events are the "foam on the surface" of the sea of history.* This of course reflects the Marxian diagnosis of institutions and ideas as "superstructure" to the forms and relations of production, which are seen as fundamental.†

---

* Braudel, *The Mediterranean*, vol. I, p. 21: Braudel refers to *"l'histoire événementielle"* (the history of events) as "surface disturbances, crests of foam that the tides of history carry on their strong backs."

† V. I. Lenin, *The State and Revolution: The Marxist Theory of the State and the Tasks of the Proletariat in the Revolution* (Moscow, 1972), which relies heavily on Engels's *Anti-Dühring.* See also Ralph Miliband, *The State in Capitalist Society: The Analysis of the Western System of Power* (London: Quartet Books, 1969).

For the liberal historian it is not enough, therefore, to show that human history is not the history of the state. In fact, the specific contribution of the liberal historian can be, paradoxically, to draw attention to the state and stress its fundamental importance in human affairs. To imagine a society without pervasive state influence, it is essential to know how the state developed and came to dominate all other forms of political organization. Conversely, to understand how the state came into being is to understand that its existence and present nature are not inevitable.

Such assertions may surprise the nonhistorian. Surely, he will think, coercive political organization is universal, and has always been with us. This commonplace view misses the critical point that coercion is context-specific; it can be identified and corrected only in a specific institutional context. To believe that coercion is endemic to *all* forms of human organization is both pessimistic and untestable—and only the darkest cynic would say that there are no differences between human societies in this respect. These differences, if one believes in them, are institutional differences, and we simply do not know how far coercion can be reduced under different institutional forms.

The specific institution through which most political coercion is presently mediated is the national state, the characteristic political structure of modernity. It came into existence at a specific time, the fifteenth and early sixteenth centuries, and in a particular place, western Europe. Like industrialization, the national state was in its origins a uniquely European phenomenon.

Historians have only recently focused on the state itself (rather than the group of which it is a "superstructure," or the history of particular states) as a subject of research. Like economists who have made the state itself a focus of research in recent years,[‡] they have found that the state has its own dynamic, independent of those in whose interests it is supposedly run. Niels Steensgaard, in a remarkable article criticizing the debate about the mid-seventeenth-century "General Crisis" (a phenomenon well known to contemporaries, but which was then forgotten until the 1950s because historians were so narrowly focused on individual national states) was perhaps the first to point out that the growth of the state was in itself the dominant historical trend of early modern Europe:

> Behind the conflict we find the same thing everywhere: the State's demand for higher revenues . . . in every case it was the governments that acted in a revolutionary manner: the tax demands disrupted the social balance. They did not create a revolutionary situation: they were in themselves a revolution.[*]

Though this approach has not yet found a wide following, it does provide the framework for what could be a fruitful research

---

[‡] See George Stigler, "The Economics of Regulation," *Bell Journal of Economics and Management Science* (Spring 1971); Richard A. Posner, "Theories of Economic Regulation," *Bell Journal of Economics and Management Science*, (Autumn 1974); Sam Peltzman, "Towards a More General Theory of Regulation"; Gary S. Becker, "A Theory of Competition among Pressure Groups," and, of course, the works of the Public Choice school, for instance J. M. Buchanan, *The Limits of Liberty: Between Anarchy and Leviathan* (Chicago: University of Chicago Press, 1975).

[*] Niels Steensgaard, "The Seventeenth-Century Crisis," in Parker and Smith, *The General Crisis of the Seventeenth Century* (London: Routledge, 1978), p. 44.

program for economic and social history—even for political and institutional history. In fact it provides a framework for integrating these different "kinds" of history—economic, political, social, intellectual—that is potentially much more powerful than the rigidly deterministic approach of the *Annales* schools' "*histoire totale.*"[†]

Other Sources of Coercion

While modern western societies represent a great improvement over the past in many respects, coercion, privilege, and oppression survive and flourish. The new schools of history have captured the imagination of so many dynamic and critical young historians precisely because they insist on looking at the oppressed rather than the oppressors. The task of the historian with clear and critical liberal principles must now be to ensure that *all* the sources of oppression and coercion in past societies are laid bare, not only those that proceed from the state. The libertarian historian must have the courage to recognize and proclaim the existence of social injustice and oppression wherever he sees it, rather than merely celebrate historical "progress." Furthermore, he must be willing to test his theories about the true causes of oppression, by taking up the new and demanding methods (historical demography, computer analysis of long documentary series, microsimulation) that classical liberal historians have hitherto in their folly left to the statists.

Only by doing so can the libertarian show that the state is not the instrument of a particular class, but an entity with its own,

[†] As outlined in the "Preface" to Braudel's *Mediterranean* (see note on page 297).

self-perpetuating, rationally self-serving dynamic, often horrifyingly independent of both ruler and ruled, but in pursuit of whose support many groups in society will always be willing to make large investments. Only so can the liberal historian show that the systematic oppression of certain groups in the past (such as women) did not result from the free operation of markets, but from specific, male-dominated legal and social institutions: the state, corporations such as guilds, merchant cartels, communities of male citizens, and trade unions.[‡] By questioning traditional assumptions concerning the alleged capitalist oppression of women, the libertarian historian can show in quite a new way that the state and protective corporate groups were not sources of liberalization and progressive social justice, but rather operated to protect established (in this case male) interests.

Freedom is not served by complacency with existing states of society, the results of historical progress, and the continued dominance of traditionally dominant powers. Rather, it arises from skepticism and criticism of accepted assumptions and inadequate theories, and an aspiration toward a better state of society in which the institutions that perpetuate established evils and entrenched privileges and abuses shall be abolished. The role of the liberal historian in the next decade must be to be *seen* to be defending capitalism against the abuses even of "capitalists"—against

[‡] This argument is put forward in my article "Women, Proto-Industrialization and the Corporate Society: Württemberg Woollen Weaving, 1590–1740," in *Women's Work, Family Income and the Structure of the Family in Historical Perspective*, ed. W. R. Lee and P. Hudson (Manchester: Manchester University Press, 1987).

private monopolies as well as public ones, against "capitalist" cartels, against the purchase of bureaucratic and legislative favor by *anyone*, even those who identify themselves politically as "in favor of capitalism." Liberal historians have not sufficiently dissociated capitalism from entrenched privilege and the abuses arising from the existence of regulatory initiatives, which can be "purchased" by business.

My own research has shown that what German historians of all political persuasions have blindly accepted as the "transition to capitalism" in Germany was in fact something very different from the mobile and relatively unregulated commerce enjoyed by western European societies such as England. It was in fact a transition to "state monopoly capitalism" (*Stamokap*) in which the state licensed out monopolistic privileges to merchant cartels, producer-monopolies, and professional corporations.* Small wonder that Central Europeans (most eloquently but by no means uniquely Marx and Engels) saw the "transition to capitalism" as bringing with it the economic and political oppression of industrial workers by a privileged few.

It is the task of the classical liberal historian to show the importance of investigating and identifying *all* barriers to the free operation of markets: both the state and individuals and groups that have, historically, frequently benefited from state support and

---

* This argument is put forward in my "Corporatism and Regulation in Rural Industry: Woollen Weaving in Württemberg 1590–1740" (PhD diss, Cambridge, 1985). It is corroborated by numerous studies of the overweening role of the State in German industrialization, among which (for Württemberg), Friedrich-Franz Wauchkuhn, "Die Anfänge der württembergischen Textilindustrie im Rahmen der Staatlichen Gewerbepolitik 1806–1848" (diss., Hamburg University, 1974).

have in turn helped to strengthen the state. It is imperative that the liberal historian find the courage and ingenuity to identify *all* sources of coercion and market distortion, lest he or she seem to the critical and Utopian intellectual to be more a political apologist than a seeker after truth.

I have argued that the new "scientific" historians have set off a revolution, which liberal historians would do well to adopt as their own. In demonstrating the fruitfulness of cross-cultural comparisons, the new historical schools have rejected the nation-state as the unit of analysis. In turning to hitherto-unplumbed documents and to "history from below" they have shown that there is a great iceberg of social behavior underneath the level of the central state that is impervious to the explicit initiatives of those who claim to control or guide it, and which always has confounded and always will confound political programs.[†] What the liberal historian must bring to this is the perception that precisely for this reason the official versions of history (recorded from above by officials and intellectuals) are likely to be misleading. He must also, however, bring the perception that although state action often fails in achieving the results it *intends*, it can seriously distort markets, and have far-reaching *unintended* consequences. He must show that there are other powerful coercive institutions at work in most societies which, so long as they benefit from *some* state enforcement, can also seriously distort markets, and perpetuate inequalities and abuses.

[†] It is well known, for instance, that state birth control programs in India and other third-world countries experience a marked lack of success as long as the "demand" for a large quantity of children persists.

The uniquely powerful perception of the liberal historian is that behind the enduring corporate institutions, and behind all entrenched privilege, lies the state. With the rise of interdisciplinary approaches to "scientific" history in the last two decades, historians have been searching in vain for a new focus for history: what, ultimately, is history "about"? The nineteenth-century nationalist-liberal research program is played out; the *Annales* and Cambridge schools ignore the institutional dimension; the classical-liberal research program should be a candidate to fill the vacuum. The history of national states would then be replaced by the history of the state.

Individual Rationality

One of the props of coercive regimes and one of the favorite arguments of Utopian socialists is that the state is necessary to protect people from the harmful results of their own irrational choices. The assumption that many human decision-making mechanisms are irrational is based on innumerable studies by social scientists who have fallen back on "human nature" when they have found a social structure or a pattern of behavior too complex for their explanatory models.* Historians have contributed to this in two ways. They have explained the economic and other choices of pre-industrial Europeans in terms of concepts such as "the moral economy of the peasant": according to this, the peasant was not concerned with rational maximization, but with achieving some

---

* A number of studies advancing "nonrational" or outright "irrational" explanations for human behavior are rightly castigated in Gary Becker, *The Economic Approach to Human Behavior* (Chicago: University of Chicago Press, 1976), p. 7.

culturally or economically determined standard of "limited good," which would not deprive his neighbors in the peasant commune of their slice of a "cake" of a fixed size.[†] Rational maximization, according to a second, concomitant assumption of many historians, came into being only with the rise of a "capitalist mentality" in the seventeenth or eighteenth century.[‡] Thus a majority of historians joins the many social scientists outside the field of economics who hold that hunting societies, or peasant societies, or western societies before a certain date, or the "worker" sector of emergent capitalist societies, lack the mentality required for the economist's tools to be applicable to them, and for the political theorist to be able to expect that they will make choices that are in their own best interests.

One of the most vital tasks of the libertarian historian is to refute this patronizing assumption that human beings in the past were incapable of rational calculation. It is possible to advance explanations of human behavior and social structures in the past that are consistent with individual rational choice rather than collective irrationality. The belief of many historians—even among classical liberals—that rational maximization was invented in

[†] The idea of the moral economy attitude is put forward by James C. Scott, *The Moral Economy of the Peasant: Rebellion and Subsistence in Southeast Asia* (New Haven, CT: Yale University Press, 1976). The classic evocation of "the peasant" in anthropology is in E. C. Banfield, *The Moral Basis of a Backward Society* (Glencoe, IL: Free Press, 1958); and G. M. Foster, "Peasant Society and the Image of Limited Good," *American Anthropologist* 67, no. 2 (1965): 293–315.

[‡] See Joyce Oldham Appleby, *Economic Thought and Ideology in Seventeenth-Century England* (Princeton, NJ: Princeton University Press, 1978), which was written to explain the "puzzle" of "how Adam Smith was able to assume that human beings possessed an innate commercial mentality," p. ix. But see also a myriad of precursors, among whom R. H. Tawney, *The Acquisitive Society* (London: Bell, 1921), p. 17 and *passim*.

Europe only in the seventeenth or eighteenth century is one of the more damaging injuries to the liberal recognition of the dignity and worth of individuals.

In my own doctoral research I succeeded in falsifying a new and powerful historical theory by showing that the economic and demographic behavior of proto-industrial workers in Central Europe in the eighteenth century did not follow the theory's assumption of peasant and artisan irrationality, but rather was wholly consistent with the rational behavior of individuals in markets seriously distorted by social and legal institutions.* This led me to prefer the formulation of Sutti Ortiz, an anthropologist who studied peasant corporatism in modern Colombia:

> The peasant's goals and aspirations are not altogether different from our own; his behavior can be explained without having to resort to a different logical framework; his uncertainties are phrased differently, perhaps, but his response to them is similar to ours. Peasants are not endowed with a different soul or a different perception of the world from ours. If they behave differently, if they shy away from recommended policies it is because they are either less informed about certain events, or perhaps better informed about the realities of their physical, social and economic world than we are.†

---

* Sheilagh C. Ogilvie, *Early Proto-Industry, Corporatism, and the State: Wildberg Weavers and Calw Merchant-Dyers 1600–1740* (fellowship diss., Trinity College, Cambridge, 1984).

† Sutti Reissig Ortiz, *Uncertainties in Peasant Farming: A Colombian Case* (London: Athlone Press, 1973), p. 1.

Thus, even more important than the recognition that the state is *not* the inevitable unit of historical analysis is the recognition that the individual—however lowly his status or undeveloped his education—*is* the proper unit of analysis. He probably will not be pursuing pecuniary maximization (as caricatures of classical liberal principles try to portray), for most markets in the past— as in the present—are distorted by political coercion, and since every individual, nowadays as well as in the past, also maximizes nonpecuniary values (esteem, security, and so forth).[‡]

The recognition that the individual *is*, and historically always has been, equipped to make the best of his situation in the light of his own values is not only a necessary step in recognizing his dignity and worth. It is a radical and Utopian reinterpretation of social developments in the past, and an indispensable component of the belief in voluntarism in human relations.

Three possible approaches have been suggested by which a sound understanding of classical liberal principles could revolutionize the academic practice of history. By pursuing any of these approaches (as well, no doubt, as many others I have not mentioned), liberal historians can help their readers to understand the nature and origins of coercion in human societies. To an academic profession searching for a role in modern life, this is a brilliant prospect.

[‡] George J. Stigler and Gary S. Becker, "De Gustibus Non Est Disputandum," *American Economic Review* 67, no. 2 (1977): 76–90.

Notes

1. For an early example of inevitability in liberal history, see Bishop William Stubbs, Regius Professor of Modern History at the University of Oxford (1866–1884). J. W. Burrow, *A Liberal Descent: Victorian Historians and the English Past* (New York: Cambridge University Press, 1981).

2. George Macauley Trevelyan, *Clio, a Muse, and Other Essays Literary and Pedestrian* (London: Longmans, Green, 1913), p. 12.

3. Joseph Schumpeter, "The Creative Response in Economic History," *Journal of Economic History* 7, no. 2 (1947): 150.

4. Benedetto Croce, *History as the Story of Liberty* (New York: Meridian Books, 1955), p. 49.

5. Charles Victor Langlois and Charles Seignobos, trans. G. G. Berry, *Introduction to the Study of History* (New York: Henry Holt and Co., 1903), p. 289.

6. Croce, *History as the Story of Liberty*, p. 23.

7. Samuel Hammond, "The Future of Liberalism and the Politicization of Everything," January 25, 2017, https://niskanencenter.org/blog/future-liberalism-politicization-everything/?fbclid=IwAR1yUyOq4mLL_gzXaez_7X-WLlFKuufQeH_U8zdpCizbj98iWbKIFgUwXEQ.

8. Carl L. Becker, *The Heavenly City of the Eighteenth-Century Philosophers*, 2nd ed. (New Haven, CT: Yale University Press, 2003), p. 98.

9. Julia Markus and J. Anthony Froude, *The Last Great Undiscovered Victorian* (New York: Scribner, 2005); and A. L. Rowse, *Froude the Historian: Victorian Man of Letters* (Gloucester, UK: Alan Sutton, 1987).

10. See, for example, John Mackinnon Robertson, "The Anti-Scientific View of History," in *Buckle and His Critics: A Study in Sociology* (London: Swan Sonnenschein & Co., 1895), pp. 293–323.

11. F. W. Maitland et al., *Essays on the Teaching of History* (Cambridge: Cambridge University Press, 1901), p. xix.

12. Henry Sidgwick, a philosophy professor then at the University of Cambridge.

13. Richard D. Mosier, "The Educational Philosophy of William T. Harris," *Peabody Journal of Education* 29, no. 1 (1951): 24–33, specifically p. 30.

14. Writings about Harris include Charles Franklin Thwing, "William Torrey Harris," *Journal of Education* 95, no. 26 (1922), 719–21; Edward Leroy Schaub, *William Torrey Harris 1835–1935: A Collection of Essays, Including Papers and Addresses Presented in Commemoration of Dr. Harris' Centennial at the St. Louis Meeting of the Western Division of the American Philosophical Society* (Chicago: Open Court, 1936); and Kurt F. Leidecker, *Yankee Teacher: The Life of William Torrey Harris* (New York: Philosophical Library, 1946).

15. And it is found in textbooks of the era, sometimes with racial overtones, like Samuel Eagle Froman's *Advanced American History* (New York: Century Co., 1914), where the author writes: "The three greatest achievements of the American people have been these: they have transformed a continent from a low condition of barbarism to a high state of civilization; they have developed a commercial and industrial system of vast proportions; and they have evolved the greatest democracy the world has yet seen. In this text, therefore, it has been my aim to present fully and clearly these three aspects of our growth: to show the forces of civilization pressing ever westward upon the wilderness and extending the boundaries of the white man's domain; to show an industrious and ingenious people moving ever forward to make new conquests in the economic world; and to show a liberty-loving nation struggling with new problems of government and advancing ever nearer to a complete realization of popular rule" (p. v).

16. The U.S. Centennial of 1876.

17. Entry for "Charles George Crump" in the *Oxford Dictionary of National Biography*, January 5, 2012 version, www.oxforddnb.com.

18. WorldCat, www.worldcat.org, accessed on May 14, 2019.

19. Tommaso Campanella was an Italian philosopher and poet in the 16th and 17th century.

20. Ferdinando Galiani was an 18th-century Italian economist and Enlightenment thinker.

21. *Les Rougon-Macquart* is the title given to a collection of 20 novels by Émile Zola.

22. Victor Cousin was a 19th-century French philosopher and Jules Michelet was a 19th-century French historian.

23. Giambattista Vico was a philosopher and polymath in the 17th and 18th centuries. A century after his death, his book *Scienza Nuova* (New Science) became influential in conceptualizing social science history.

24. Vittorio Alfieri was an 18th-century Italian dramatist and tragic poet.

25. Christopher Lloyd, "Realism and Structurism in Historical Theory: A Discussion of the Thought of Maurice Mandelbaum," *History and Theory* 28, no. 3 (1989): 302.

26. Max Scheler (1874–1928) was a German phenomenologist, ethicist, and anthropologist, while his contemporary Ernst Troeltsch (1865–1923) was a German theologian, philosopher of history, and liberal politician.

27. Georg Simmel (1858–1918) was a leading German sociologist.

28. In the original, Hayek quoted Democritus in the original Greek.

29. Herbert H. Rowen, "The Historical Work of Pieter Geyl," *Journal of Modern History* 37, no. 1 (1965): 49.

30. For more on this, see Michael J. Douma, "Why Historians Have Failed to Recognize Mises's *Theory and History*," *Review of Austrian Economics* 31, no. 1 (2018): 359–72.

31. Henry Steele Commager, "The Constitution: Was It an Economic Document?," *American Heritage* 10, no. 1 (December 1958): 58, https://www.americanheritage.com /constitution-was-it-economic-document.

32. R. W. Davis, ed., *The Origins of Modern Freedom in the West* (Stanford, CA: Stanford University Press, 1995); R. W. Davis, "The Center for the History of Freedom," *The Historian* 55, no. 4 (1993): 629–34; Louis Mink, "The Theory of Practice: Hexter's Historiography," in *After the Reformation: Essays in Honor of J. H. Hexter*, ed. Barbara C. Malament (Manchester, UK: Manchester University Press, 1980), pp. 3–24.

33. Copyright 2004 by Reason Foundation, 3415 S. Sepulveda Blvd., Suite 400, Los Angeles, CA 90034: www.reason.com. Originally delivered as a speech before the first convention of the Society for Individual Liberty, University of Pennsylvania, November 15–16, 1969, http://praxeology.net/RC-BRS.htm.

34. Jeff Riggenbach, "The Story of Roy A. Childs Jr. (1949–1992)," *Mises Daily*, January 21, 2011, https://mises.org/library/story-roy-childs-jr-1949%E2%80%931992.

35. This article (published as a pamphlet by the Institute for Humane Studies) is based on lectures delivered in the United States and Canada in April 1974, under the auspices of the Institute for Humane Studies. It was also presented as a paper at the 25th anniversary meeting of the Mont Pelerin Society in Montreux, Switzerland, in 1972. It was reprinted in the journal *Modern Age* in its fall 1974 issue, pp. 380–89.

36. See, for example, E. J. Hobsbawm, "The British Standard of Living, 1790–1850," *Economic History Review* 10, no. 1 (1957): 46–68; R. M. Hartwell, "Interpretations of the Industrial Revolution in England," *Journal of Economic History* 19, no. 2 (1959): 229–49; E. J. Hobsbawm, "The Standard of Living during the Industrial Revolution: A Discussion," *Economic History Review* 16, no. 1 (1963): 119–34; and Jonathan Hughes, "Professor Hobsbawm on the Evolution of Modern Capitalism," in *Essays in Contemporary Fields of Economics: In Honor of Emanuel T. Weiler*, ed. James P. Quirk and George Horwich (West Lafayette, IN: Purdue University Press, 1981), pp. 168–86.

About the Editor

Michael J. Douma is an assistant research professor at Georgetown University's McDonough School of Business, where he is also the director of the Georgetown Institute for the Study of Markets and Ethics. He is a coauthor of *What Is Classical Liberal History?* (Lexington Books, 2017) and the author of *Creative Historical Thinking* (Routledge, 2018).

Libertarianism.org

Liberty. It's a simple idea and the linchpin of a complex system of values and practices: justice, prosperity, responsibility, toleration, cooperation, and peace. Many people believe that liberty is the core political value of modern civilization itself, the one that gives substance and form to all the other values of social life. They're called libertarians.

Libertarianism.org is the Cato Institute's treasury of resources about the theory and history of liberty. The book you're holding is a small part of what Libertarianism.org has to offer. In addition to hosting classic texts by historical libertarian figures and original articles from modern-day thinkers, Libertarianism.org publishes podcasts, videos, online introductory courses, and books on a variety of topics within the libertarian tradition.

Cato Institute

Founded in 1977, the Cato Institute is a public policy research foundation dedicated to broadening the parameters of policy debate to allow consideration of more options that are consistent with the principles of limited government, individual liberty, and peace. To that end, the Institute strives to achieve greater involvement of the intelligent, concerned lay public in questions of policy and the proper role of government.

The Institute is named for *Cato's Letters*, libertarian pamphlets that were widely read in the American Colonies in the early 18th century and played a major role in laying the philosophical foundation for the American Revolution.

Despite the achievement of the nation's Founders, today virtually no aspect of life is free from government encroachment. A pervasive intolerance for individual rights is shown by government's arbitrary intrusions into private economic transactions and its disregard for civil liberties. And while freedom around the globe has notably increased in the past several decades, many countries have moved in the opposite direction, and most governments still do not respect or safeguard the wide range of civil and economic liberties.

To address those issues, the Cato Institute undertakes an extensive publications program on the complete spectrum of policy issues. Books, monographs, and shorter studies are commissioned to examine the federal budget, Social Security, regulation, military spending, international trade, and myriad other issues. Major policy conferences are held throughout the year, from which papers are published thrice yearly in the *Cato Journal*. The Institute also publishes the quarterly magazine *Regulation*.

In order to maintain its independence, the Cato Institute accepts no government funding. Contributions are received from foundations, corporations, and individuals, and other revenue is generated from the sale of publications. The Institute is a nonprofit, tax-exempt, educational foundation under Section 501(c)3 of the Internal Revenue Code.

CATO INSTITUTE
1000 Massachusetts Avenue NW
Washington, DC 20001
www.cato.org